Alistair Moffat was born and bred in the Scottish Borders. A former Director of the Edinburgh Festival Fringe, Director of Programmes at Scottish Television and founder of the Borders Book Festival, he is also the author of a number of highly acclaimed books. From 2011 to 2014 he was Rector of the University of St Andrews.

WAR PATHS

WALKING IN THE SHADOWS OF THE CLANS

ALISTAIR
MOFFAT

BIRLINN

First published in 2023 by
Birlinn Limited
West Newington House
10 Newington Road
Edinburgh
EH9 1QS

www.birlinn.co.uk

ISBN: 978 1 78027 824 7

British Library Cataloguing-in-Publication Data
A catalogue record for this book is available from the British Library

Designed and typeset by Hewer Text UK Ltd, Edinburgh
Printed and bound by Clays Ltd, Elcograf S.p.A.

*To my sisters, Barbara and Marjie,
with thanks for a lifetime of love and kindness*

Contents

Acknowledgements   ix

Prologue Barbarians
Prestonpans, 21 September 1745   xii

1 High Tide
  Glenfinnan, 19 August 1745   1

2 The Stockade and the Scaffold
  Lewis, Edinburgh, 3 April 1613   28

3 The Year of Great Alasdair
  Tippermuir, 1 September 1644   47

4 The Snow March
  Inverlochy, 2 February 1645   75

5 The Perfect Ground
  Mulroy, 6 August 1688   91

6 A' Dol Sios
  Killiecrankie, 27 July 1689   105

7 The Godly Commonwealth
  Dunkeld, 21 August 1689   131

8 Blaeberries
  Sheriffmuir, 13 November 1715   153

9 Rain, Sleet and Speed
  Falkirk, 17 January 1746   167

10 The Army of the Dead
    Culloden Moor, 16 April 1746   183

11 The Old Road
    Arisaig to Morar   197

    Epilogue
    Charles III   210

Further Reading   214
Index   217

Acknowledgements

I would like to thank the team at Birlinn. We have worked together over the years on many books and projects. Visits to West Newington House are always made a pleasure by Hugh Andrew, Jan Rutherford and Andrew Simmons, consummate professionals and thoroughly good eggs all. When we sat down together to talk about the striking cover of this book, it felt like the nightmare of Covid was coming to an end as we exchanged positive, creative ideas. Thanks also to the lovely Patricia Marshall for her editing, and also to Debs Warner for helping with the maps and much else.

My agent, David Godwin, master of the one-liner (sometimes one-word) email and the art of getting straight to the point, was as ever a joy to work with. The other day I worked out that David had shepherded no fewer than thirty-one of my books to publication. How he survived these repeated ordeals, I have no idea.

I spoke to many people as I walked the war paths, and most were very helpful. At Falkirk Muir I met someone who was even inspirational, full of kindly insights and happy to share them. But perhaps my most constant companions were never quite visible, although I never ceased to hear their whispers, and sometimes the distant echo of their war cries on the Highland winds. The warriors whose ghosts I followed on my journeys back into the darkness of the past were always with me. Having walked where they charged, I was in awe of their physical courage and their unhesitating will to defend their beloved home-places. It was a privilege to walk beside them.

Alistair Moffat
July 2023
Selkirk

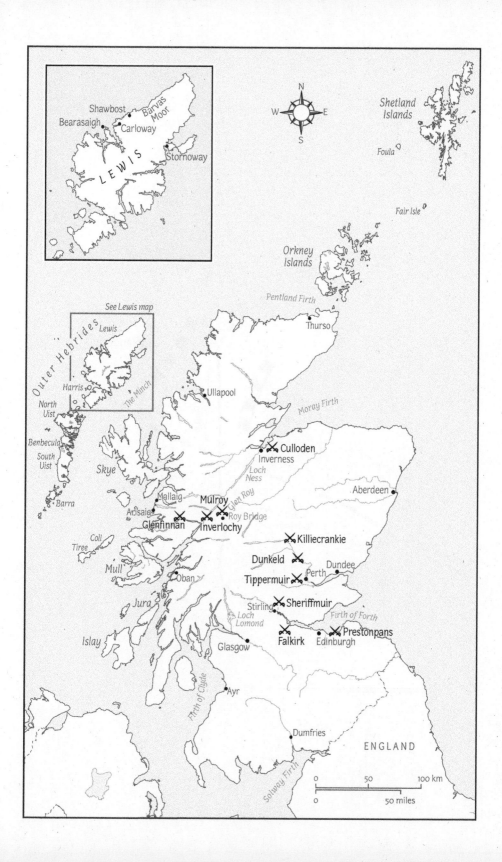

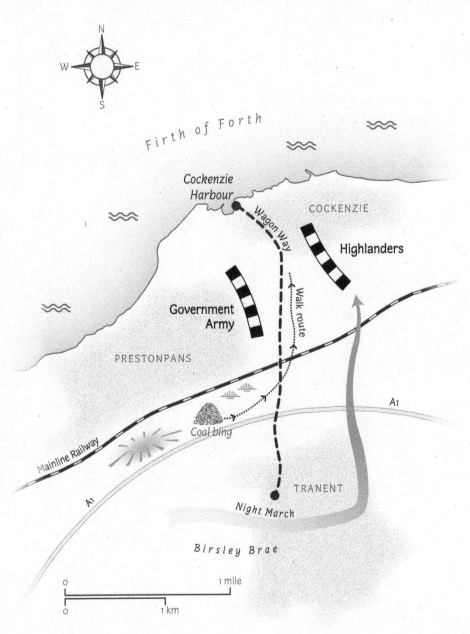

N W E S

Firth of Forth

Cockenzie
Harbour

Wagon Way

COCKENZIE

Highlanders

Walk route

Government
Army

PRESTONPANS

Mainline Railway

Coal bing

A1

A1

TRANENT

Night March

Birsley Brae

0 ——————— 1 mile

0 ——————— 1 km

Prologue

Barbarians

Prestonpans, 21 September 1745

Burned off by the sun rising over the North Sea, the haar lifted in moments. As quickly as the mist had rolled in over the cornfields before dawn on 21 September 1745, the wisps of its grey veil dispersed and revealed what the soldiers in the ranks of the government army thought at first was a black hedge. Peering into the chill morning light, shading their eyes against the growing glow of the low sun, no one was certain what it was. But it did seem to some that the black hedge was moving.

Having marched his force of clansmen south from the muster at Glenfinnan, Prince Charles Edward Stuart, the Young Pretender, had taken Edinburgh without a fight, a party of Camerons having forced entry at the Netherbow Port at dawn on 17 September. When news came of the landing of General Sir John Cope and his army at Dunbar on the southern shore of the Firth of Forth, the Jacobites moved quickly eastwards to meet him, eager for battle. But, when scouts reported that government troops had taken up a strong defensive position near Prestonpans by a run of protective walls on their right, placed cannon on a high embankment behind their ranks and had marshy ground below them to the south, there was disagreement.

Lord George Murray, the Jacobites' most effective and experienced general, sent Colonel Harry Ker of Graden to look more closely at the terrain between the two armies. Here is a passage from John Home's *History of the Rebellion in the year 1745*:

He came down from the Highland Army, alone; he was mounted on a little white pony; and with the greatest deliberation rode between the two armies, looking at the ground on each hand of him. Several shots were fired at him as he went along. When he came to a dry stone dyke that was in his way, he dismounted, and, pulling down a piece of the dyke, led his horse over it. He then returned to Lord George Murray and assured him that it was impossible to get through the morasse and attack the enemy in front without receiving several fires.

Nevertheless, the prince wanted to attack immediately but, after a fierce argument, was persuaded by Lord George Murray and the cool appraisal of Ker, also an experienced and professional soldier who had served in the armies of the kings of Spain, to seek better ground. The Highland charge, the Jacobites' sole tactic, would have been much impeded by the morass in front of Cope's lines and more importantly it would slow the charge and allow 'several fires', the opportunity for the government soldiers to reload and fire more than one volley. The ground had to be right.

A local farmer's son, Robert Anderson, knew of a safe and hidden track through the marsh that would allow the clansmen to move east around the government army and confront them across sloping, well-drained and recently cropped cornfields. A keen wild fowler and sure footed, Robert was able to find his way through the half dark and the enveloping mist in the hours before dawn. Only three abreast and keeping very quiet, the Highlanders were led by the boy and 100 men from the Clanranald regiment. George Murray followed immediately behind them with the rest of the army, men keeping close contact with each other but moving only slowly. One of his officers remembered that 'it was so difficult that every step men made they sunk to the knee in mud. This made them pass in some disorder.'

Through the dense, foggy hour before dawn, James Drummond, the Duke of Perth, led the three MacDonald regiments across the fields towards the sea to take up position on the right wing. Clan

Cameron, a company of MacGregors and the Stewarts of Appin followed him to make up the centre and the left while the Atholl Brigade, the Menzies and the MacLauchlan regiments, other smaller companies of Robertsons and Glencoe MacDonalds and Viscount Strathallan's small cavalry force took up positions as a second line. With his lifeguards, Prince Charles sat on a grey horse, trying to make out his enemy's lines.

Behind the prince, out to the east, a pale dawn had begun to rise over the North Sea. But the mist still hid the small Highland army. Murray and the chiefs who led the clan regiments ordered their men to keep absolutely silent and with the front rank both commanders crawled slowly through the stubble of the cornfield to get as close as possible to Cope's lines. The black hedge had begun to move.

As the sun warmed and the haar lifted, lookouts were at last beginning to detect some substantial activity and government officers informed their commander that the Jacobites appeared to be moving around to the east. Another report had them wheeling to the north-east. Immediately realising what was happening, General Cope quickly turned his army to face their enemy, disposing them in lines three deep with his dragoons and cavalry in two ranks.

Then it suddenly began. The *claideamh mor*, the order to charge, came as the war pipes skirled, echoing through the morning air. Erupting from the mist-strewn stubble field like an army of spectres rising from the bowels of Hell, the Highlanders began to run towards the government army. And then they broke into an all-out charge. Howling like wolves, roaring their war cries, they came on very fast, closing quickly. Many paused to fire their muskets or pistols, immediately threw them down and raced towards the ranks of redcoats.

Running as quickly as they could, low to the ground, their small, round shields covering their heads and their broadswords drawn, the brave Camerons hit first, smashing into Cope's troops on the right of his line, scattering them instantly. Leading from the front, Lord George Murray and the Duke of Perth ploughed on into the murderous melee, knocking aside bayonet thrusts with their targes, swinging their razor-sharp swords, furiously hacking and cutting, knocking men down, driving the red-coated soldiers backwards. Momentum was everything.

The MacGregor regiment rushed towards the mounted dragoons and the cavalry. Some of these clansmen had no swords and so they had lashed the blades of farmers' scythes to long poles to make primitive halberds. A few weeks before this first experience of battle, young James Johnstone of Edinburgh had volunteered to join the prince's army and he left a vivid record of what happened on that blood-spattered morning as the MacGregors raced out of the rising sun across the yellow stubble field.

> They had been frequently enjoined to aim at the noses of the horses with their swords, without minding the riders, as the natural movement of a horse, wounded in the face, is to wheel round, and a few horses wounded in that manner are sufficient to throw a whole squadron into such disorder that it is impossible afterwards to rally it. They followed this advice most implicitly, and the English cavalry were instantly thrown into confusion. Macgregor's company did great execution with their scythes. They cut the legs of the horses in two, and their riders through the middle of their bodies.

Many redcoats panicked at the sight of the Highlanders coming on 'like a living torrent' and did not wait for the driving shudder of impact. James Johnstone again:

> The panic-terror of the English surpassed all imagination. They threw down their arms that they might run with more speed, thus depriving themselves by their fears of the only means of arresting the vengeance of the Highlanders. Of so many men in a condition, from their numbers, to preserve order in their retreat, not one thought of defending himself. Terror had taken entire possession of their minds.
>
> I saw a young Highlander, about fourteen years of age, scarcely formed, who was presented to the Prince as a prodigy, having

killed, it was said, fourteen of the enemy. The Prince asked him if this was true. 'I do not know,' replied he, 'if I killed them but I brought fourteen soldiers to the ground with my sword.' Another Highlander brought ten soldiers to the Prince, whom he had made prisoners, driving them before him like a flock of sheep.

Prestonpans was a rout, a profound shock, a disaster for George II and his government. Many more men died in flight than in the battle 'without firing, or being fired upon, and without drawing a sword', according to a redcoat officer. The stubble of the cornfield was awash with blood and rang with the appalling agonies of the dying. Bladed weapons rarely kill quickly and the screams of the badly wounded rent the early morning air before the clansmen used their dirks and swords to put enemy soldiers out of their misery.

Even across two and a half centuries, the shock felt by James Johnstone is palpable: 'The field of battle presented a spectacle of horror, being covered with heads, legs, arms and mutilated bodies: for the killed all fell by the sword.'

*

On a bright and unseasonably warm March morning, I parked next to a pair of giant pylons, their six arms carrying electricity south to the towns and cities of Lowland Scotland and, when I got out of the car, I heard the whoosh and whine of a high-speed train racing along the main line from Edinburgh to London. Behind me was the incessant hum of traffic on the A1. It seemed that the 21st century had the Battle of Prestonpans surrounded.

Battles not only make history, they can be submerged by it. I had come to look at the fields of blood – the place where the carnage that had so shocked James Johnstone had played out. Next to the road rose a high coal bing, a man-made mountain of mining waste that had been reshaped into a more or less conical hill. It was a very good vantage point, close to where the night manoeuvres around from the morass had forced Cope to turn his army, and it was also a grandstand that rose to the south of the stubble fields where the Highlanders charged. Despite all the upheavals the landscape had suffered during the Industrial Revolution and on into the 21st century, the nature of the ground, what obsessed Lord George Murray, could be much better understood.

From the top of the coal bing, I could see Birsley Brae rise up to the south, the first position taken by the Highland Army. It is now all built up with what looks like a large council estate that commands long vistas over the place where General Cope deployed his redcoats. Had it not been for the morass at the foot of the brae, it would have been an excellent position from which to attack. Geography made sense of the fierce arguments between Prince Charles and Murray the night before the battle.

The boggy ground found by Colonel Harry Ker has not quite disappeared. When the cutting was made for the railway line, it must have been drained because the trains now run just below where the government army had been drawn up. But, under the pylons to the east, I noticed several deep-cut drainage ditches and a large area, disfigured by fly-tipping, that looked soggy even though there had been no rain for a week. Telltale clumps of marsh grass grew in several places.

Brown direction signs at the foot of the coal bing would have been understood by those of Prince Charles's clansmen who could read. Their Gaelic pointed me along *Slighe Blar a' Bhatail*, the Battlefield Trail. The worn paths were black with the compacted dust of old coal waste and recent storms had blown down many trees, some fallers forcing detours, making it difficult to make sense of the Jacobites' movements. But, when I reached the road from Longniddry to Prestonpans and crossed it, I began to understand the events of 21 September 1745 much better. A path between two ploughed fields with a wall on either side traces the route of a waggonway that took coal down the brae from the pits at Tranent to be loaded onto boats in Cockenzie harbour. Cope's redcoats had re-formed their lines just to the east of it when they realised that the Jacobites had changed their position. I stopped and realised I was probably close to where the government general sat on his horse in the rear, looking over the heads of his soldiers, watching the black hedge suddenly become a furious charge. When Cope's men broke and ran, the charging Highlanders streamed across the waggonway. As they roared their ancient war cries and raised their claymores, it was as though the past was unknowingly crossing the future. The old way would become a railway, as more and more coal was mined, and eventually a huge coal-fired power station would be built at Cockenzie, its tall chimneys a famous landmark on the Forth coast. Long since closed and its chimneys toppled, the huge pylons remembered how much electricity it produced.

Their rich, chocolate earth freshly ploughed, the fields of blood on either side of the old tracks were waiting to be planted, probably with barley or wheat. Screening out the rush of the trains and the grinding traffic, I found myself walking around the walls listening for echoes, to the fury of the clansmen and the panic of the redcoats as they turned and fled, streaming past me. I've sometimes found that places have memory and, against all expectations, these empty fields in the midst of busy roads and the thunder of speeding trains seemed to me to remember the slaughter, the chaos and the shock-waves that spread down the length of Britain like a tide. History was turned upside down at Prestonpans when an army from the past defeated the future.

The battle probably lasted less than ten minutes but its impact was enormous. Not only did it make Prince Charles master of Scotland, it brought to life an image that terrified all Britain. Out of the morning mist at Prestonpans, monsters had raced into history. Savages who howled and roared their war cries in a barbarous tongue had scattered and slaughtered a modern army in moments. Wielding ancient weapons with dazzling and deadly skill, they had cut to pieces modern soldiers who were equipped with musket and cannon and flanked by cavalry. When Clan Cameron smashed into the lines of redcoats, the government army all but collapsed, fear turning to panic in an instant. Men trained to aim and shoot their muskets so that they could kill at a distance were engulfed by the chaos of hand-to-hand fighting as the prince's army surged through their ranks. In the bright morning sun, blood spattered the yellow corn stubble. But more than anything, what made the difference at Prestonpans was that the Highlanders were possessed of an atavistic physical courage that could sweep all before its fury. It was a courage that never faded.

*

At the end of May 1940, the Camerons found themselves at the edge of another cornfield. After breaking through the Maginot Line in their spectacular dash to defeat France, the Germans had crossed the River Somme and established a bridgehead. The Cameron Highlanders were ordered to mount an infantry advance to help drive them back. Even though there was no cover in the cornfield, B Company did not hesitate as they charged over the open ground, taking heavy casualties.

Suddenly, two German companies who had been lying flat, hidden by the high stalks of growing green corn, rose up when the Camerons were within 100 yards of the river. They quickly set up Spandau machine guns and the losses were severe as fire raked across the field. But the Highlanders kept coming. When they reached the riverbank only forty-six men out of the 126 who began the charge had survived.

In the days that followed, the panzer divisions broke through all along the front, crossed the Somme in force and made spectacular inroads as they raced towards the French coast. Coordinated with the Luftwaffe, blitzkrieg had succeeded beyond even Adolf Hitler's wildest expectations. After the grinding, static trench warfare of the First World War, the speed of the advance amazed everyone. German panzers refuelled at roadside petrol stations as they rumbled on across the old battlefields of 1914–18 and far beyond them. As France quickly fell and its armies surrendered, the British Expeditionary Force was encircled at Dunkirk and evacuations began on 26 May and ended on 4 June. Meanwhile, the Cameron Highlanders, along with the rest of the 51st Highland Division, were still fighting a desperate rearguard action, hoping to reach the port at Le Havre and be evacuated from its quays. But General Rommel's 7th Panzer Division quickly swept around from the south-east to cut off the retreat.

For eight days, there was fierce fighting around the small port of St Valery. Hemmed in by the encircling German army, the Camerons, the Seaforths, the Gordons and the Black Watch held the line with the support of the French IX Corps in the south. But evacuation proved impossible, the ships unable to get close enough to the shore. On 12 June, the 51st Highland Division was forced to surrender and 10,000 brave men were led away to four years of captivity.

Injured pride and incomprehension rippled through the ranks of the Camerons on that day. Donald John MacDonald remembered that the order to lay down arms, seen as a dishonour, was at first disobeyed and had to be forcefully repeated, even enforced. In 1999, interviewed at the age of eighty-nine, Archie MacPhee recalled it as 'the saddest day of [his] life'. When Rommel himself appeared with three panzers and battalions of infantry marching behind them to invite the Camerons to surrender, a French liaison officer stepped forward to agree to the proposal. Gregor Grant MacDonald from Highland Perthshire remembered the humiliation and the anger in the ranks and the fact that 'the island boys reverted to Gaelic to express their opinion of him'.

The old Highland regiments and the clan armies and companies that preceded them are all gone now, their identities fading, their war glory, their prowess and pride remembered by too few. What follows is a series of journeys back into that martial past and its traditions, an attempt to understand something of these remarkable warriors, the most feared in 17th- and 18th-century Europe: how they fought, why they fought and perhaps where that famous and much-feared physical courage came from.

Losers rarely write history. But, in the case of what Gaelic speakers call *Am Bliadhna Thearlaich*, 'The Year of Charles', they certainly did. The defeated had a stirring story to tell. The '45, the rising of the clans between the summer of 1745 and the rain-soaked catastrophe of Culloden in April 1746, was remembered and recorded by many Jacobite sympathisers. They knew and intuited it was the last act in a century-old tragedy and, more than that, the passing of a world. When the Highlanders charged across Drumossie Moor, they disappeared into the smoke of history, their fading war cries echoing across the turning world. And, as they summoned their courage and raised their broadswords, they roared the names of their places – *Craig Elachaidh*! *Creagan an Fhithich*! *Loch A' Mhoigh*! *Dun Mac Glais*! It was for their land and their clan and each other that these men fought like furies. It was the loss of their identity that broke their hearts when many were forced into exile after 1746 and during the infamous Clearances of the following centuries.

War Paths is a record of twelve journeys I made in the course of a year. All remember conflict, courage, hardship, change and loss as I tried to get closer to what sped the Highlanders into the charge, how it was they almost toppled the British state, what they looked like in their war splendour, why their prowess terrified those who faced them. But I did not make these journeys alone. As I sailed up Loch Shiel to Glenfinnan or climbed up to Glen Roy or waded through the bracken to a ruined shieling, the ghosts of warriors walked beside me, whispering their stories, remembering the glories of an immense past.

I

High Tide

Glenfinnan, 19 August 1745

On 22 July 1745, the French frigate *Le du Teillay* dropped anchor off the tiny Hebridean island of Eriskay. It was mid-morning on a day of high summer. In the shelter of the Wooded Bay, the bright shimmer of the sea was blinding and a warm breeze blew out of the west, over the sheltering shores of the neighbouring island of Barra. Under the shade of an awning on the foredeck, two remarkable men were talking animatedly to each other. They had agreed on English although it was the native tongue of neither. On that glad morning of brilliant sun, both were excited about the same thing – even though they had not met until that moment and had little or no idea of each other's identity.

Alasdair Mac Mhaighstir Alasdair had probably studied at both Glasgow and Edinburgh Universities before returning to his native Clanranald country to teach in Ardnamurchan and to compose some of the greatest Gaelic lyric poetry ever heard in the western Highlands. Nominally a Protestant, he had nevertheless come out to fight for the rightful king in the Jacobite Rising of 1715 even though he was only seventeen or eighteen years old. In 1745, he became the captain of a company in the Clanranald regiment. At Prestonpans, he and his clansmen had led the charge into the ranks of a startled government army and torn them to pieces with ferocious and dazzling swordplay. Less than a year later, he had raced across the heather on Culloden Moor as his dreams disappeared into the roar of cannon fire and the darkness of history.

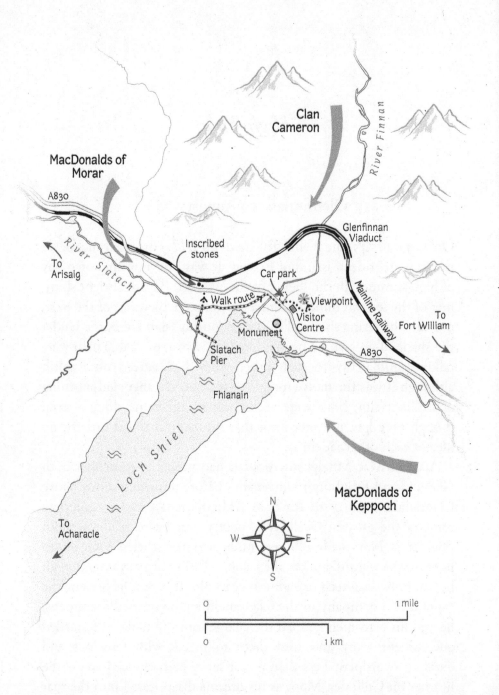

Clan
Cameron

River Finnan

MacDonalds of
Morar

A830

River Slatach

To
Arisaig

Inscribed
stones

Glenfinnan
Viaduct

Car park

Walk route

Viewpoint

Visitor
Centre

Mainline Railway

To
Fort William

Monument

A830

Slatach
Pier

Fhianain

To
Acharacle

Loch Shiel

MacDonlads of
Keppoch

N
W   E
S

0   1 mile

0   1 km

Mac Mhaighstir Alasdair was a gifted poet, university educated and aware of the classical tradition of Greece and Rome. At the same time, he was a ferocious swordsman whose slashing blade inflicted horrific wounds as the terrified redcoats ran for their lives at Prestonpans. Modern sensibilities might find those contrasting attributes in the same man disconcerting but, in the context of the clans and their ancient culture, poetry and carnage, great lyric writing and a feral courage were part of the same tradition – the one often the subject matter of the other. Warriors were poets and poets would raise their claymores, roar their war cries and race into the charge. Who better to hymn the prowess of the Highlanders than a Highlander who knew how to fight, to wound and to kill without mercy in the ruck of vicious hand-to-hand combat?

On the frigate bobbing at anchor in the sunshine of the Wooded Bay, Alasdair Mac Mhaighstir Alasdair had sat down beside a tall young man half his age and begun immediately to engage him in conversation. After a few minutes, they were interrupted by a courtier who sniffed and pointed out that formalities were not being observed, to say nothing of a distinct lack of deference. The tall young man was formally introduced as His Royal Highness the Prince Charles Edward Stuart, the son and heir of James III of Great Britain and Ireland, the eighth of that name to be king of Scotland.

Perhaps because of the confusing length of his name – it uses the Gaelic patronymic and means 'Alasdair, the son of Master Alasdair', a title usually given to a priest or a minister and the equivalent of 'Reverend' – Alasdair is often referred to as Alexander MacDonald. A supremely gifted writer, he seems also to have had a passionate, independent spirit that did not always please his father. When the young man arrived late to a Presbytery meeting attended by other ministers, one of them asked where he had been. 'Alasdair was in Hell,' said his father, knowing the disreputable company he had been keeping. 'What did you see when you were in Hell?' asked another minister. 'I saw nothing there but what I see here,' said the bold Alasdair. 'I could not get near the fire for ministers.'

He composed drinking poems and was at one point accused of much worse. The ministers of the Presbytery of Mull reported that Alasdair was wandering through the countryside 'composing Galick songs stuffed with obscene language'. But he also created verse of great power and beauty. 'The Birlinn of Clanranald' harked back to the great sea culture of the Gaelic west, the Lordship of the Isles and the fast, trim little warships that were rowed by clansmen. Here is a short excerpt where the crew is urged to take hold of:

The smooth-handled oars, well-fashioned,
Light and easy,
That will do the rowing stout and sturdy,
Quick-palmed, blazing,
That will send the surge in sparkles,
Up to skyward,
All in flying spindrift flashing,
Like a fire-shower!
With the fierce and pithy pelting
Of the oar-bank,
That will wound the swelling billows,
With their bending.
With the knife-blades of the white thin oars
Smiting bodies,
On the crest of the blue hills and glens,
Rough and heaving.

The poet's father, Maighstir Alasdair, was the Episcopalian minister of the ancient church on Eilean Fhionain, a small island in Loch Shiel where Irish missionaries had founded a monastery in the 7th century. In 1729, his son was appointed to the island school to teach children their letters and also the catechism. Long before then, he had begun to compose poetry but not in the sense of using pen and paper. In the Gaelic bardic tradition, Alasdair first created the verses in his head, lying on the grass, it was said, with a stone on his chest. He would recite them over and over until rhyme and metre fell into place. Only then would some of the poems be committed to paper.

In 1745, when he was probably about fifty years old, Alasdair sent three new poems to Paris, to Aeneas MacDonald, banker and adviser to the court of the exiled Stuarts. He translated '*Oran Nuadh*' ('The New Song'), '*Oran do'n Phrionssa*' ('A Song to the Prince') and '*Oran nam Fineachan Gaidhealach*' ('The Song of the Highland Clans') into English and read them to Prince Charles. Apparently they were inspirational, helping to persuade the Young Pretender that the time was right to come to Scotland and raise his father's standard in the Highlands.

When Alasdair met the prince, he was twice as old as the young man he didn't recognise but it seems likely that they had attitudes in common, if little else. Charles Edward Louis John Sylvester Maria Casimir Stuart was named Charles after his great-grandfather, Charles II, Edward after Edward the Confessor, an 11th-century king of England, Louis after fourteen kings of France, John after his great-grandfather, king of Poland, Sylvester because he was born on 20 December, the feast day of St Sylvester, Maria after his mother, the Polish noblewoman, Maria Clementina Sobieska, and Casimir after Casimir III, another king of Poland. History was heaped on the young man's shoulders – a great weight of expectation and a need to hold on tight to the aura if not the fact of royalty.

Charles was born in Rome. He spent much of his early childhood there in the close, even claustrophobic atmosphere of an exiled court – a group of people yearning for somewhere else, probably deeply resentful of their fate, bored, frequently engaged in meaningless rituals, enduring what they saw as snubs and slights and insisting on empty titles. The young prince's parents appear to have argued constantly and, in 1725, when the boy was only five years old, his mother walked out, moving to live in a convent for two years. Charles was raised as a Catholic and spent much of his time not with other children but mainly in the company of older men, many of them Jacobite exiles, some of whom were with him on *Le du Teillay*. In addition to his fluency in Italian, the boy learned to speak English and French. With courtiers in attendance, he became an accomplished horseman who took an enthusiastic part in hunting in the countryside around Rome. It might have been a blessed release from the atmospheres and tensions at home.

When only thirteen, Charles joined his cousin, James FitzJames Stuart, on a military expedition. The son of an illegitimate son of James II and VII, James was Duke of Liria and Berwick, the sort of exotic and unlikely titles sometimes collected by well-connected exiles who had made a career in soldiering in Europe. In 1734, Charles III of Spain had moved to reconquer the kingdom of Naples and the young prince was given the nominal and more than faintly ridiculous title of General of Artillery at the siege of Gaeta, a port on the coast of Lazio, south of Rome. Watching the Spanish and French storm the city on 6 August was Charles's first exposure to war. With his honorary rank, perhaps the boy felt he glimpsed his destiny as his guns pounded the ancient walls of the city and troops poured through the rubble-strewn gaps. What he was seeing was not a fantasy but real fire, smoke, death and the din of battle. Perhaps the foundations of belief in himself were laid that day – an ability to translate fancy titles and portentous middle names from a pretension into a reality as he witnessed men die for their kings.

Three years later, Charles's father sent him on a tour of Italy and the courts of the northern duchies, statelets and principalities, and the Republic of Venice. He expected to be received as a royal prince but most of the Italian nobility, not wishing to sour relations with George II of Great Britain, addressed him by a courtesy title, the Duke of Albany. Only the Doge of Venice accorded him his rank. These rebuffs must have stung the young man. At the same time, perhaps to look the part ever more emphatically no matter what anyone called him, Charles began to spend money, much of which he borrowed, on fine clothes and also fine wine. Even at that early age, he began to drink to excess. But all of the early portraits show a very good-looking young man, confident, straight backed with brown eyes and a fresh complexion. The biscuit tin lid title of Bonnie Prince Charlie was more than a posthumous legend.

In late 1743, the Old Pretender – a title now freighted with various meanings but, in the 18th century, it meant a claimant – made Charles his Prince Regent, giving him complete authority to act in his name – a king in all but title. From that time on, the young man began actively to plot and make plans for an expedition to Britain and the restoration of the Stuarts.

The War of the Austrian Succession certainly presented an opportunity. To force the British to pull troops away from the main theatres of war in the Low Countries and Central Europe, the French agreed to mount an invasion of southern England in February 1744. An army was equipped and mustered at Dunkirk. Charles travelled to join the fleet, no doubt believing that destiny beckoned. But a spring storm scattered the ships in the Channel and eleven were lost. This disaster was followed by a British blockade that effectively closed off any future prospect of another expedition. But it seems that Prince Charles refused to be discouraged or deflected even when the French tried to force him to return to Italy by refusing to pay him an allowance. When he could no longer afford to rent a grand house in Paris, the prince moved as a guest to the country house of Anne, Duchess of Berwick, the wife of the man who had taken him along on the expedition to Gaeta and made him a teenage general.

The Young Pretender was determined that pretence should be translated into action and he became convinced that he did not need the French. To add to the emotional encouragement from the poems of Alasdair Mac Mhaighstir Alasdair, an old exiled courtier, Sir Thomas Sheridan convinced the prince that support for him in Scotland was significant and Sir Hector MacLean, chief of the clan, sent a petition that listed sympathisers and stated that at least 5,000 clansmen would flock to his standard if Charles came. It was enough to persuade him and to prompt action. He borrowed the huge sum of 180,000 French livres to pay for weapons and to fit out two ships, the *Elizabeth* and *Le du Teillay*. But almost from the moment they set sail, things began to go wrong. In an engagement with a Royal Navy ship off the southern coast of Ireland, the *Elizabeth*, carrying most of the weapons and cannon as well as company of French marines, was damaged and forced to return to France. But Charles pressed on and *Le du Teillay* sailed north to the Hebrides to drop anchor in the Wooded Bay off Eriskay.

Knowing that events of great moment were likely to unfold after the arrival of the prince, Mac Mhaighstir Alasdair began to keep a diary. It has survived in a collection of documents known as 'the Lockhart Papers' and was cryptically entitled the 'Journal and Memoirs of P----- C------ expedition into Scotland, by a highland officer in his army'. Here is an early extract of what happened after Alasdair had met the prince and they had gone on to make landfall on the mainland:

> After we had all eaten plentifully [in the house of Angus McDonald of Borradel in Arisaig] and drunk cheerfully, H.R.H. drunk the grace drink in English which most of us understood; when it came to my turn I presumed to distinguish myself by saying audibly in Erse (or highland language), 'Deochs laint-an Reogh'; H.R.H. understanding that I had drunk the King's health made me speak the words again in Erse and said he could drink the King's health likewise in that language, repeating my words; and the company mentioning my skill in the highland language, H.R.H. said I should be his master for that language, and so was made to ask the healths of the P. and D.

The Gaelic lessons seemed to have stuck for, when Alasdair Mac Mhaighstir Alasdair passed close to Prince Charles at Prestonpans moments before the clans broke into the charge across the cornfield, the poet records in his diary that the prince 'with a smile said to me in Erse, "*Gres-ort, gres-ort.*", that is, "Make haste, make haste."'

With only a handful of followers on board, *Le du Teillay* had weighed anchor and sailed the short voyage from Eriskay to the mainland and the hospitality of Borrodale House. The prince's immediate retinue was not an inspiring group. The so-called 'Seven Men of Moidart' were mostly old, ill and peripheral. The eldest son of the Duke of Atholl, William Murray, the Marquis of Tullibardine, was a genuine Highland aristocrat and the brother of Lord George Murray but he was fifty-eight and suffered badly from arthritis and gout. With Colonel John O'Sullivan, a professional soldier who had fought in the French army, were three other Irishmen – the sixty-eight-year-old Sir Thomas Sheridan, Sir John MacDonald or MacDonnell who, according to George Murray, was 'old . . . and much subject to his bottle' and the Reverend George Kelly, who appears to have been a secretary for the prince and would later draft a manifesto. Having been involved in the 1715 rising, Colonel Francis Strickland had also seen military service on the Continent in his younger days but he too was in his fifties and in declining health. Considerably younger than the others, the seventh man was Aeneas MacDonald, who acted as the prince's banker and fundraiser.

From the shores of Loch nan Uamh, Prince Charles and his retinue then eventually made their way south to Dalilea, a Clanranald house on the northern shore of Loch Shiel and the birthplace of Alasdair Mac Mhaighstir Alasdair. With the help of the poet, who had the rare gift of being able to write in Gaelic and English, a stream of letters went out to the chiefs of the western clans. Some of those whom the prince had met off Eriskay had advised him to return home to France. There was no French support and the chiefs rightly believed that that was vital for a rising to stand any chance of success. 'I am come home' was the young man's reply and he persisted with his efforts to gather support. Only twenty-five years old, Prince Charles was handsome, tall and glowing with charisma. But he knew he spoke too little Gaelic and most of his men knew no other language so, over the days at Dalilea, Alasdair Mac Mhaighstir Alasdair taught him as much as he could.

Meanwhile, in contrast to some of the chiefs, the Clanranald ladies showed faith. Using silk from their finest gowns, they sewed the royal standard, a white square on a red ground. A good, strong-voiced singer, Alasdair Mhor, as the ladies called him, composed a hymn to the prince, '*Tearlach mac Sheumais*', 'Charles, Son of James'. A final flurry of letters was dispatched to the chiefs with an ultimatum – a call to arms. An hour after noon on Thursday 19 August

1745, the royal standard would be raised at Glenfinnan, at the head of Loch Shiel, and they were summoned to come there and do their duty for their rightful king.

Early that morning, boats were cast off from the jetty at Dalilea and, with fifty clansmen from Clanranald as an escort, the prince began to make his way to the head of Loch Shiel to meet with what he hoped would be his destiny. In the prow of the leading boat sat Colonel John O'Sullivan, the prince and Alasdair Mhor. After staying the night at Glenaladale, they rowed on towards Glenfinnan.

*

It had rained so heavily overnight that the little River Slatach was roaring, foaming white as it tumbled over boulders and poured into Loch Shiel. I'd found a place to park by its banks and was reassured to see that it ran through a rocky gorge. I'd come to Glenfinnan to see, as much as was possible, what Prince Charles and his group of old courtiers saw when they sailed up the loch on the morning of 19 August 1745 and to trace what happened when they came ashore. The mountains had not moved, the shape of the shoreline was no different and perhaps I would be able to intuit what the young man raised in the sunshine of Italy would have seen on his first glimpse of the elemental grandeur of Highland Scotland, the place where his destiny and that of his dynasty would be settled, for good or ill.

A few weeks before, I'd contacted Loch Shiel Cruises and booked a passage down the loch to Acharacle and then back up to Glenfinnan, the direction the prince had travelled. But the rain was so heavy that I'd called the day before to check that the MV *Sileas* would be making the journey.

'Och, yes,' said the cheerful young woman on the phone. She was somewhat distracted – one of her spaniels had run off and she was looking for it, calling its name as she spoke to me.

'We'll be going. I won't but Jim will skipper the boat. He's a good man – knows the loch better than anyone.'

When I walked down to the pontoon quay, I was consoled by the fact that I could see the far side of the loch. When I looked down it, south-west towards Acharacle, it seemed that the mountains rose up even more massive, dark, vast, glowering, the rain-mist clinging to their tops, their flanks very steep, diving almost sheer into the water. Loch Shiel looked like a Norwegian fjord.

Moored out on the loch, someone was on board the MV *Sileas*, no doubt making all ready. That was encouraging but there was nowhere to shelter while I waited. A new building labelled The Jetty Hut was locked and I stood in its back doorway, hoping the lintel would keep off some of the rain. I found that the most efficient arrangement in this sort of relentless weather was a long-brimmed baseball cap to keep my specs dry and then the hood of my GORE-TEX coat pulled up over it to stop the rain from running down my neck. To my surprise, I was joined by an older couple, both well wrapped in waterproofs and wearing warm hats. A car appeared and another elderly man – Did that make three of us? Possibly – emerged, immediately pulling on over-trousers as well as a long waterproof coat and a broad hat. I looked at my already damp jeans and wondered.

The back end of the boat – 'Aft,' said the man in the over-trousers – was covered in a green canopy with plastic windows so streaked with rain it was impossible to see more than a blur out of them. A table in the middle was piled with books – 'To pass the time,' said the man who might have been thought of as the first mate – and a lot of blankets. Oh dear.

It was clear from the questions from the older couple that the principal attraction of the voyage down the loch was to see wildlife – sea eagles and golden eagles in particular. Not this morning, I thought. Even if they are flying, the cloud is so low that there would be little or no chance of spotting them. Up on deck, there were slatted wooden boards where hopeful birders might sit patiently looking up at the sky with their binoculars and cameras at the ready.

Jim, the skipper, managed some introductory commentary after we cast off and began to chug south-west. Eighteen miles long, Loch

Shiel is the fourth longest freshwater loch in Scotland and, at 400 feet in places, very deep. 'The catchment area for rain is very wide,' said Jim, with no hint of irony, 'at 350 square miles.' It felt like it was all falling on the loch.

After several brief visits on deck, enough to soak my jeans below the knee, I retreated into the green canopy, sat on one blanket, draped another over my knees and used a third as a muff. The older couple smiled at me but I was numbed to the bone. There was no heating, of course, and a breeze flapped at the entrance to the canopy. At least it might dry my jeans, I thought. It was only 10 a.m. and the voyage had another six hours to run. Breakfast had been a couple of slices of toast and, even though I wasn't hungry, I reckoned I needed calories. Relying on a half-forgotten and mostly misunderstood classical education, I remembered that the word derived from *calor*, Latin for 'heat' – internal heat. Rummaging around in my rucksack, I found a delight – a slice of Marks & Spencer's millionaire's shortbread – and devoured it. At least it tasted good.

'The pier at Acharacle is under water,' announced the first mate. 'The level of the loch has risen by about six or seven feet in the last few days,' he went on. 'We've passengers to pick up. If I can get ashore, then maybe I could tell them to go around to Dalilea and we could possibly get them on board there.' This man had told me earlier that he was the 'wrong side of eighty'. Clearly agile, though.

I looked around the green canopy and saw a plasticised notice on how to inflate the life raft that was attached to the back of the boat – the aft, that is. There seemed to be plenty of lifebelts but, if it kept raining so hard, maybe the quay at Slatach would be underwater by the time we got back there. I found a suspiciously old, half-eaten bar of Cadbury's Fruit & Nut in one of the many pockets of my rucksack. I thought about saving it for an emergency but then ate it, sucking the rock-hard chocolate like a boiled sweet. More calories.

The rear of the green canopy was open to the elements and I sat looking at the wake of the *Sileas* and the steep mountainsides unspooling behind us as we chugged down the grey loch. The first mate pointed out a white cottage on the shore at a place called

Gaskin – 'Seven miles from any road, only reachable by boat.' It was usually occupied only in the summer. On the eastern side, at Scamodale, hidden by trees, was the only cottage on the shore with a permanent resident. 'All you can see is the smoke from his chimney,' he added. We had sailed at least three-quarters of the way down the loch before we saw the first houses near Dalilea. Jim, the skipper, pointed out the stumps of old quays just showing above the water. When a steamer service had plied up and down Loch Shiel, carrying supplies and the post, it had stopped at these little piers to deliver packages and letters, and take on passengers. Where there was nowhere for the steamer to tie up, people rowed out to it. The service ceased in 1967 as a new road was built from Acharacle up to Arisaig and gradually the cottages and houses by the loch were abandoned. All they left behind were the names they had given their places, empty names on a map.

When we finally reached Acharacle, its scatter of white houses only just visible through the rain-mist, Jim showed great skill as he manoeuvred the *Sileas* so that the first mate could moor it on the upper part of the sloping quay, where it was not under water. It turned out that the passengers waiting were going on an hour-and-a-half trip around the southern part of the loch to look at wildlife. Most of them appeared to have brought their own. There were five dogs and one of them – a terrier, of course – had to be restrained from attacking the others.

'See anything?' asked one of the embarking passengers.

'Nothing,' I said. 'Sorry.'

The first mate told me I was welcome to stay aboard or I could go ashore at Acharacle and find some lunch. I immediately shook my head. A warm fire, hot soup, a soft seat – all of these delights danced in front of my imagination as I climbed on to the slippery quay. The rain was definitely easing and, at the top of the track leading to the village, I saw a promising large house with a sign outside. It was indeed the Loch Shiel Hotel and it was indeed closed – not open until 4 p.m. The rain seemed to thicken. The word 'bleak' seemed apt. At least the village shop across the road was open. I asked another customer if there was anywhere I could get some lunch. She shook her head and so with my packet of crisps and a pork pie, I joined the queue at the till. Beside it was a small hot cabinet with a tired looking sausage roll in it. Wonderful! It was as close as I was going to get to a hot lunch if only I could find somewhere out of the rain to eat it. The shop was warm. Maybe they'd let me sit in the corner. Maybe not. Perhaps there was a bus shelter?

When I set down my purchases on the counter and just before I asked for the sausage roll, I enquired again about the remote possibility of a place being open for lunch.

'Yes,' said the lady at the checkout. 'Two minutes up the road. Turn right out of here.'

Hallelujah! Hosanna in excelsis! Deo!

I walked quickly. Perhaps it was a mistake or a mirage. Perhaps it closed soon. But no! There it was – a sign for Cafe Tioram. And, at the bottom, a Gaelic exhortation – '*Thigibh a-staigh*', 'Come on in!' Yes! Above a busy car park was a cheery-looking, blue and white wooden building. I ignored the community defibrillator attached to the wall by the entrance and tried not to rush in. Warmth, the irresistible aroma of home baking and the smiling faces of three young women waiting on the tables greeted me. There was a big table by the fire that was free and I claimed a corner, plonking down my sodden rucksack. But then I was quickly followed in by two couples with six children and so I reluctantly gave it up. Only for Christian charity to intervene as a young couple at a small table on the other side of the fire stood up and said they were leaving. I must have looked bedraggled, needy, forlorn.

Prompted by the exhortation on the sign and perhaps in a pathetic effort to ingratiate myself, I asked one of the waitresses if she had Gaelic. She did and was fluent. Hooray! When I asked, '*Co as a tha thu?*' – loosely translated as 'Where do you come from?' – her reply was even more cheering. She'd gone to the primary school in Acharacle where Gaelic was widely used – I couldn't discover if it was a Gaelic medium school or perhaps bilingual – and it turned out that at least one of the other young women who worked in the cafe was also fluent.

I told her it was '*uamhasach fuar air a' bhata*' – 'terribly cold on the boat' – and asked what she recommended from the menu. Carrot and courgette soup followed by eggs Stornoway. Why not? Both were wonderful, the soup appearing in moments, the latter turning out to be a brilliant and better version of classic eggs Benedict with Stornoway black pudding under the poached eggs instead of ham and under that a thick, home-made scone instead of the usual characterless bun. I was enormously comforted by the food and the knowledge that there was a defibrillator close at hand. It was also very warming to hear young people speaking in Gaelic naturally while running a great business. Courgette in Gaelic turns out to be *courgette*.

The sole downside was the racket coming from the family group at the large table I'd given up. The six children, even the youngest, a toddler, were fine. Most of the noise came from a show-off, look-at-me, what-a-modern-father/husband-I-am dad. His accent – no doubt acquired at one of the capital's extortionate fee-paying schools – would have been audible on the other side of the loch and his smug, self-important face was one you would never tire of slapping.

I'd agreed with the first mate that I'd be back on the Acharacle pier at 1.15 p.m. sharp for the return journey up the loch. I congratulated the sparkly young women on their business and their superb food, while they were kind enough to say that, for a learner, I had a very good *blas* – a credible Gaelic accent. When I stepped outside, the clouds were clearing, revealing the mountain tops in the north, and the sun had begun to peep out.

A party of people from Manchester, judging by their *blas*, boarded the *Sileas*. Their plan was to sail up to Glenfinnan and then catch a bus back down to Salen on Loch Sunart, where they had taken a holiday cottage. Wildlife was also their interest and one man had a camera with a huge telephoto lens attached. Talkative and with a plentiful supply of bottled beer, they were welcome, cheery shipmates.

Jim swung the *Sileas* into the bay at Dalilea, close to the large, white estate house. It had been much enlarged since 1745 when the

Clanranald ladies had cut up their silk gowns and sewed Prince Charles's red and white standard and Alasdair Mac Mhaighstir Alasdair strode around the countryside declaiming smutty 'Galick' poetry. Very different from the north-western end of the loch and its steep, fjord-like shores, Dalilea was green and fertile, its undulating fields suggesting good natural drainage, and, in many places, there grew stands of sheltering oak and larch, with birch flourishing down by the edges of the loch. Close enough to the sea, the estate probably benefitted from the warmth of the Gulf Stream and the coastal microclimates it creates.

Up ahead were more memories of the life and times of Alasdair Mac Mhaighstir Alasdair. Eilean Fhionnain or Fhianain, also known as the Green Isle, rose up out of the middle of the loch and Jim slowed his engine and let the *Sileas* get closer. Some time in the 7th century an Irish holy man, later canonised as St Finan, came to the islet to found a *diseart*. Like Columba and others, he had been much influenced by the exemplary lives of a group of early Christian ascetics known as the Desert Fathers. So that they might commune more closely with God and practise mortifications of the flesh such as fasting, as well as prayer and contemplation, they retreated from the cities of the Roman Empire in Egypt, Palestine and Syria. Many founded lonely hermitages in caves in the desert but their pious solitude was often disturbed by other Christians who admired them or wished to join them. It was in the desert that the practices and traditions of monasticism were founded.

Western European ascetics replaced the sands of the desert with the waves of the sea and, on islands such as Iona, Lismore and Eileach an Naoimh, at the mouth of the Firth of Lorne, the first monasteries were founded in Scotland. When St Finan came to the little island in Loch Shiel, he saw what he had been looking for – a place cut off from the secular world, a place that might become holy ground, sanctified by the prayer and sacrifice of generations of monks, men who had given their lives to God.

As Jim slowed the *Sileas* and edged closer to the rocky shore of Eilean Fhionnan, I could see thickets of stone crosses and headstones on the higher ground of the islet. Also just visible were the rubble-built walls of a small chapel. Alasdair Mac Mhaighstir Alasdair's father had care of the islet in the early 18th century and burials, if not services, continued beyond that time. Clanranald chiefs claimed the right of interment on Eilean Fhionnan, and for a very particular reason. Some of these men were ruthless, particularly in the 15th century. Allan MacRuari, the 4th chief of Clanranald, was feared as 'the dread and terror of all neighbouring clans'. He was buried on the islet along with many of his ancestors and descendants. This right of interment mattered very much because it was widely believed that holy ground such as Eilean Fhionnan had the divine power to cleanse bodies of their sins. As the corpses of ruthless chiefs who had lived by the sword and committed many carnal acts rotted in the earth that had been walked by saints and sanctified by generations of prayer, their mortal sins fell away with the flesh off their bones.

As Jim steered the *Sileas* around the little island, he pointed out a pungent historical detail. A smooth shelf of moss-covered, grey stone jutted a little into the loch and he told me that it was known locally as the Priest's Rock. After the Reformation of 1560 in Scotland, Catholicism persisted for a long time amongst the clans even though formal worship was banned. Clanranald chiefs and their clansmen and families cleaved to the old religion and a priest used to come to Eilean Fhionnan to say mass from the little shelf of rock on the holy island. After he raised the host, he blessed his congregation, all of whom knelt in their boats, moored around the rock, bobbing with the gentle swell of the waves on the loch. It is an elegiac image and no doubt one that will have prompted biblical analogy with the New Testament stories of the Sea of Galilee and the disciples as fishers of men.

It seemed as though the sun was following us up the loch. It lit beautiful Dalilea, the big white house glowing luminous and the water below its pier glinting. Beyond Eilean Fhionnan, the butter-coloured sunlight climbed the flanks of the high mountains to the north, revealing the subtleties of their pale greens and browns and

the seams of grey, craggy corries as it chased the rain clouds eastwards. The bleakness of the journey down the loch had entirely fled
but the stillness remained for the people had also fled.

When Prince Charles set out from Dalilea with his new silken
standard on the morning of 18 August 1745, he sailed through a
much busier landscape. The small settlements that speckled the
lochside grew what they could on the lower ground, fished in the
waters below and tended their cattle, sheep and goats on the high
summer pastures. We sailed past several places where I could see the
remains of the strip fields known as runrig and the later lazy beds
that grew potatoes. There was an old sheep fank, its rubble walls still
visible close to the shore. In the 18th century, woodland was also a
rich resource and not only for timber for building and firewood for
burning. I enjoyed a fascinating conversation with Jim, the skipper.
His knowledge of different styles of boats and their history was long
and deep, as well as practical. Clanranald, he told me, was famous
for its boat-building skills and, along the shores of Loch Shiel, ship-
wrights cut and shaped timber to make all sorts of craft. Jim is
certain that the royal party sailed up the loch in ships known as
birlinns.

Hymned by Alasdair Mac Mhaighstir Alasdair in 'The Birlinn of
Clanranald', these little ships were perfectly designed for Highland
and island waters. They were driven both by sail and oars. Derived
from the Viking longships but equipped with a hinged rudder
attached to the sternpost rather than a long steering oar on the star-
board or steerboard side, they were very agile. In Loch Shiel and in
long stretches of coastal waters, rocky reefs can be very dangerous,
especially close to shore. Steersmen could turn and manoeuvre these
small ships, as they are known in Gaelic, into bays and anchorages
where larger boats feared to follow them. And, for that reason, the
fleets of clan birlinns and those of the Lord of the Isles were, for
centuries, successful fighting ships, especially in their home waters.

Jim and I discussed how many birlinns may have sailed up the
loch with the prince and agreed on two, perhaps three, no more. In
addition to his small retinue, the so-called Seven Men of Moidart,

Alasdair Mac Mhaighstir Alasdair and some others, Charles was escorted by fifty Clanranald men from Dalilea and more might have been taken on at Glenaladale, further up the loch.

'On a day like this,' said Jim, 'with a following breeze, they'd have unfurled their sails, seen them billow out and moved quickly over the top of the water.'

Shafts of sunlight sent streaks of yellow up the grey mountain-sides and brought their muted colours alive. If 18 August 1745 was as good a day, how could the young, twenty-four-year-old prince not have felt his spirits lifted by the elemental beauties, the glories of the kingdom he claimed for his father? It is likely that the communities on both shores of the loch watched history sail past as the prince's birlinns ploughed on towards Glenfinnan, towards rebellion, what they would call a rising, the restoration of the rightful king and also the dissolution of the much disliked union with England. Perhaps some will have rowed out in their curraghs, the light hide boats commonly used for fishing and transport in 18th-century Highland Scotland and long before. Jim told me he'd sailed a curragh in southern Ireland and we discovered we had a friend in common, the curragh builder from Cork, Padraig O'Duinnin.

Like the little hide boats, the birlinns will have glided soundlessly up the loch, and unlike the loud chug of the *Sileas*'s engine, the only noise was the snap and billow of their sails or the creak of the oars as they were pulled against the rowlocks. In the late afternoon, the little flotilla weighed anchor in the shallow bay at the mouth of Glenaladale, the territory of Alexander MacDonald. At his house, the prince and his people spent the night. Glenaladale is a classic U-shaped valley and, when we sailed closer to its wooded shore, I could see the long, white foaming fingers of cascades tumbling down through the rocks and crags of Croit Bheinn, the Humped Mountain, at the head of the glen.

Jim reckoned it was about an hour from Glenaladale to the quay at Slatach and Glenfinnan beyond it. It may be that the prince hoped more men would join him, having gathered at Glenaladale, but it seems they did not. On the following morning, the muster having been called for an hour after noon, the flotilla cast off and made their way north.

Ahead of us was a small sandy inlet. Known as the Prince's Bay, it hardly seemed to merit the name, being only a few yards long, but it was an example of history naming geography. Tradition holds that Prince Charles ordered his flotilla to pause there. Around Eilean Dubh, the promontory beyond the little beach, those in the prows of the birlinns would be able to see Glenfinnan, see how many clans had come to the muster, make out their banners fluttering in the breeze. It may be that before the little ships rounded the promontory, the prince wished to compose himself.

Royal dignity mattered at that moment for, when Glenfinnan at last came into view, all anyone could see was disappointment. Probably using a telescope, the prince's adjutant, Colonel John O'Sullivan, could make out only fifty or so men waiting by the shore. Only fifty. There was no army, scarcely even an escort. Ignominy loomed, an immediate return to France, the death of hope, the consignment of the Stuart dynasty to history, to permanent, bitter exile.

When the birlinns moored at Slatach, some way south of the mouth of the glen, where the waters of the loch are deeper, the prince at last came ashore. It was said that O'Sullivan and others took him immediately to a nearby barn so that his men would not see him weep. A short time later, lookouts reported men approaching on the western trail, from Arisaig. Allan MacDonald of Morar had come, marching at the head of 150 men. He was made most welcome but the muster had brought only a few more than 200, still no more than an escort and very far from an army that could challenge the might of the British state.

Around the middle of the afternoon, from somewhere to the north, came the music that changed everything. Just audible, floating clear above the trees at Glenfinnan, the sound of the war pipes turned every head. It seemed to be coming from the top of the narrow valley, from the flanks of Sgurr Thuilm. The men waiting by the loch recognised the music. '*Taing gu Dia*!' – 'Thanks be to the Lord!' Clan Cameron had come.

Men strained to see, counting when they could make out more clearly the lines of clansmen snaking in single file down tracks on the mountainside. Perhaps 600, maybe 700, maybe more! At last, an army was mustering and one of the prince's courtiers, Sir John MacDonald remembering the immense relief, wrote, 'Never have I seen anything so quaintly [meaning piquantly] pleasing as the march of this group of Highlanders as they descended a steep mountain by a zigzag path.'

They were led by their chief, Sir Donald Cameron of Lochiel, who had, at first, been reluctant to rise in rebellion, advising the prince to return to France. He had apparently then changed his mind when given certain guarantees. There were 700 Camerons, men who were counted amongst the bravest of all the clans. It was a beginning, a good beginning.

More men came – 200 led by Jeanie Cameron of Glendessary and behind them trotted a herd of cattle, almost as welcome. An observer left a memorable description of the arrival of this remarkable woman. She rode 'a bay gelding with green furniture [harness] trimmed with gold, her hair tied behind in loose buckles, with a velvet cap and a scarlet feather, carrying a naked sword in her hand'.

Jeanie Cameron not only had a sense of the formal drama of the occasion but also the courage to come in place of her nephew, who was unwell. At about 6 p.m., 350 MacDonalds of Keppoch came from the east with surprising company in tow. At High Bridge, not far from Spean Bridge, Donald MacDonnell of Tiendrich and his men had ambushed and captured two companies of the Royal Scots. Amongst them was a Captain Swettenham. He turned out to be invaluable to the Jacobite cause. After extracting the chivalrous promise that he would desist from fighting against the prince's forces for a year and a day, he was allowed to go free and, crucially, to tell others what he had seen at Glenfinnan. Here is what Colonel O'Sullivan remembered:

This officer behaved very gallantly, he frightened the governors of those garrisons he passed by, and even [General John] Cope. For he told them all that the Prince had 6,000 men, and that neither arms nor money was wanting to them: he gave everywhere the most favourable account that could be given of the Prince's activity and person. It is said the Elector [George II] sent for him when he arrived in London, and asked him what kind of a man the Prince was, [and] he answered that he was as fine a figure, as clever a Prince as a man could set eyes on, upon which George turned his back and left him there.

Clearly the wrong answer. But, in an age without rapid or mass communication, witnesses like Swettenham were avidly listened to and widely believed. Almost before it had begun in earnest, the 1745 Rebellion had already acquired an air of glamour.

Early in the evening of 19 August, a piece of necessary theatre was acted out. On high ground at Glenfinnan, where every clansman could see and hear what was happening, somewhere above the marshy area at the head of the loch, the royal standard was unfurled by the Marquis of Tullibardine. Stripped of the dukedom of Perth for supporting the Jacobite cause in 1715 and 1719, William Murray was fifty-eight years old but contemporaries thought he looked much older. Suffering badly from gout and arthritis, he needed the help of two men to hold up the flagpole as the breeze tugged at the red and white silk banner made by the ladies at Dalilea. Despite that display of obvious weakness, Tullibardine's central role and symbolic act were important. Many of his former tenants in Atholl still regarded him as the legitimate duke and the prince hoped that they would follow his lead and rise with him in rebellion. Tullibardine then read a declaration, dated 23 December 1743, in Rome. It proclaimed Prince Charles's father as James VIII, King of Scotland and James III, King of England and Ireland. There was also a commission from James VIII appointing his son as Prince Regent and finally a declaration of intent from the prince himself.

Almost all the clansmen listening would have understood little of what was said, their native tongue being Gaelic. It seems highly likely that Alasdair Mac Mhaighstir Alasdair translated Tullibardine's words and then brought proceedings to a close by singing his composition, '*Tearlach mac Sheumais*'. And then the Highlanders were exhorted to cheer, throw their blue bonnets in the air and, surely in Gaelic, shout, 'Long live King James the Eighth and Charles, Prince of Wales. Prosperity to Scotland and No Union.' Barrels of brandy were breached and each man given a tot to toast the prince. Many had come to the muster without much in the way of provisions and cheese, milk and perhaps oatcakes were also distributed. As parties of clansmen began to make bivouacs for the night, there must have been a buzz, an excitement, a keen sense of anticipation. They knew they were making history and so did Alasdair Mac Mhaighstir Alasdair. He wrote:

The reckless, active, splendid Gaels
Will rise with silken banners,
In hundreds they'll encircle him,
Keen to prepare for action.

*

Glenfinnan looks and sounds very different now. The road from the quay at Slatach is lined with mature hardwood trees and new houses encroach on little fields by the loch side that would have once been cultivated. Tourism is now far and away the biggest industry in the Highlands and it has encouraged the building of holiday homes and I noticed two pods – one labelled ash, the other oak. They seemed odd, like rigid wooden tents, and they looked like something from a film set – homes for hobbits rather than human beings.

The peace broken only by Alasdair Mac Mhaighstir Alasdair as his anthem rang out on the clear air of the glen and the cheering that followed is now gone as trucks and buses rumble day and night through Glenfinnan. The A830 takes them and a regular stream of cars to the sea at Arisaig and on up to the Skye ferry at Mallaig. I had to remember my Green Cross Code when crossing the main road.

Beyond it is a vast car park and beyond that, the reason for it. In the enormously popular *Harry Potter* films, the trains that travel to the wizard school at Hogwarts run across the Glenfinnan viaduct. Beautifully curved, it arcs around the head of the valley, offering stunning vistas of the loch and its steep mountainsides before the track plunges into the western woods. One of the car park attendants who patrol constantly, making sure everyone pays their £3.50, told me that many more people walk up to the viaduct than go down to the monument on the loch shore that commemorates the muster. In the National Trust for Scotland shop next to the car park, there is a 'Platform Nine and Three-Quarters' section of *Harry Potter* merchandise. It's the first thing visitors see when they enter the shop.

I did not go to the viaduct or down to the shore but instead climbed a steep path to a viewpoint. It was magnificent looking down the sunlit loch, the pencil-like monument in the centre of what seemed like a very painterly composition framed by the mountains and with a vanishing point where the sky met the blue water far in the distance. I pulled a plastic bag out of my rucksack so that I could sit down on a damp bench. In perhaps half an hour, more than thirty people came up, stayed for a minute or two, took photos of the view with their mobile phones and then immediately left. There was a sense not so much of looking at a beautiful, unique, atmospheric place but of somehow collecting it, ticking a box.

From the high vantage point, I wanted to try to make sense of how the geography shaped the history, the defining events of 19 August 1745. Men had come to the muster from all directions – the prince and his Clanranald escort up the loch, Allan MacDonald of Morar from the west, Clan Cameron had descended from the mountains behind me and the Keppoch men with their captives marched from the east. What was the focal point, the place where the standard was unfurled and raised by Tullibardine and his two supporters, the point from which history began to unfold?

Despite the claims carved into the tomb-like stones set into its surrounding wall, the ceremony cannot have taken place down at the monument. The ground is flat and boggy. When I walked around the perimeter, I saw that the rain-swollen waters of the loch lapped at the foot of the wall. It had to be somewhere higher up, a place where all could see and hear, perhaps the viewpoint where I was sitting? But I'd come across another story that suggested a more likely place. Behind the church at Glenfinnan, on high ground, there were said to be inscribed stones that marked the exact location. A helpful young woman working at the National Trust centre had told me that they were 'behind people's houses' and hard to find. And visitors were not encouraged to look.

The A830 runs uphill, close to the church, and I could see three houses on the other side of the road and a thickly wooded hill behind them. A very pleasant man who ran a coffee wagon in the lay-by told me that the stones lay behind the house on the right, 'the blue one'. No one answered the doorbell and there was no one at home in the other two houses either. The hill behind them looked difficult, inaccessible, with a boggy area at the bottom on one side and a dense barricade of rhododendrons on the other. I couldn't see an obvious path.

The bog was definitely not an option and so I plunged into the damp jungle of the rhodies and managed to zigzag my way up to the top of the hill. It was thickly covered in tall ferns but off to my left I spotted a forlorn-looking, rotting old bench, and then as I thrashed through the ferns towards it, I suddenly came to an open area, a rocky outcrop. Scuffing away the leaves with my boot, I was able to make out *Caroli*, the genitive case of the proper name, *Carolus*, the Latin version of Charles.

Kneeling down, something of a business these days, I brushed off all the fallen leaves and other debris to find an inscription in large, rather crudely carved, capital letters:

MDCCXLV
IN NOMINE DOMINI
HIC VEXILLA TANDEM TRIUMPHANS [? – the last few
  letters were hard to make out]
CAROLI EDUARDI STUART ERECTA

Next to the letters were what might have been footprints carved from the rock, perhaps those of the Marquis of Tullibardine and possibly Bishop Hugh MacDonald, the Vicar Apostolic of the Highlands, who was said to have blessed the standards. It appears that there was more than one and it may be that the clans brought their own banners up the hill. I had imagined that the inscription had been chiselled on a stone tablet or upright memorial of some kind, like those that surrounded the monument, and not into the living rock. That somehow made it more powerful and persuaded me that it might have been done either at the time of the muster or soon after. Here is a rough translation:

1745
IN THE NAME OF THE LORD
HERE WERE THE STANDARDS
OF CHARLES EDWARD RAISED
TRIUMPHANT AT LAST

Some classical scholarship may have been at work here. Lewis & Short, the best single-volume Latin dictionary, notes that a *vexillum* was a military flag that was always red and hoisted on a general's tent as a signal for battle. A student at both Edinburgh and Glàsgow universities, it may be that Alasdair Mac Mhaighstir Alasdair had advised the Clanranald ladies that red silk would be appropriate.

Even though the larches and other pines around the summit of this rocky hill screened some of the prospect, it was certainly possible to judge how prominent it was in 1745, especially if there were many fewer trees at that time. The ceremony could have been seen clearly by clansmen gathered at its foot, near where the church is now. The sole reservation that occurred to me was the Marquis of Tullibardine. I'd found the climb up the steep hill difficult enough and I don't suffer from gout, at least not yet. Perhaps the Clanranald men sat him on a pony and led it up.

Even though the claims made by the inscriptions on the wall around the monument by the shore are clearly the stuff of wishful thinking, there are two poignant details that point to authenticity of a different sort. On top of the tall column stands a statue of a kilted Highland soldier. He wears a long feather in his bonnet and perhaps he is meant to represent a chief, for they often wore an eagle feather. With one hand, the figure clutches a basket-hilted sword and in the other is what looks like a rolled-up scroll, perhaps the formal declarations made when the standard was raised. Almost all of the guidebooks are certain that the sculpture is generic, not a representation of Prince Charles. But I'm not so sure. Who else would be carrying the declarations and proclamations from his father than the prince? And why not crown the column with the most important man at Glenfinnan on that day? It seems perverse to do otherwise.

There is one more reason to believe that the prince stands on top of the monument. He does not look out over the noble prospect of the loch and its steep-sided mountains. Instead his body is half-turned in the opposite direction and his eyes are fixed on the head of Glenfinnan. It seems to me that the sculptor has commemorated a freeze-frame, a moment in history, when Prince Charles turned because he heard the war pipes of the Camerons and saw the clansmen coming down the mountainside. It was the turning moment of the great enterprise, when everything suddenly seemed possible. If Clan Cameron had not come, the standard would not have been raised and there would have been no rebellion.

2

The Stockade and the Scaffold

Lewis, Edinburgh, 3 April 1613

There is nothing now to be seen, no trace of a remarkable, defining series of events in the history of the Highland clans. In the decades either side of 1600, these events took place on the Isle of Lewis and in Stornoway and what happened cemented attitudes, creating an even wider cultural divide between northern, western Gaelic-speaking Scotland and the Scots of the lowland south and east.

By far the largest town in the Western Isles, Stornoway surrounds the reason for its existence. The placename derives from the Norse *Stjornavagr*, 'the steering bay', meaning a good, wide but sheltered harbour. When I first came to Lewis thirty years ago, it was raining and the wind blowing off the sea was buffeting the taxi from the airport. I remember my hotel as a modern building on the northern edge of the town that looked less like a warm, welcoming, blazing-fire, dram-in-your-hand, Highland lodge sort of a place and more like an office block.

Bleak was the adjective that came to mind as I drove around the island. I was working in television at the time and, for reasons no one could quite fathom, the Conservative government of Margaret Thatcher had given £8m for the production of programmes in Gaelic. This surprising provision formed part of the Broadcasting Act of 1990 that was designed to introduce a new regulatory system for ITV. Some of this output was to be broadcast in peak time and, since I was Director of Programmes at Scottish Television, I thought I should try to understand something of Gaelic culture, of the Highlands and Islands.

According to everything I'd read and been advised, Lewis and the Western Isles were the heartland of the language – what seemed like the last redoubt after centuries of retreat. I had proposed that we produce a soap opera in Gaelic and locate it on Lewis. This presented great difficulties of all kinds, both creative and logistical, and so I thought I should go and see for myself.

Stornoway seemed unremarkable then and, for reasons I couldn't quite put my finger on, it felt like a temporary sort of place, somewhere hanging on the edge, peripheral, a frontier town whose Wild West was not plains and mountains but the wastes of the Atlantic Ocean. Beyond the office block hotel and a straggle of villages and townships, the middle of the island of Lewis seemed like a vast, featureless brown bog studded with lochans. On the road across the Barvas Moor to the Atlantic shore and its string of small settlements and crofts on the edge of the ocean, I don't think I saw a single house or farm and not many other vehicles. Unrelieved bleakness.

But slowly during that first visit, I found my attitude changing, the mood lifting. As we made contacts and I met more and more people, first impressions, usually so adhesive, began to shift. Perched on what seemed to me to be the edge of the world, between the Atlantic breakers and the moor, the people I met on the west side of the island had warmth and some optimism about what we were trying to achieve. Some had left the island to go to university in Aberdeen or Glasgow but had decided to return home to see if they could live a life in Gaelic, carry on the crofting traditions of their families and patch together a living. I admired that. Especially when the wind drove the never-ending rain horizontally across the moor.

It also quickly became clear that I had to learn the language, to have at least some Gaelic to help me find a way into what appeared to me, a Lowland Scot raised speaking Border Scots, to be a very different set of sensibilities. Back in Glasgow, I did a six-week immersion course and had weekly lessons thereafter. I managed a B grade in my Higher Gaelic for Learners. It would have been an A but I made a mess of the listening comprehension test – my excuse was that the old lady who read out the passage was from Mull and I'd never heard that accent and while she was reading the passage an oil lorry drove into the playground to fill the tank and I couldn't hear much of it. OK? And I began to be able to make short speeches in the language as a matter of courtesy when I was in the islands, which was often at the beginning of this enterprise. Some were kind enough, like the young women in Acharacle, to say that I had a good *blas*, a good accent. But more than that, I could see how Gaelic would help me better understand *Alba,* all of Scotland, all of my native land.

Even though I left my job in television more than twenty years ago, I've never lost my love for the Highlands and Islands and never quite lost all my Gaelic, although it is now in a poor state. 'Use it or lose it' is the well-worn mantra, and living in the Scottish Borders, as far away in Scotland from the Western Isles as it is possible to be, I speak and listen to the language all too rarely. But the rhythms and rhymes of music can sometimes bring it back. Many years ago, when I began to think seriously about how we might approach putting more Gaelic TV programmes on the screen and persuade English-speakers not to switch off, I quickly realised that the music and songs of the Highlands and Islands might make a cultural bridge. I didn't want to return to the kitsch and the cringe of *The White Heather Club* and all that tartan-clad, accordion-accompanied fakery. We needed something of the moment, something new and authentic.

By accident, I came across an album called *The Cutter and the Clan* recorded by Runrig, a band whose principals were three Gaelic speakers from Skye. Most of the songs were in English but all of them seemed to me to be stories, a series of impressionistic images that struck me as springing out of real experience, out of the Highland landscape and way of life. 'The Cutter', one of the featured tracks, was about an emigrant from Lewis who had done well in Canada and sent gifts of items like a fridge or a television to his widowed mother in her croft house. She told her son that she didn't really want all of this newfangled stuff and it would be much better if he could spend his money on a plane ticket to come home every spring to cut peats for his old mother.

But it was the songs in the Gaelic language that appeared to me to have heft, real power, even more authenticity. I produced an hour-long film based on a Runrig concert in Glasgow and it was broadcast in peak time on Scottish Television in 1990. We were astonished to discover the following morning that a million people had watched it. It was a turning moment, the first time Gaelic music and culture had enjoyed mass exposure and, with the raft of popular TV shows that followed, it helped to move the language from the periphery and make it, if not mainstream, then an accepted part of Scotland's sense of itself.

When I caught the plane to Lewis at Glasgow Airport, I realised it had been twenty years since I'd made the journey north to the islands. The older I get, the more I find myself remembering snatches of music, finding it replaying in a loop in my head, what are known as earworms or sticky music. It wasn't Runrig I was listening to when I fastened my seatbelt, but the crystal voice of Karen Matheson singing *'Canan nan Gaidheal'*, 'The Language of the Gaels', by Murdo Macfarlane from Lewis. Its chorus, endlessly repeating as we took off and flew high over the mountains and sea lochs, seemed appropriate.

> *Thig thugainn, thig co' ruim gu siar,*
> *Gus an cluinn sinn an canan nan Gaidheal.*

> Come to us, come along with me to the west,
> Until we hear the language of the Gaels.

When I arrived in Stornoway, I found the town much changed. Walking along the harbour road at South Beach, past the splendid new An Lanntair arts centre, I felt the place was no longer peripheral, more a centre. Television had helped make that happen and the Gaelic language channel, BBC Alba, is based in Stornoway as well as production companies and much else. I was glad and proud to have been part of the stimulus that had made that happen and brought jobs, self-confidence and prospects to the town.

But I had come back to Lewis to look for the past rather than to the future.

*

In the early winter of 1599, a small army invaded the island. Having cast off from St Andrews and the Forth ports, a flotilla sailed through the Pentland Firth, rounded Cape Wrath and dropped anchor in the steering bay at Stornoway. Six hundred soldiers and many civilians disembarked and immediately set about defending themselves from the natives. They hurriedly dug a perimeter ditch on the foreshore at South Beach and, on the upcast piled up inside it, they rammed in hundreds of posts and tied them together to make a stockade. Perched on a rocky outcrop in the harbour, Stornoway Castle was seized and secured by one of the leaders of the invading army, James Learmonth of Balcomie, a laird from Fife.

Two years before, the Macleod clan chiefs of Lewis and part of Skye had been served with legal documents that asserted the Crown's ownership of the island and their other lands. In a process that had been applied all over the Highlands and Islands, the clan chiefs had been required to prove that they had legal title to their estates; documentary evidence. Most of course had nothing but their ancestry and their hereditary rights – traditions that were nowhere written down. After a great deal of rummaging around and some outright forgery, many were able to prove ownership of land that had belonged to their families for centuries. However, the Macleods of Lewis failed to produce anything and so their possessions became automatically forfeit to the Crown, exactly the outcome that James VI of Scotland wanted.

His attitude to the clans bordered on the genocidal. In 1598, ignoring centuries of tradition, generations of Macleod chiefs and their hereditary rights, the king granted the island to a consortium of Fife lairds known as The Gentlemen Adventurers for the Conquest of the Isle of Lewis. The details of their commission were far from gentlemanly. If necessary, the king allowed them to use 'slaughter, mutilation, fyre-raising or utheris inconvenientes' to subdue the natives and bring civilisation to the wilds of the west. Even though the people of Clan Macleod and the other inhabitants of Lewis were his subjects, the king saw them as illiterate, ungovernable barbarians who spoke an incomprehensible babble of a language. It was said that James VI had to be dissuaded from a much more radical plan – the extermination of the entire native population.

South Beach is now of course all built up – the site of the stockade and what was called a 'pretty little towne' completely obliterated. But I thought I might be able to locate it more precisely if I could find any trace of the castle on the rocky outcrop in the harbour. Photographs from the 19th century exist of what looked like the gable end of a square or rectangular tower on a long reef that rose up out of the bay not far from the shore. A survey of 1846 showed two rectangular fragments of buildings on different outcrops but, after decades of stone robbing, the remains were greatly reduced. In 1882, Sir James Matheson, a wealthy businessman who made his fortune in the opium trade, bought the island of Lewis, had the old castle summarily swept away and a wide, modern pier built over it.

From the harbour wall to the east of the Matheson pier, I could see nothing below it, no sign of an outcrop in the shadowy, dark water. All trace of the invasion of 1598–99, an extraordinary and defining incident in the history of the clans, seemed to have disappeared. Only the attitudes endured, a series of related, unattractive mindsets that informed how much of the rest of Scotland saw the peoples of the Highlands and Islands. And these attitudes were not confined to Scotland.

Sir Walter Raleigh is perhaps most famous for an extravagant episode of sucking up to Queen Elizabeth I when he is said to have laid his cloak over a puddle she was in danger of walking into. His sycophancy paid handsome dividends. The queen knighted Raleigh and granted him a royal patent to explore Virginia, what would become the first English colony in North America. A native of Devon, he formed a company known as The West Country Men that included Francis Drake and Richard Grenville. Wisely, Raleigh did not join the expedition of 1585 that founded a colony at Roanoke

Island in Virginia, now North Carolina. On arrival, the colonists immediately built a stockade to protect themselves from the Native Americans, just as the Gentlemen Adventurers did at Stornoway. Upon receiving reports, Raleigh compared them to 'the Wild Irish'. The colony at Roanoke ultimately failed but successive expeditions did establish a more permanent defended settlement which they named Jamestown after James VI, who was by that time also James I of England and Ireland.

Profit and exploitation motivated Walter Raleigh and many others. He finally did risk crossing the Atlantic in search of a great prize, the fabled city of Eldorado. It turned out that the Gentlemen Adventurers of Fife were also in pursuit of a myth. In order to attract colonists to Lewis, a prospectus had been published that spoke of fertile fields and abundant fisheries. While the latter claim had some substance, the former was clearly false and as they looked out over the apparently featureless brown bog beyond the settlement, the soldiers and settlers who built the stockade at Stornoway were desperately disappointed not to find broad acres of prime farmland there for the taking. Instead they encountered immediate hostility. And a very different culture.

Old Rory's marital problems were the cause of many of the difficulties that beset the island of Lewis in the second half of the 16th century and they led directly to the arrival of the colonial army in 1598. Chief of Clan Macleod, Ruaridh Macleoid may have lived into his nineties, an immense age for the times, almost the span of the century, but it seems that in all that long time he never ceased to be the cause of disastrous difficulties for himself, his family, his people and his island.

Rory's uncle Torcuil had managed to annoy James IV of Scotland sufficiently to get himself deposed as chief of Clan Macleod in 1506. But his brother, Rory's father, Malcolm, had then persuaded the king to return the island and the territory at Trotternish on Skye to the Macleods in 1511. Presumably he made the usual promise of better, more loyal behaviour. The genealogy and the chronology can be complex and confusing, with illegitimate sons suddenly staking claims and other relatives making fleeting appearances, but the twists and turns in the story of the Macleods of Lewis are important because they were not unique in the Highlands and Islands and they informed the attitudes and actions of Lowlanders.

Rory's story began as it went on. When his father, Malcolm, died, his son was too young to take over his inheritance. Instead, Torcuil's son, John, seized Rory's inheritance, probably sometime after 1520 – or perhaps 1530. Reliable records are scant in this long, drawn-out sequence of events, perhaps not surprisingly in a non-literate society. History and genealogy were very important in Gaelic-speaking Scotland but instead of being committed to paper, they were remembered and recited.

The story quickly became more complicated and confused. John Macleod, son of Torcuil and cousin of Rory, had allied himself to Donald Gorm – meaning 'blue', probably blue-eyed – chief of the MacDonalds of Sleat in Skye. He had married John's daughter and sole heir, Mairi. But something important happened, recorded in no source that has survived, and Rory, still claiming his inheritance of the island of Lewis, reached an agreement with Donald Gorm. In return for keeping the territory of Trotternish, the most northerly peninsula of Skye, and for receiving military aid in fighting off the Macleod chief of Harris, Rory would become the sole inheritor of Lewis. He would finally inherit the chiefdom of the Macleods.

Behind this unlikely alliance swirled dreams of olden glory. Donald Gorm MacDonald was the male heir to the Lordship of the Isles, the grandson of John of Islay, the last to hold the ancient title, and who had been deposed after 1483. With Rory Macleod's help, Donald began to campaign against those clans who opposed him. But when he attacked Eilean Donan Castle in 1539, allegedly defended by only two men, he was fatally felled by an arrow. A year later, James V's fleet dropped anchor at Stornoway and Rory Macleod was forced to submit. But having given assurances, he was pardoned rather than suffering the horrific death of a convicted traitor. The attempt to revive the ancient lordship should have fizzled out on the foreshore at South Beach.

Instead, Rory continued to ignore the king and his government until, in 1554, a Letter of Fire and Sword was granted to the Mackenzies of Kintail on the mainland. This commission allowed them to hunt down and kill 'Roderick of the Lewes' and his clan, as well as take their property and their land. The letter specifically allowed the Mackenzies 'to administer justice upon them and execute them to the death; and if need be, to raise fire and sword to burn their houses and slay them in case they make opposition or resistance in the taking and apprehending'.

These sweeping, draconian powers were in fact an admission of weakness. The effective reach of central government in the far north and west was very limited and sporadic and so power was delegated to loyal clans who could act quickly and decisively. There was, of course, a great deal of abuse and the immunities granted by letters of fire and sword became a legal means of carrying on private feuds, settling old scores and annexing the territories of rival clans.

The letters of 1554 also sanctioned the killing of John of Moidart, Chief of Clanranald, and Donald Macdonald of Sleat, the son of Donald Gorm. Their possessions were part of the old heart of the Lordship of the Isles and, much later, Clanranald would be the first to support Prince Charles in 1745.

Behind the scenes even more instability was beginning to bubble up. Old Rory had married Siobhan, a daughter of Iain Mackenzie of Kintail. They had a son, Torcuil Connonach, so named because he lived as a foster son with the Mackenzies of Strathconon in Easter Ross – fosterage was a traditional means of making and sustaining alliances – except in this case. But was he really Old Rory's son? Adultery was alleged between Siobhan and Hutcheon Morison, a lord who held land in the north of the island. Morison was also a hereditary judge and, as such, known by the title 'the Brieve of Lewis'. Behind the walls of Dun Eistean, a spectacular fortress built on a sea stack off the north-east coast of Lewis, they were difficult to dislodge and the Morisons governed a significant part of Lewis without much interference from the Macleod chiefs.

Believing Torcuil to be no son of his, Rory disowned him. No doubt all the while the chief himself had been committing adultery – several illegitimate sons surface later in the tale. In any case, Siobhan seems to have had a mind of her own and been a restless soul for she abandoned Hutcheon Morison, fled from Dun Eistean and eloped with John of Raasay. This spasm of domestic drama allowed Old Rory to formally divorce Siobhan.

His second wife was Barbara Stewart, a widow from Orkney and perhaps a safer bet. She was the daughter of Andrew Stewart, Lord Avondale, a distant relative of the king. A son was born, some time after 1541, and to cloud the foggy picture even further, he was also christened Torcuil. For the avoidance of doubt, he was given the byname *Oighre*, 'the Heir', and it was often repeated. But that did not ensure the smooth succession Old Rory so desperately wanted. In 1566, Torcuil Oighre was drowned in the Minch as a storm blew up on the voyage between Lewis and Skye. This accident prompted the original Torcuil, Torcuil Connonach, to recruit the help of the Mackenzies in reclaiming his inheritance. Having landed at Stornoway with a powerful force at his back, he took Old Rory prisoner and shut him up in a damp and freezing dungeon in Stornoway Castle. Perhaps Torcuil hoped that old age would take its toll. The deposed chief was then in his sixties but he must have been extraordinarily resilient because he endured four years of captivity as the winter winds and storm tides whipped around the rocky reef in Stornoway harbour. The old man was released only when he at last agreed to appear before the Privy Council to renounce his claim to Lewis in favour of Torcuil.

Except he did no such thing. Over seventy by this time, Old Rory sailed back to Lewis, repudiated all he had agreed, probably truly claiming he had been coerced, and resolved to ignore central government. The picture blurs for the following four years before sharpening into focus in 1576 when the Regent Morton – James VI was only ten or eleven years old at that time – brokered an agreement between Old Rory and Torcuil that installed the latter as the lawful heir to Lewis and other territories.

But once again, the old man ignored what he had agreed and then, amazingly, he took a third wife, a sister of the Maclean chief, Lachlan Mor. And then, even more amazingly, he fathered two sons with his new wife. One can only marvel at how durable his powers were – all his powers. Inevitably, the eldest boy was named Torcuil and he was immediately declared the sole heir of the Macleod patrimony. Equally inevitably, Torcuil Connonach arrived in Lewis to contest yet another betrayal. This armed conflict flushed out no fewer than five illegitimate sons of Old Rory. Three of them, including *Niall Odhar* – probably meaning that Neil had a sallow complexion – supported the chief and two others stood with Torcuil Connonach. Once again, the old man was captured and imprisoned in Stornoway Castle. It was then attacked by a force led by Ruaridh Og, another of Rory's natural sons. Then, it seems, to everyone's surprise, peace broke out. Perhaps they were all exhausted. The old man continued to rule over Lewis until he died in 1595, almost certainly over ninety years old.

Torcuil – the third Torcuil, that is – became chief and he seemed determined to carry on the family tradition of warfare, destruction and score settling. But a year after Old Rory's death, an old enmity surfaced when Torcuil was betrayed by the son of Hutcheon Morison, the Brieve of Lewis, the former lover of Siobhan. The captive young chief and several of his henchmen were beheaded on the orders of Kenneth Mackenzie of Kintail in July 1597.

This endless, repeating pattern of feud, double-cross and unhesitating violence in pursuit of power on the part of the Macleods of Lewis was by no means unusual in the 16th century. Known in Gaelic as *Linn nan Creach*, 'the Age of the Forays', these prolonged spasms of disorder followed the final forfeiture of the Lordship of the Isles in 1493. The unity and stability of the MacDonald principality was fractured as chiefs sought to protect their own interests and more pressure was piled on an already combustible situation by the involvement of the Stuart kings and their determination to impose their authority.

Seen through southern eyes and filtered by Lowland prejudice, the Highlands and Islands were synonymous with trouble, the resort of squabbling, bloodthirsty savages. A steady trickle of atrocity stories were repeated and no doubt embellished. In 1588, there was a massacre on the island of Eigg. Probably part of a long-running feud between Lachlan Mor Maclean of Duart and the chiefs of Clanranald, it seems that many islanders who had hidden from his men in a cave were trapped there and asphyxiated by the smoke from fires laid at its mouth. Earlier the same year and presumably as part of the same feud, Lachlan Mor had no fewer than eighteen men of Clanranald killed while they were guests at the wedding party of his mother, Jonet Campbell, and his new stepfather, John MacKane, at Torloisk on the island of Mull. Big Lachlan was clearly not much taken with his mother's new husband because he imprisoned him after the wedding and had him cruelly tortured. It was rumoured that MacKane would thereafter not make much of a husband.

All that and more in only one year. Lachlan Mor Maclean was eventually captured by government forces and imprisoned. But when he escaped, no further action was taken against him.

These and many other episodes painted a lurid picture of lawlessness and blood-spattered atavism. Highlanders and Islanders, babbling their incomprehensible language, were seen as lesser beings, uncivilised, almost sub-human, with savagery all they understood and respected. These attitudes persisted at least until the Jacobite risings of the 18th century and their bitter aftermath. When the Clearances began, the clansmen and -women deserved little consideration as the glens and straths emptied and the process was seen by some in the south as a series of deliberate acts of enfeeblement. Images of savagery were then quickly obscured by the mists of romance as Walter Scott and others wove tales of derring-do, fortitude and even humour around figures like Rob Roy and episodes like the '45. Savagery became noble. And history was hidden.

*

It was a wild, roaring morning when I drove out over the Barvas Moor to the west coast. *Fiadhaich* is what Gaelic speakers call a wind like that – savage, like a rampaging animal. At home in the Borders, the gusts bend the winter trees as they wave their bare branches like flailing arms in a strong sea. But here on Lewis, the whining, whipping wind is invisible on the bleak moor. There are no trees for it to savage – only the tall tussocks of marsh grass snap this way and that.

I was driving out to Loch Roag on the Atlantic shore, a sea loch that cuts deep into the north-west coast of the island, the place where the last, desperate episode in the story of Old Rory's family took place.

I'd chosen to take the long way round, to drive down through the crofting townships and tiny villages of the west coast for old times' sake. When I first came to Lewis, I had enjoyed the welcoming company of several families, people who lived their lives in Gaelic and had chosen to stay on the island so that their children might have the same choice as they had – to remain or to leave for the mainland. As I passed Bru and Shawbost, I remembered not only an unforced conviviality but also having the good sense to ask questions and then listen closely to the answers. With their backs to the ocean, these warm and thoughtful people were quietly determined to remember and honour their past, their language and culture and make them part of the future.

Pilgrimage also brought me down that spectacular road. More than thirty years ago, in an exhibition in Edinburgh, I had seen a photograph that intrigued me. It showed a land and seascape, part of a wide, horned bay where the breakers thundered in off the ocean and washed against the dark cliffs and small sea stacks. In the foreground were the white tombstones of a graveyard and amongst them a funeral was taking place. Dalmore never fails to move me. When I first came to this place, I marvelled not only at the grandeur of the bay but also the power of belief. There are no houses, no neighbouring community – only the dead inhabit Dalmore. And it is difficult to reach, at the end of a single-track road, and there is nothing beyond it – only the ocean and the deeps of the world.

Spirits soar above the spray, swirling and spiralling on the whistling winds as their earthly bodies sleep beneath the sandy turf, buried on the edge of the world in this elemental place where the land, the sky and the ocean meet. Dalmore is not for those who seek comfort or even solace. It is where the journey across the snows of eternity begins.

There was no funeral that day. Dalmore was deserted. I sat down on one of the huge, rounded, wave-worn boulders that had long ago rumbled onto the beach, rolled in by the tides of the mighty Atlantic. I thought about how the land and the sea form the character of the people and how much those who were born here love this hard, dramatic, unyielding place and how its moods moulded them.

After the death of his half-brother, Torcuil, and the arrival of the Gentlemen Adventurers at Stornoway, Neil Macleod and his brother, Murdo, led the resistance to those who would take their native place from them. At first, they tried peaceful means. Having been trained as a lawyer, Murdo served the settlers in the stockade with papers that clearly showed that their actions were not legal. Clan Macleod had legitimate if not formal title to Lewis. Only after the leaders of the colonists ignored Murdo's arguments did he resort to force, attacking the settlement, capturing their ship and seizing their leader, James Learmonth of Balcomie. He was imprisoned for six months.

Neil Macleod appears to have commanded his own force of clansmen and he attacked the settlers, killing twenty of them and driving away their livestock. There then followed a classic outbreak of internecine feuding. Neil turned on Murdo, captured him and agreed to hand his brother over to the settlers in return for a guarantee that his own actions would be pardoned by the Edinburgh government. But the agreement failed to stick and Neil and his men killed sixty of the settlers when their plan to ambush him, take him prisoner and hand him over to the authorities was uncovered. Neil Macleod then retreated to the rocky islet of Bearasaigh off the wild Atlantic coast of Lewis.

That was my destination on that windswept morning. I knew I'd not be able to sail out to this formidable redoubt but I wanted to see where it was. As the road reached Carloway, I branched off it on a bumpy B road, parked and walked down to the shore. Having brought binoculars, I could make out the steep cliffs of the little island.

Bearasaigh was a last resort. All the time he had been resisting the settlers, Neil Macleod had sent provisions to the little island, building up reserves of salted herring, beef and other items that would keep. He had his men dig a wide depression on its flat plateau – a place where rainwater could collect. Although the defeat and expulsion of the Gentlemen Adventurers appeared to be Macleod's goal, Clan Mackenzie was moving behind the scenes, and he knew it. In the 1590s they had acquired, probably from Torcuil Connonach, what little legal paperwork there was on who had title to the island. And so it was clearly in their interests to see the colony fail. When it finally did, in 1609, and the last of the settlers left, Neil Macleod recognised that Clan Mackenzie were his deadly rivals. And they would prove to be ruthless.

The blearing wind off the ocean discouraged me from lingering at the mouth of Loch Roag. As I walked back to the shelter of my car, I tried to imagine how a warrior like Macleod would have seen it. As a man schooled in the seafaring traditions of the Hebrides, he would not have shared my instinctive view of Bearasaigh as an isolated, remote, wave-lashed rock in a hostile, seething ocean. For Neil, the sea was a highway, safe and fast. A great volume of traffic moved up and down the coasts of the islands and the mainland in the 16th century and long before, and the islet made a natural, formidable and convenient redoubt. Derived from a Norse placename, Bearasaigh means 'Precipice Isle' and its rocky ramparts made it very difficult to assault.

Sometime around 1609, perhaps after the departure of the settlers, Neil Macleod seems to have made the islet his permanent base with about forty men, apparently abandoning the mainland of Lewis to the Mackenzies. Instead, he became a pirate. Preying on passing ships, Macleod and his band made a great nuisance of themselves. But when the sails of the *Priam* were seen on the horizon, events took a dramatic turn. Peter Love, the captain of the ship, was a notorious English pirate and on board was a looted cargo of spices, hides, silver plate, a chest of gemstones and coins and many muskets. Macleod must have been impressed and, having made an agreement with Love, they set up a base, perhaps on Bearasaigh, from where they attacked, boarded and looted passing ships, even making some of their prisoners slaves.

But deceit and duplicity were never far from Neil Macleod's thoughts. He still hankered after a legitimacy of sorts, a pardon for his crimes and excesses. During a feast, his men attacked the pirates, made Peter Love their prisoner and took over the *Priam*. Saying that he himself had not been present when the Englishmen had been surprised and captured, Neil sent a message to the Privy Council in Edinburgh offering to hand them and their ship over. Perhaps he hoped that distancing himself from the deed but facilitating justice would show him in a more favourable light and secure his bona fides with the government. Love and his shipmates were sent south and all of them were hanged on Leith Sands.

Meanwhile, Ruaridh Mackenzie had arrived in Lewis. After the departure of the colonists, his clan had been granted title to the island and issued with a Letter of Fire and Sword. He was empowered to act with impunity against a 'number of thevis, murthouraris, and ane famous byke ['nest', meaning Bearasaigh] of lawless lymmaris, under the charge and commandiment of the traytour, Neil McCloyd, who hes usurpit upoun him the authoritie and possessioun of the Lewis'.

Acting in the name of his nephew, Colin, the chief of the name but too young to lead his clan, Mackenzie was known as the Tutor of Kintail. Ruthless and effective, he subdued the islanders and his name became a byword for severity on Lewis. There were said to be only two things worse than the Tutor of Kintail – *reothadh Cheituin agus ceo san uicharr*, 'a frost in spring and mist in the dog days [of high summer]'.

Ruaridh Mackenzie was determined to bring Neil Macleod and his byke of pirates to justice. When he arrived on the shores of Loch Roag, the Tutor had no intention of attacking Bearasaigh. Instead, he ordered his men to take prisoner all of the families of the men on the islet, those who had remained on the mainland. Women and children were rowed out at low tide to a small reef that was close enough for Macleod's men to see and hear them. And they were left there. As the incoming tide lapped around their feet and small children were picked up by their mothers, the cries for help were pitiful. Neil Macleod and his men quickly surrendered.

On the morning of 3 April 1613, a huge crowd had gathered at the Mercat Cross in Edinburgh. Despite the chill east wind blowing up the High Street, there was a carnival atmosphere as food and drink sellers mixed with the throng and the ale houses emptied. It was a Gala Day – a Gallows Day. When the doors of the Tolbooth opened and the prisoner was led out, a momentary hush fell as people craned to see the man who was about to die. Shivering in his linen sark, Neil Macleod had his hands tied in front of him and not behind, so that when he had climbed the ladder to the scaffold, he might pray and die 'very Christianlie'.

When at last he stood under the beam, beside a chaplain, the hangman and two soldiers, Neil Macleod fell to his knees and prayed once more. The crowd bayed as he took his time. 'Come on, *Bhodach*,' said the hangman, 'We haven't got all day!' Neil understood some English but when he heard the Gaelic word *bodach*, 'old man', he roared, '*Nam bithin air deck luinge far am bu duilich do fhear seasamh, stiuireadh na mara gu tric, cha bhodach dhuit mis' a mhacain!*' 'If I were on the deck of a ship, steering over the billows, trying to stand steady, you would not call me an old man!' Even though his hands were tied, Macleod lunged forward and head-butted the hangman, knocking him down.

The crowd gasped, erupted and jeered at the barbarian, the savage Highlander who would dance a jig on the end of the rope, the urine running down his kicking legs, his feet frantically searching for solid ground. The soldiers pinioned Neil by tying his arms, the bloodied hangman slipped the noose over his head and they began to haul the prisoner off his feet as he choked and retched and his face turned purple. No coins had been given to hangers-on to pull at his legs and make death come more quickly. The agony of strangulation might have lasted for a quarter of an hour. But when Macleod's body stilled at last and the hangman cut him down, the indignities did not cease.

The corpse was dragged over to a block and an axe raised high. The severed head of the barbarous, bloody, wicked Highland man was held up by the hair and shown to the roaring crowd before it was taken down to the Netherbow Port and rammed onto a spike. It would be a fell warning to all who passed under it and a reminder of the fate of those who treated the king's authority with contempt. Macleod's would not be the last head of an executed Highlander to be displayed as a grisly trophy.

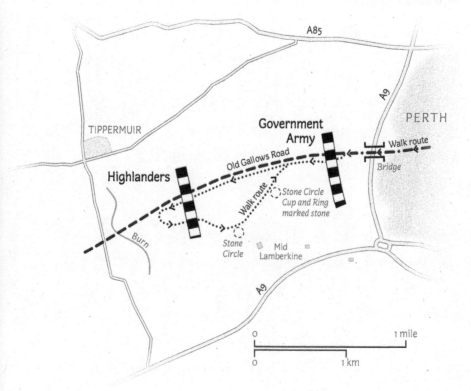

3

The Year of Great Alasdair

Tippermuir, 1 September 1644

Alasdair Mhic, o ho,
Cholla Ghasda, o ho,
As do laimh- 's gun, o ho
Earbainn tapaidh, trom eile.

Alasdair the son, o ho,
Of Gallant Colla, o ho,
Into your hand, o ho,
I would entrust heroic command, *trom eile*.

This is the opening verse of '*Alasdair Mhic Cholla Ghasda*', an ancient song made famous beyond the *Gaidhealtachd* by Capercaillie, a much loved and listened-to Scottish band from Argyll. It was included in their very successful album, *Sidewaulk*, released in 1989, and they often perform it on stage. To an insistent, almost thumping beat, the lyrics rise above on the crystal voice of Karen Matheson as she punctuates the melody with piercing, pure notes. '*Alasdair Mhic Cholla Ghasda*' is usually described as a 'waulking song', one of many sung by groups of women as they 'waulked' or thickened a bolt of homespun cloth. Often sitting along the long sides of a table, facing each other, their sleeves up, the women pounded and pummeled the cloth to felt it slightly and thereby make it denser, warmer and more waterproof. This needed to be done in a rhythm as they moved the cloth around the table – always to the left as the other direction was thought unlucky – and the beat of the music helped this process as well as making a dull and repetitive job more interesting.

It turns out that the song is also a story, a historical record made soon after the end of a remarkable year. It is also a battle song. At the end of each line are what musicologists call vocables, nonsense words like *o ho* or *hi ri*, whose role is to fill out the metre and keep the insistent beat going. At the end of the last line of each verse is *trom elie*, also thought to be a vocable. But these are not nonsense words. They mean something – something specific to the story of the Year of Great Alasdair. *Trom* can mean 'a charge' and *eile* means 'another'. And so the last two words of the last line of each verse may be seen as an incitement – 'Another charge!'

Between 1 September 1644 and 15 August 1645, the warrior general, Alasdair Mac Colla, charged at the head of a small army of Highlanders and Irishmen and defeated his enemies again and again, in no fewer than six battles. The clansmen who raced across the corn stubble at Prestonpans owed their dramatic victory not only to their commitment and courage but also to Great Alasdair. He invented the Highland charge and it had its origins in Ireland.

The first two lines of the song recite the warrior's genealogy and hint at what fired his passion and determination. First and above everything, he was a MacDonald. Born around 1610 on the little island of Colonsay, Alasdair was, as the song and his patronymic say, the son of Colla, also know as Colkitto. The latter is an anglicisation of Coll Ciotach Mac Dhomnhaill and the nickname usually translates as 'left-handed'. But the word can also mean 'crafty, devious or under-handed'. It was said that Coll became Lord of Colonsay by an act of betrayal, although the details are hazy and confused. He was descended from the line of southern MacDonald chiefs who based themselves at Dunyvaig on Islay, the old centre of the Lordship of the Isles. The placename means 'the Fortress of the Little Ships', the fast and highly manoeuvrable birlinns celebrated by Alasdair Mac Mhaighstir Alasdair in his magnificent epic, 'The Birlinn of Clanranald'.

Coll was born in Northern Ireland, probably in 1570, and, like his son, he retained strong links, becoming involved in the blood-soaked politics of Ulster. The MacDonalds of Dunyvaig had, through marriage, become Earls of Antrim in the early 15th century and their holdings in the southern Hebrides were closely connected by the busy sea roads that linked the harbours of the Ulster coast with the islands to the north. But after the failure and break-up of the great MacDonald principality of the Lordship of the Isles at the end of the 15th century and the subsequent growth of the power of Clan Campbell, whose lands encompassed much of mainland Argyll, Coll Ciotach and his Irish kinsmen were under great pressure. Even then, as early as the 16th century, battle lines in Ulster were drawn on either side of a sectarian divide, much hardened by the outbreak of civil war in England in 1642. It quickly involved Ireland and Scotland and the conflagration is now known not as the English Civil War but more properly as the Wars of the Three Kingdoms. And nowhere was it fought more viciously than in Ireland.

In 1641, rebellion flared in Ulster and what became known as The Association of the Confederate Catholics of Ireland recruited and organised campaigns all over the island. Later, the Catholic armies fought against the forces of Protestant settlers, Scottish Covenanters and English Parliamentarians. The Catholics were led by Owen Roe O'Neill, a scion of the ancient O' Neill dynasty of Ulster, who could claim High Kings of Ireland in their genealogy. As campaigns ebbed and flowed, Alasdair Mac Colla became one of the most important lieutenants of Owen Roe O'Neill's cousin, Phelim O'Neill. But, as ever, he was also fighting on behalf of the interests of his clan and kinsmen. Randal MacDonnell, his surname the Irish rendering of MacDonald, had become the second Marquis of Antrim and he raised a company of soldiers. Alasdair was appointed as an officer. At that point, events took a surprising turn.

On 11 February 1642, part of the garrison defending the Protestant town of Coleraine sallied out to scour the countryside for provisions. It had been a difficult, long and hungry winter. At Laney, near Ballymoney, a small detachment of Confederate soldiers deliberately encountered the force of defenders and quickly retreated, luring them into an area of boggy ground where Alasdair Mac Colla and his men were waiting. In the ensuing ambush, the young officer ordered the use of a new tactic, something that must have been drilled into his men, perhaps even rehearsed. Here is a contemporary source:

> having commanded his murderers [clearly a description written by an enemy] to lay down all their firearms . . . they [Alasdair's men] fell in amongst them (with swords and dirks and knives) in such a furious and irresistible manner that it was reported that not a man of them escaped of all the eight hundred.

It seems that, after Alasdair gave the order to charge the soldiers of the garrison, his men suddenly stopped, fired a single volley from their muskets or pistols at close quarters, dropped them, drew their swords and charged again. Great slaughter did indeed follow and only the Protestant commander, Archibald Stewart, and a handful of his men escaped.

This incident is not well documented but it seems to have been very significant, especially in light of what happened the following summer in the north of Ireland.

In June 1642, Phelim O'Neill led the Confederate Catholics west to Donegal to confront the Protestant forces known as the Laggan Army. The battle at Glenmaquin was a disaster. On one side of a valley near the village, the Laggan men dug defensive ditches and may have rammed stakes into the upcast. Confronted with this, Phelim O'Neill halted, arrayed his army on the slopes of the other side of the valley in a rank two deep and waited. Eventually the Protestant commanders sent out a sally of sharpshooters to fire at the enemy and goad them into reacting. Which they did and Alasdair Mac Colla and his men led the charge. Sir Robert Stewart, commander of the Laggan Army, left a record:

> [They] came on with a furious and swift march, making a terrible outcry on their march according to their manner . . . Coll Kittagh's

sons, cried up for their valour as invincible champions, with their Highlanders and some others assaulted my brigade fiercely in so much that they were not far from coming to push of pike [i.e. getting close enough for hand-to-hand fighting].

Stewart noticed the valour of the leader of the charge: 'A stout, brave fellow charged up alone to the [earth]work but was shot, and after a very smart skirmish, the Irish fell back.'

One of his lieutenants, Manus O'Cahan, moved quickly to reach Alasdair and 'brought him off in a horse-litter'. When the Confederates reached close to the defensive line, the Laggan Army had fired a series of deadly volleys and the Catholics were mown down. And then they fled. Alasdair was probably distinctly unimpressed with Phelim O'Neill's feckless leadership but Glenmaquin taught him a valuable lesson. Courage and resolve in the charge were not enough. The ground had to be right. It had to be open, not boggy or rocky, and an enemy that had built defensive works or were protected by fortifications of any sort could not be successfully assaulted by charging men, no matter how brave they were.

After the debacle at Glenmaquin, the young warrior promptly agreed a truce with Alexander Leslie, the great Covenanter general who was so influential in the outcome of the Wars of the Three Kingdoms. In the event, nothing came of their negotiations but it seems likely that Alasdair never forgot what he saw in Donegal and was determined not to see it happen again.

The picture blurs after the battle at Glenmaquin. A year or so later, Mac Colla rejoined the Confederate Army but almost certainly not out of principled support for the royalist cause or Catholicism. As ever, the interests of Clan Donald were at the front of his mind. At first, Alasdair met with abject failure. In late 1643, he sailed from Ulster with 300 men to the Southern Hebrides to harry and raid the properties of the Campbells. At that time, Archibald Campbell, Marquis of Argyll, was the effective ruler of Scotland, a role he retained for the most of the course of the Wars of the Three

Kingdoms. He dispatched a much larger force and they drove Mac Colla and his men back to their birlinns, back to Ireland.

No doubt also motivated by MacDonald antipathy for Clan Campbell as well as royalist and Catholic sympathies, the Marquis of Antrim suggested to the Council of Confederate Ireland that Alasdair should return to Scotland but this time with a much more substantial force at his back. Strategically, war vigorously prosecuted in Scotland might draw Covenanter support for the English Parliamentarians back north, thereby aiding the royalist cause. Mac Colla took three regiments with him and almost all appear to have been Irishmen. Many had fought as mercenaries for the King of Spain as he attempted to hang onto his colonies in what is now Belgium and Holland. Mac Colla's brigade of about 1,600 soldiers had also fought in Owen Roe O'Neill's Northern Army and many were described by John Spalding, a contemporary historian and lawyer from Aberdeen, as 'brought up in West Flanders, expert soldiers, with a year's pay'. In other words, some of them were hardened professionals.

Colonel Manus O'Cahan, the brave and loyal comrade who rescued his general at Glenmaquin, commanded a regiment as did Colonel Alexander MacDonnell and Colonel James MacDonnell, kinsmen of the marquis and distantly related to their brigadier general. An analysis of the names of the soldiers suggests that many were related. Manus O'Cahan appears to have had five brothers or cousins in his regiment. The origins of others were surprising. Sergeant Major Ledwitch's company were Palesmen, men of English descent whose families had settled around Dublin, and they carried names like Dease, Newgent and possibly Cooper – although Cooper may have been one of only a handful of Scots in the brigade. Priests accompanied each regiment as padres and these professional soldiers also brought their women and sometimes their children with them. Although they had no uniform, many men wore a coat and brightly coloured trews. As a distinguishing badge, very important in the ruck of hand-to-hand fighting, they pinned stalks of oats to their bonnets. Acting as lifeguards to protect Mac Colla, three companies of Islemen were recruited from the Hebrides. And he also had two bodyguards who never left his presence, Calum Mor MacInness and Dubhaltach MacPhee. The small invasion force set sail from the southern port of Waterford on 27 June 1644.

Mingary on the Ardnamurchan peninsula was one of a string of sea castles that had held together the Lordship of the Isles. Like others at Ardtornish and Castle Tioram, it was located very near the coast so that it was accessible by ship rather than by road and below it there was a safe anchorage. After dislodging the Covenanter garrison in July 1644, Alasdair Mac Colla first engaged in family business, attacking and raiding Campbell holdings in Argyll.

Two years before the birlinns dropped anchor below Mingary Castle, another young man, also a gifted, courageous and charismatic soldier, had been wrestling with competing loyalties. General Alexander Leslie led the Army of the Covenant into England at the end of August 1640 and took the city of Newcastle from the royalists. One of his most able and effective officers was James Graham, Earl of Montrose. A graduate of St Andrews University and a signatory of the National Covenant, he proposed that the army should wear blue bonnets and blue sashes for the officers – the colour of militant Protestantism ever since. But he was becoming more and more uneasy at the pace of change in society, at how parliaments and assemblies were asserting themselves over kings. In May 1641, Graham was charged with plotting in favour of Charles I and imprisoned in Edinburgh Castle.

After an amnesty, he was released but, by that time, his loyalties had indeed changed. In 1644, the king made him Marquis of Montrose and appointed him Lord Lieutenant of Scotland. They were grand titles but, at first, they had little substance and it proved very difficult to recruit men to the royalist cause, so much so that Montrose was forced to travel in secret with only two companions. In August of 1644, he was hiding in Methven Wood, north-west of Perth. By chance, it seems, Montrose encountered a clansman carrying a fiery cross, the dramatic device used to call out men to war. The Perthshire clans were alarmed at the news of the coming of Alasdair

Mac Colla and his Irish and Clan Donald warriors. They were seen as ruthless, no better than raiders – men who would devastate the countryside if the clans did not rise with them to support the cause of the king. The bearer of the fiery cross was raising a force to oppose them. It may well be that he told Montrose that Alasdair Mac Colla's small army had reached Blair Castle.

The sequence of events is not clear from such scant sources as exist but it seems that a force of Atholl clans, Robertsons, Stewarts and others, had indeed mustered and marched to Blair Castle while Montrose was hiding in Methven Wood. Alasdair Mac Colla was much vexed by what was unfolding. He had hoped to recruit the very clansmen who opposed him and not to fight them. But then fate or good timing intervened. Three riders appeared at Blair Castle and one of them wore Highland dress. He asked to see Alasdair Mac Colla and then told him he was the Marquis of Montrose, the King's Lieutenant in Scotland. On receiving the news, the Irishmen and the Highlanders threw their bonnets in the air and some let off a celebratory volley of musket shot – which nearly misfired. The Atholl clansmen mistook the gunfire for an attack and battle was only averted when Montrose's arrival was revealed.

What the marquis brought to Blair was legitimacy, the king's commission, and he was able not only to prevent an unnecessary battle but also to persuade the Atholl men to join with Mac Colla's in the royalist cause. There were around 700 and, at a stroke, it converted an Irish incursion seeking to further the interests of Clan Donald into a Scottish rebellion in support of the rightful king.

A series of remarkable events began to unfold – what became known as 'the Year of Miracles'. The two men complemented each other. Mac Colla had raised more men from his Clan Donald kinsmen and his fearsome military reputation went before him. Montrose was also seen as an excellent soldier and tactician whose courage and resolve were not in doubt. And his royal appointment conferred legitimacy on Mac Colla's expedition and also solved the issue of leadership. One clan chief would never submit to the leadership of another but a neutral and prestigious aristocratic figure with a high military reputation could command all. At Blair, it was decided to march on Perth and confront the Covenanter forces stationed in the city and that Montrose would lead the army.

*

The Old Gallows Road stops only 100 yards after it begins, reappearing out of the suburban sprawl of Perth. Near a street on the western edge of the city that had borrowed its name, I found the real thing, its line flanked by an avenue of mature hardwood trees. Their canopy was so dense that the old road was shaded from the slanting morning sun and, despite the grey, industrial railings around a large electricity substation only a few yards away, the old road suddenly seemed otherworldly, atmospheric. Its metalled surface was still hard, largely unbroken and nothing but grass and weeds had grown up through the irregularly shaped pavers and rammed gravel I was walking on. But very abruptly the road disappeared into the 21st century and the roar of traffic broke into my reverie. At the foot of a very steep bank, the dual carriageway of the A9 carried thundering lorries and cars whooshing to and from the Highlands.

I had come looking for the Old Gallows Road because, in 1644, it was the main western road out of Perth and the route its garrison took when it marched out to defend the city against the army of Montrose and Alasdair Mac Colla.

Not anxious to embark on a lemming-like descent down the steep cutting and dash across the dual carriageway, I retraced my steps to the new Old Gallows Road. A bridge took me over the rumble of the traffic and into the car park of Noah's Ark, an oddly named golf driving range. It wasn't flooded with visitors. Only one vehicle was parked and I noticed three people working on the roof of the building. Perhaps it was closed for maintenance. After asking the workmen if it was OK to leave my car, I went off in search of management.

'No,' said a pleasant man who had been gathering up hundreds of yellow golf balls on the range using only, it seemed, a golf club. I suppose it meant he didn't have to bend down.

'Professional dog walkers,' he added by way of explanation. 'Before we put up signs, we could have as many as thirty vans parked here – people who walk dogs while their owners are at work. So. No.'

Right. OK. 'I'm looking for the Old Gallows Road,' I said and the golf ranger pointed to a strip of mature trees beyond the practice greens and the bunkers.

'That's it but watch where you're walking. Dog mess. They don't all pick it up.'

When I told him I was looking for the site of the Battle of Tippermuir, he looked at me for a moment and said, 'Right.'

Having driven back across the bridge over the A9 and found an uncontentious place to park by the electricity substation, I began my walk at last. Next to a large sign for the Perth Dog Park – 280 metres off to the right and, anyway, what is a dog park? A much smaller sign was attached to a gap in a breeze-block wall. It said 'Public Right of Way'. Watching carefully where I was stepping, I was about to pass through the gap when two very large people barred the way, forcing me to move quickly backwards as they steered themselves and two equally burly Labradors into the car park, across the bridge and back into the suburbs of Perth. Despite a sunny, windless morning, the countryside fresh and glistening after a welcome night of rain, I was beginning to feel unwelcome. Perhaps I should have brought Maidie, my West Highland Terrier. She has a good deal in common with Alasdair Mac Colla.

Just inside the gap in the breeze-block wall I found yet another sign, this one attached to a tall screen of metal mesh of the sort used to keep people off building sites. It was something about how to object to planning permission. But at least I was in the right place, the old road stretching in front of me, leading arrow-straight into a welcoming, shaded avenue of dappled light filtering through tall broadleaf trees. When I came across more metalling, the smooth, irregular pavers I had seen on the other side of the A9, and saw that many of the trees were old, I was certain I'd rediscovered the line of the Old Gallows Road.

All my research and the excellent Historic Environment Scotland website had convinced me that the Battle of Tippermuir had been fought on the ground I was walking through. The army that mustered to defend Perth from Mac Colla and Montrose had marched out of the city and arrayed themselves across the line of the Old Gallows Road and my plan was to walk westwards into the heart of the fighting, to where Alasdair Mhor and his men made history.

After 100 yards, it suddenly struck me that, amongst the many signs, I'd seen nothing about the battle. There was no information board, no indication at all that, in the late summer of 1644, the royalist army had clashed with a large force of Covenanters in this place. History turned at Tippermuir, what happened exactly where I was walking had changed Scotland and Britain and its effects had rippled on for a century and more. Had the outcome been different, our past would have been different and so would our present. Nothing is inevitable. And yet there was nothing to mark what happened along the line of the old road. No wonder the nice man at the golf range had looked at me blankly.

When I did at last find a sign, it gave directions to the Old Gallows Road Woodland Circuit and an alternative, shorter route for walkers that led off to the right. With the fields on either side mostly screened by tall trees and their brambly and thorny undergrowth, it was difficult to get a sense of what the land might have looked like to Montrose, Mac Colla and Lord Elcho, the commander of the Covenanter army that marched out of the city to meet them. Shelter belts of tall pines ran from north to south and fence lines were made more emphatic by the bushy growth of hawthorns and rowans. One thing was clear, however, something that is not readily evident from maps, and that is the gradient. The Old Gallows Road ran gently but appreciably downhill and Elcho would have liked that – he'd have been more comfortable on higher ground.

In the middle of the 17th century, the landscape was much more open. The sloping ground offered good drainage and the old runrig system needed that. These long strips of ploughed ground were slightly mounded and had ditches between them to carry away

rainwater and prevent water logging. And there were many fewer
trees. Wood was a vital, well husbanded and much used resource.
On my right, I could see the ancient fertility was still there. A vast
field of flowering potatoes seemed to be defying the summer's
drought and had obviously had enough rain, perhaps because these
fields lay in the rain shadow of the mountains. On either side of the
old road, the thick and burred oaks had produced many clusters of
acorns, all still green, waiting for the autumn before they fell, fat and
brown, to be gobbled up by foraging pigs in the not very distant
past. Tangles of brambles and raspberries added to the wild harvest
that formed an important part of the diet of people who lived on the
land in the centuries before urbanisation.

I came across many rosehip bushes and the red, oval-shaped fruits
remembered annual childhood riches, the first money I ever earned,
the first time coins jingled in my pocket. Waiting until late in the
autumn, perhaps even after a first frost, we gathered ripe rosehips in
sacks that were provided by our primary school. Rich in vitamin C,
the hips were first harvested on a countrywide scale during the
Second World War to be made into syrup that was spoon fed to
growing children. We were paid 3d or 4d a pound and each full sack
and its weight was marked and stamped on a yellow card with my
name at the top and it had to be closely guarded. The reason for that
was a badge. If you were busy and gathered a lot – I've no idea how
many pounds – you were given a badge as well as the extra cash. The
rosehips were sent to a factory in Newcastle, I think, to be made into
a gloopy syrup called Delrosa. I've not seen a jar of it for years.
Perhaps it contained too much sugar, for the hips could be bitter.
Now, it all strikes me as a very fragile basis on which to base a business – many thousands of little kids thrashing around the countryside yanking the essential ingredient of your product off bushes that
might not have been theirs.

But it wasn't by any means unusual. At the end of every summer
in the late 1950s and early 1960s, my mum and dad took us out to
pick wild berries, mostly raspberries. 'Never let the bush beat you,'
my dad used to say, every time, as we complained about being

pricked and scratched by the thorny stems. On roadsides and in copses and woods, we picked wild rasps – 'before the birds get them' – and it must have been a weighty harvest. My mum made a lot of jam, enough to last several months. I remember sitting on the draining board of the kitchen sink, next to the gas cooker watching her stir the blood-red mixture and enjoying its aroma. The taste, sweet, fruity and somehow red, has stayed with me, completely unlike even expensive bought stuff. As a child I consumed many jam pieces – jam sandwiches made with Scottish plain loaf, the bread and jam of heaven. I read the other day that, since childhood, the queen used to eat a jam piece every day, the jam made from berries picked at Balmoral. Lucky her.

Beyond the signpost, the Old Gallows Road narrowed to a path and the avenue of old trees began to thin out. Eventually, I came to a burn running across the line of the road. Its ditch was deep enough to need care crossing. It ran into another, larger burn, one that would have slowed an advancing army. On the far bank, someone had built a shelter out of branches, something soldiers in a Highland army would have done routinely as they moved though the landscape and needed a bivouac for the night. The shelter marked the end of the Old Gallows Road for me. It looked as though it extended down a series of field ends but there was simply no way through the tangle without a machete. According to the excellent maps on the Historic Environment Scotland website, which I could access on my phone, I'd come to the approximate place where Montrose and Mac Colla halted and positioned their small army. I didn't need to go much further.

*

During the Wars of the Three Kingdoms, the government of Scotland was mainly in the hands of a body known as 'the Committee of Estates'. When news of the royalist muster at Blair Castle reached Edinburgh, its members ordered the Earl of Lothian to gather forces and that Perth and Stirling should at all costs be defended so that they did not fall to the rebels. Not only was Perth the second city of

Scotland at that time, Stirling and control of its bridge over the River Forth were the key to the Lowlands. Montrose and Mac Colla moved quickly. Neither wanted to meet a combined Covenanter army that would certainly hugely outnumber them in battle. But Montrose did not march down Strathtay, the fastest route to Perth.

From Blair Castle they turned west and followed the Tay upriver to Aberfeldy and Castle Weem, the principal fortress of Clan Menzies. Montrose sent a messenger to the chief, Sir Alexander Menzies, but the old man was badly treated, attacked and severely wounded. He refused to join the rising. When he went further and sent out skirmishing parties to harass Montrose's army as it marched through his land, the Lieutenant General retaliated and, in the fighting, Menzies was fatally wounded. From Aberfeldy, the Highlanders and the Irishmen climbed up through Glen Cochill, and, in the shadow of the great mountain of Meall Dearg, they made their way south. It appears that they planned to attack Perth from the west.

Tradition holds that the royalists had a chance encounter with a party of 500 clansmen led by Lord Kilpont and Sir John Drummond. They were marching to Perth to join the government army but it was later said that Montrose's eloquence persuaded them to change sides. The reality is that secret messages had probably been exchanged. Lord Kilpont, Henry Grahame, was a kinsman of Montrose and both he and Drummond were royalist sympathisers. They had almost certainly used the ruse of pretending to support the government so that they could muster a substantial force without raising suspicions. Montrose had taken a circuitous route to Perth so that he could join with Kilpont, who was marching from the west.

It was 31 August when the two men met, and events were beginning to move quickly. That night, the royalist army, now almost 3,000 strong, camped at Fowlis Wester, less than fourteen miles from Perth.

Behind the walls of the city another army was gathering. Between 4,000 and 5,000 men had come from Angus, Perthshire, Dundee, Fife and Forfarshire. A store of provisions had been brought and distributed, the fields around the city commandeered for grazing cavalry horses and places found where troops could set up camp. All the army lacked was a general. The Earl of Lothian was still in Edinburgh and would not reach Perth in time. Scouts had returned to the town with news of Montrose's approach and it became clear that a new commander was needed.

Lord Elcho, John Wemyss, the Earl of Wemyss, came from an old Fife family but he had had little military experience. And, at fifty-eight, he was old for the times – not a man who might inspire his troops or lead them into battle. But, if Elcho could hold Perth and drive off the smaller army of Montrose and Mac Colla, then he would buy precious time. Archibald Campbell, Earl of Argyll, was in the field with an army of hardened soldiers who had been campaigning in the west. If the royalists retreated north, back towards Blair and into the mountains, they might run into Argyll's advance. And that would surely settle matters.

At dawn on 1 September 1644, when the sun's rays streaked low along the undulating ridges above Strathearn, Montrose will have sent out mounted scouts. If they had followed the Old Gallows Road eastwards to the village of Tippermuir, they would have been able to watch Lord Elcho and his captains march the Covenanter army out of Perth to beat of drum and with standards flying. Rather than heraldic devices, the banners carried their beliefs – 'For Christ's Crown and Covenant'. Some bore a yellow saltire on a blue ground with the words 'Covenants', 'For Religion', 'King', 'And Kingdomes' in the four segments between the arms of the cross. Others had more chilling slogans – 'No Quarter For the Active Enemies of the Covenant'. The scouts will also have been counting, estimating the size of Elcho's army as companies took up positions across the Old Gallows Road – how many cannon were being emplaced and how much cavalry he had.

The deployment of the Covenanter army led Montrose's men to look closely at something else – something that might be decisive for the outcome of the battle. What was the ground like? Below the position taken by Elcho, was it boggy? Were there burns to be crossed? Was it open? And, crucially, how much of a slope was there? At Glenmaquin, where he had been badly wounded, Alasdair Mac Colla had seen great slaughter as his men charged up a slope to assault well-entrenched defences. At Tippermuir, the scouts reported that it was different – much better ground, a place where the charge might succeed even though there was a slight incline. And Elcho's men were not digging ditches.

By mid-morning, Montrose had led his heavily outnumbered army to a position about a mile west of where the Covenanters were arrayed across the road, barring the way to Perth. Anxious that the wide and open farmland might allow Elcho to outflank him, the Lieutenant General stretched his forces into a long, 1,000-yard line, perhaps only two men deep. On the left was Lord Kilpont and his clansmen, many of them bowmen, in the centre was Alasdair Mac Colla's Irish and MacDonald brigade and, with his tiny force of cavalry and the Atholl regiment, Montrose took up position on the right.

He almost certainly spoke Gaelic. Before battle was joined, Montrose rode up and down the line exhorting his troops, many of whom will have had no English. Not all the men had muskets either and those that did were short of powder and ammunition. And so Montrose told them to pick up stones and throw them at the ranks of the Covenanters before they charged. To be able to give such an order, acknowledging weakness and the enemy's superior firepower, without damaging morale, is testament to the general's eloquence.

Up on the Old Gallows Road, it was not their commander's words that mattered. God spoke to the Covenanters. With their bibles in hand, ministers walked up and down the lines, their sonorous voices carrying in the morning air. The words of the Reverend Carmichael of Markinch in Fife were later recorded. 'If ever God spoke certain truth out of my mouth,' he declared, 'in His name, I promise you today a certain victory.' The battle cry would be 'Jesus and no quarter!'

Formalities came first. Under a flag of truce, Montrose sent the Master of Madertie to parley with Lord Elcho. David Drummond was his son-in-law and had joined the rising at the same time as Lord Kilpont. The young man read out a declaration from his commanding officer. Here is a later account of what was said:

> All he desired was that in God's name they would at length give ear to sounder councils, and trust to the clemency, faith and protection of so good a king . . . If notwithstanding they persisted in rebellion, he called God to witness that their stubbornness forced him into the present strife.

This form of words neatly turned the tables as it asserted that Lord Elcho and his men were in rebellion against the legitimate authority of the rightful king. Montrose went on to ask, through David Drummond, if it was right and Christian to wage war, to fight and kill on this day – for 1 September 1644 was a Sunday, the Sabbath. The Covenanter ministers cut him short and replied that the Lord's Day was a fine day for doing His work. At that moment, clearly nettled at what he saw as effrontery as well as treachery, Lord Elcho defied all convention, had the young man seized and sent to the rear. As soon as the battle was won, Drummond would be hanged as a traitor.

Watching from a distance, Montrose must have been outraged but he did not react. Instead, it was Elcho who made the first move. He sent out a squadron of cavalry under the command of Lord Drummond to attack the right wing and Montrose's division. Moving forward at a trot, it was supported by a company of infantry. This may have been a diagonal movement across the face of the royalist lines for it encouraged Alasdair Mac Colla to roar out the order to charge. And what happened in the following few minutes was devastating.

The clansmen and the Irishmen shouted their war cries, the names of their places and broke into the charge. When they had raced to within twenty yards of the Covenanters, the waves of warriors suddenly stopped and fired a single volley at point-blank range. As the clouds of gun smoke billowed, the line broke up into small, compact wedges, formations of between twelve and fifteen men. Many were related – brothers, cousins, fathers, sons, uncles and nephews fought alongside each other and for each other. Often the older, more experienced and battle-hardened men were set at the point of the wedge. The Gaels believed that courage flowed down the generations and the older men knew what was coming. They then all threw down their muskets, drew their swords and, clutching their dirks and targes in the other hand, they charged once more out of the smoke, roaring their war cries, howling like ravening wolves.

At the moment of impact, all sorts of emotions and instincts must have been churning through the minds of the charging Highlanders and the men facing them. Courage has many forms but the raw, physical bravery needed for hand-to-hand fighting is surely the most elemental. Racing out of the billowing smoke of their musket volley, those at the leading point of the wedges did not know exactly what they would meet – another volley at point-blank range, muskets with bayonets fixed, levelled pikes or halberds? What they were sure of was momentum. Lord Elcho's lines were largely static, like Cope's at Prestonpans, and, when the clansmen hit, the ranks of their enemies would certainly move. In that split second of impact, momentum mattered more than anything. The charging Highlanders wanted the opposing lines to buckle and then break. They wanted to get in amongst them with sword and dirk. Their skill and determination in hand-to-hand fighting was far greater, far more telling than that of most soldiers in the government armies. From a young age, with wooden weapons, boys were taught the physical arts of war, how to swing, parry, cut and thrust with a sword, stab at close quarters with a dirk and deflect a bayonet or a blow with their targes. Because their chiefs expected military service as part of what clansmen owed as rental for their land, training in these warlike skills was as important as learning herdsmanship and all the others arts of farming.

In the 1860s, an old man recalled how young boys were trained in fighting techniques and also how their stamina, something they would need on campaign, was encouraged:

It was the custom in the Highlands of Scotland before the year 1745, that the gentry kept schools to give instruction to youths in sword exercise, and the laird of Ardshiel [in Appin, the mainland between Ballachulish and Connel Ferry] kept a school for the instruction of youth in his own district. He stored the cudgels [wooden staffs or staves] behind his house and the lads and laddies went every day to receive instruction on the cudgel from the laird. After the laddies had received their day's instruction, each got a bannock and lumps of cheese. They were then sent to try who would soonest ascend a mountain and eat the bannock and cheese; and whoever was first got another bannock and lumps of cheese home with him.

Modern armies mostly fight at a distance with rifles, artillery, missiles, air strikes and drones. During recent conflicts in Iraq, Afghanistan and elsewhere, those distances could be vast. Drones can be launched and directed to targets by operatives looking at screens thousands of miles away on a base in the continental USA. And once a target has been destroyed, the screen flashes and smoke and dust billow, these people complete their shift, shut down their machines or hand over to a colleague, go home to supper and perhaps an evening watching TV.

Nevertheless, technology has not taken over warfare entirely. Particularly in the war against the Taliban in Afghanistan, the order to fix bayonets was shouted several times as British soldiers prepared to engage in what is now known as melee fighting. Retired servicemen and women have told me something of what it is like and it seems that little has changed over the centuries since Alasdair Mac Colla roared his men into the charge at Tippermuir.

Everything slows down, the former soldiers agreed, and happens in snapshots, almost unrelated, momentary vignettes of high, sharp focus. A rictus of rage or pain on a face, a blow parried, the flash and glint of a bladed weapon, another striking home, no time to think, only to react. Instead of the Highlanders' wedges of twelve to fifteen, the British Army fights hand-to-hand in groups of five. 'You can't take in more than five comrades,' said one former officer. 'You just can't see any more. All that matters is what's immediately around you.'

Control also mattered. Officers all agreed that someone who lost it, went berserk in melee fighting, was much more of a liability than an asset. 'That's not courage, just crazy stuff, and it can damage your own men as well as the enemy.'

Physical courage was not seen as the opposite of fear but something much closer, an instinct that ran alongside it. What drove men – and women – to fight hard was the fear of letting down those around you – your mates. And not in any abstract manner. Your mates were right there, in the chaos of the melee, wielding bayonets, small arms, anything that came to hand. There was also a wider imperative that gave men the steel to fight at close quarter and that was the old-fashioned concept of honour. Just as individual Highland clans celebrated their war glories in the poems and tales of their *seannachies* or 'bards', like Alasdair Mac Mhaighstir Alasdair, so the regiments of the British Army remember their history on their flags. Stitched on to them are battle honours, places, dates, the source and fount of collective pride. And that pride endures. When the war in Ukraine broke out in February 2022, the British Secretary of State for Defence, Ben Wallace MP, remembered his career as a regular soldier in the Scots Guards. At a meeting with serving officers, he said, 'The Scots Guards kicked the backside of Tsar Nicholas I in 1853 in Crimea – we can always do it again.' It was probably not the most politic remark or one whose historical context was understood by many who watched the news footage that day but the soldiers listening will have recognised the pride, the enduring sense of regimental honour.

Wallace would also have understood some of the wider context of 17th- and 18th-century warfare. When I spoke to former soldiers about the overall impact of the Highland charge breaking through a defensive line, they all mentioned operational paralysis. When a commander like Lord Elcho saw Mac Colla's wedges burst through his ranks at Tippermuir in many places, he would have been uncertain what to do, where to deploy any reserves he had. And those lost minutes at a crucial juncture of a battle could have been and often were decisive.

There were more resonances, especially with the attitudes and actions of Lord George Murray and Colonel Harry Ker at Prestonpans. Before any fighting took place, modern British Army commanders' first consideration is always the ground, the nature of the terrain on which a battle or firefight might be joined. It was and is still thought to be more than merely influential.

My conversations with former serving officers also conveyed more than a practical understanding of strategy or tactics. There was also an air of quiet dignity and no expectation of admiration for the way in which they risked their lives. Courage was certainly not seen as bravado but something born not only out of fear but also respect. Ben Wallace's remark may have sounded boastful but his awareness of his old regiment's history and pride in its battle honours was striking and by no means unusual in a soldier.

My own experience of physical courage was not military but linked to that famous substitute for war – playing rugby in Scotland's Border League. I wasn't risking death, merely injury, but I quickly learned that hanging back, standing off, was more likely to result in getting hurt, to say nothing of earning the contempt of team mates. A full-on charge into a ruck or a tackle was, counter-intuitively, a safer way to play. I'm very aware that, compared to the bravery of the British Army in Afghanistan, this may seem like a trivial comparison, even frivolous or disrespectful. But it's as close as I can get in my own experience to the emotions of the men charging their enemies. Fear and courage churn together and part of the point of playing was to hurt your opponents, beat them – within the rules – into submission.

On that bloody Sunday afternoon at Tippermuir, Mac Colla's brigade smashed through the Covenanter infantry and attacked the cavalry, driving them back up the slope and into their own ranks. Seizing the initiative, Montrose had the pipers sound a general charge and his army surged uphill to Lord Elcho's position. The wedges burst through immediately, the Covenanter line failed and crumpled as the Irish and Highland warriors' skill and ferocity in hand-to-hand fighting quickly turned Tippermuir into a rout. The battle itself may have lasted less than half an hour as panic crackled through the lines of the Covenanters. As ever, more men were cut down in flight than in the fighting. Montrose's men pursued the fleeing soldiers and also a large party of townspeople who had come out of Perth to watch the spectacle was caught up in the chaos. Blood soaked the grass on either side of the Old Gallows Road as men screamed when clansmen hacked at them, stabbing them as they fell, inflicting terrible wounds, gaping gashes that bled out quickly.

In minutes, Montrose and Mac Colla had won a stunning, shocking victory. The Irish charge had become the Highland charge and, on that day, history turned as men tore through the ranks of their enemies. For a century, when properly executed over good ground, the Highland charge would become irresistible.

*

Beyond the broadleaf trees and the tangle of their undergrowth, it seemed to me that the Old Gallows Road was a dividing line. To the north lay cultivation, the vast flowering potato field with its tall green shaws and, below it, acres of biscuit-ripe barley. On the other side, there was pasture grazed by a flock of newly shorn sheep. I noticed that, in the drought-stricken weeks with little or no new grass growing, the farmer had scattered beets for them to eat – what was usually winter fodder. Climbing the gate I could see that it was old pasture, well established with what farmers call a good mattress under it. But how old? Did Mac Colla know from his scouts that this was ground it would be good to charge over? Was this where the Battle of Tippermuir would be decided?

Most of the sheep were sheltering in the shade of tall rowans and thorns by the fence line, their ears flicking at the flies, and few bothered to stir themselves as I walked across to two wind-bent old trees near the middle of the field. Around them I came across a strange, low rampart of huge boulders, some with straight edges, others set on their edges. I wondered if it was a consumption cairn, a place where stones dug and hauled out of the ground were set to one side so that a field could be safely ploughed. Except this wasn't set to one side and there was also much more of a sense of structure, a deliberate placing of stones in a rough circle. It was too big to have been the remains of a blackhouse, a drystone-built cottage, and, in any case, most of these were rectangular. Inside the rampart there was no pile of boulders, just more big stones, many hidden in the grass or covered with moss and lichen. Most seemed clustered in the middle. I could make no sense of it, except that it looked very old.

I climbed back over the gate and found a path that led down to a burn. Beyond it stretched a gently sloping field that according to my map led up to Mid Lamberkine Farm. The Historic Environment Scotland website reckoned that that was where Montrose took up his position on the right wing of the royalist army. If that was a correct judgement, then the Covenanter cavalry and infantry had crossed the burn to attack him. And Alasdair Mac Colla had, in turn, charged them there, perhaps as they slowed to get over. Did they race across the good ground of the old pasture? If it was pasture in the summer of 1644, maybe.

I had met no one that morning after I'd passed the sign for the Old Gallows Road Woodland Circuit. And so, seized with an urgent need to pee, I didn't bother to look around first. In midstream on the side of the path up from the burn, I suddenly heard voices. Two East Asian people wearing Covid masks, a man and a woman, appeared around a thick and bushy thorn tree. There are some things in life that are impossible to interrupt, and so I turned my back on them as they passed close by. After exchanging good mornings – I didn't wave – they passed on, both of them giggling.

But over the fence I had been peeing on, something caught my eye. Half hidden in the long grass, it was another, much larger low rampart of very large stones. Similar to what I'd found in the smaller field behind me, this one seemed more intact, much more upstanding in places, its oval shape well defined and once again a cluster of big stones in the middle. Also this wide field of twenty or so acres was more or less flat. On my phone, I looked again at the Historic Environment Scotland map of the battle dispositions, and the geography seemed to fit where events had unfolded. But then – and sometimes I do wonder about my waning powers of concentration – I noticed something else. In the terrible, olde-worlde font that the Ordnance Survey use for antiquities was the legend, 'Cup and Ring marked stone', plotted exactly where I was standing. That was it – conclusive. Cup and ring marks pecked onto the surface of large stones are prehistoric, often described as rock art. Their purpose is mysterious but they are found on ancient religious sites all over Britain. What this meant was something simple. These two stone circles are very old and so massive they could not possibly be moved without enormous effort and resources. Did that, in turn, mean that these two fields had been pasture on 1 September 1644, good ground for Mac Colla's men to charge over? Very possibly.

But there were other instincts at work – not just historical logic and a (belated) reading of geography. Even before I'd looked at the OS map more carefully, I'd intuited that this might be the place where Montrose and Mac Colla's victory sparked. It had that indefinable atmosphere, a genius loci, something I've learned to trust. Did the war cries of the Irishmen and the Highlanders echo across these old fields to the south of the Old Gallows Road? There exists a little documentary support for the judgement that Tippermuir had been decided there. In the days after the battle, after the burgesses had handed him the keys of the city, Montrose had set up his head-quarters in a house in Perth. There he had heard a bitter complaint from a farmer. William Hunter of Balgayes claimed that his corn had been trampled by Montrose's men as the Covenanters fled back to the city. If his land lay to the north of the Old Gallows Road, where the potatoes I'd seen were thriving, that would make sense. By 1 September, the harvest was not yet in and Mac Colla would not have judged runrig strips with standing corn and their drainage ditches to be good ground for a charge, not a place to fight. But when the battle turned into a rout, men did not care where they ran and nor did their pursuers.

Montrose was also being pursued. Argyll's army was closing fast from the west and, after the slaughter on the Old Gallows Road, the Highlanders had acquired much plunder. Patrick Gordon of Ruthven noted: 'They could not be kept longer than they were laden with plunder for they got no other pay, and therefore could not be sworn to their colours. The Irish he [Montrose] was only sure of because they had no place of retreat.'

Immediately after the battle was won, many clansmen simply set off for home, claiming that, once the harvest was safely in, they would return to the army. Montrose sensed that these were hollow promises. After he had extracted £50 and a great quantity of cloth from the burgesses of Perth so that Alasdair Mac Colla could pay his Irishmen, Montrose led his depleted army out of Perth on 4 September. When they crossed the Tay, his men destroyed their boats behind them to slow Argyll's pursuit.

Montrose first marched to Dundee but, when his men made camp at the village of Collace, a further setback took place. The details are murky but it seems that James Stewart of Ardvorlich, an officer in the royalist army, was seen walking by a stream talking animatedly to Lord Kilpont. The latter was overheard saying that he would have nothing to do with 'that business'. The conversation grew into a fierce argument and Stewart drew a dirk and stabbed his friend in the heart. Having also killed a guard who got in his way, Stewart fled the royalist camp.

What 'that business' was remains unclear. It seems most likely that Stewart was trying to persuade Kilpont to defect to Argyll and the Covenanter army. Others claim that he wanted to assassinate Montrose and when Kilpont refused to have anything to do with that, Stewart was forced to kill him before he himself was betrayed. Before agreeing to join the royalist army west of Perth, both men had nominally mustered their clansmen to oppose Montrose. Perhaps for Stewart that opposition was more than nominal, perhaps he could not see how Montrose could possibly succeed, even after

Tippermuir. In any event, the murder of Kilpont persuaded many of his men to desert the army and return home. Montrose was left with little more than the core of his forces – Alasdair Mac Colla and his Irish brigade.

More discouragement waited at Dundee. When Montrose demanded the surrender of the town, the burgesses refused, secure behind their walls. The royalist army had no equipment and no expertise in siege warfare and they were forced to turn aside and move north. Argyll was not far behind. But Montrose hoped that he could find recruits amongst the loyal clans and families in the north-east. Aberdeen had refused to support the Covenanters.

In fact, a small Covenanter army had been raised by Lord Balfour of Burleigh and they planned to prevent the capture of the city. On the morning of 13 September, he marched his men out of Aberdeen to take up a strong defensive position on a steep ridge to the south-west. On his way north, Montrose had been able to recruit small troops of cavalry led by Sir Nathaniel Gordon and Sir Thomas Ogilvy. When deployed opposite Balfour, the cavalry were set on both wings with Mac Colla's Irish brigade once again in the centre. Perhaps Alasdair looked up at the ridge, at the lines of Protestant soldiers, and remembered Glenmaquin.

Once again Montrose sent a messenger with a drummer boy under a flag of truce to ask for the surrender of the city. It was refused, but with some courtesy. Both men were given food and drink and the boy had a coin pressed into his hand. As the envoys returned, making their way through Balfour's lines, a trooper from the Fife regiment suddenly raised his musket and shot the boy dead in full view of the royalist army. There was a great roar and Montrose was incensed. After victory was won, he shouted, his men could sack the city. It was something remembered in the verses of Alasdair Mac Colla.

Glaschu a bhith, o ho
Dol 'na lasair, o ho
'S Obair-Dheathain, o ho
'N deidh a chreachadh, trom eile.

That Glasgow, o ho
Was going down, o ho
And Aberdeen, o ho
Is being pillaged, another charge!

After a series of skirmishes on the flanks, Balfour foolishly ordered a cavalry troop to attack the Irish brigade in the centre. As the horsemen galloped ever closer, Mac Colla's men showed practised discipline. Instead of trying to stand fast in the face of charging horses, they suddenly opened their ranks, allowed them to pass right through, surrounded the troopers and slaughtered them, attacking and maiming horses and hauling riders out of the saddle.

But, when Montrose and Mac Colla's order to charge came, Major Lachlan shouted for men 'to lay down their muskets and pikes and fall on with sword and dirk'. It was exactly as they had done at Tippermuir. At the top of the ridge, the Irishmen did not scatter the Covenanters but, instead, met a much more determined resistance and battle raged for more than an hour before Balfour's infantry finally buckled, broke and fled.

It was then that Aberdeen was brutally sacked. Women were raped in the streets and more were carried off later to the royalist camp to endure terrible and repeated violence. When 'the cruel Irish' captured well-dressed men, they forced them to strip naked before killing them 'so as not to damage the clothes'. Houses were ransacked for portable plunder and, for two days, the population lived in mortal terror. The sack of Aberdeen was a rare miscalculation by Montrose. It had been a royalist city but, after his army ran amok, it forever changed allegiance.

But another emphatic victory showed that Tippermuir was no flash in the pan of a musket. A Catholic missionary working in Scotland in the 1640s, Father James Macbreck, wrote: 'The year 1644 was fruitful in new surprises and events, and an unlooked-for mode of warfare inaugurated fresh slaughter and fresh and unexpected victories.'

Soon after the pillaging of Aberdeen, Alasdair Mac Colla led his men west to continue his clan war against the Campbells and relieve the garrison at Mingary. Montrose continued to recruit and it may well be that his unexpected victories encouraged others. When Mac Colla rejoined the King's Lieutenant at Blair Castle in November, the army had swollen to almost 3,000 men. But a bitter Highland winter was coming on. What was to be done with such an army?

4

The Snow March

Inverlochy, 2 February 1645

As do laimh-s' gun, o ho
Earbainn tapaidh, o ho
Mharahadh Tighearna, o ho
Ach-nam-Bhrac leat, trom eile.

Into your hand, o ho
I would entrust heroic deeds, o ho
The Lord of Ach-nam-breac, o ho
Would be killed by you. Another charge!

Thiolaigeadh e, o ho
An oir an lochan, o ho,
Ged's beag mi fhin o ho,
Chuir mi ploc air, trom eile,

And he was buried, o ho,
At the side of the lochan, o ho,
And though small I may be, o ho,
I cast a sod on him. Another charge!

The song lyrics bring the story of Montrose's winter campaign to its climax, to its most successful, most blood-soaked moment. Having mustered a large force of clansmen, with Mac Colla's help, after the successes and the rich plunder of the autumn, the King's Lieutenant's

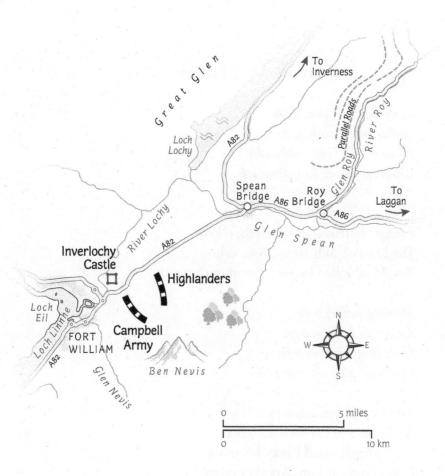

strategy was to march south, to wreak such havoc in the Lowlands that the Scottish regiments fighting in England for the Parliamentary cause would be drawn back north. Most of these soldiers were Lowlanders and their instinct to protect their families, homes and farms would have been irresistible. But Alasdair mac Colla would have none of it. He and his men wanted to march west, not south, to Argyll, to Campbell country, to the strongholds of Clan Donald's most bitter enemy. Montrose had no choice. His campaign was no longer political, part of an effort to support the royalist army in England by weakening their opposition. As the winter of 1644–45 closed in, it had become a clan war.

By December, the snow was deep. Icy winds howled down the glens and communities began to hunker down for the long Highland winter. As fires were lit and the early darkness fell, the world seemed to slow down. Men's and women's minds turned to survival, food that had been salted and stored, and how their beasts were faring in the intense cold. At Inveraray Castle, winds whistled off Loch Fyne and Archibald Campbell, the Marquis of Argyll and the most power-ful politician in Scotland, must have felt secure in the knowledge that no one with any sense would campaign in weather like this. Sitting by his glowing peat fire, he too would have to wait for the winter to end. Nothing would happen until the spring.

On 13 December, shepherds at the head of Glen Shira must have rubbed their eyes as they peered through the morning mist. Over the plateau to the south of the little Lochan Sron Mor, an army was marching through the snow. In a long column winding back into the high country, thousands of men were snaking down the slopes towards the glen. The Appin Stewarts, Clan Cameron, the MacDonnells of Glengarry, Macleans, McNeills and the MacIains of Glencoe were led by Montrose, riding a shaggy little garron pony plodding through the drifts and across the icy burns. Loch Fyne lay at the foot of Glen Shira. The town of Inveraray and the Campbell castle were less than a mile further south.

At the same time Alasdair mac Colla was leading Clanranald down Kilmartin Glen, past the ancient rock at Dunadd and then up the shore of Loch Fyne from the south. It was a classic pincer movement.

Fleeing farmers and their families, clutching what they could carry, burst into Inveraray with the astounding news that Montrose had come over the mountains and his army of savages was less than an hour from the town. Archibald Campbell was stunned, totally unprepared, and all he could do was roar for the crew of his birlinn and flee by the only route open to him. There was no time to organise a defence of the town or the castle and scarcely enough to get himself and his family to safety. There would be no mercy shown by Montrose and especially Mac Colla. Once Campbell's oarsmen had pulled their chief's birlinn out into the middle of the loch, he will have watched the royalist army march along the shore road. Perhaps their jeers and insults carried clear across the winter loch. The Marquis of Argyll knew exactly what would happen next to his defenceless town and the country around it.

Campbell should not have been surprised to have been surprised by Montrose. As much as their skill with sword, dirk and targe, endurance and strength had long been seen as martial virtues amongst the clans. At the bloody battle known as 'Red Harlaw', fought in Aberdeenshire in 1411, when the army of the MacDonald Lords of the Isles contended with the Earl of Mar for the earldom of Ross, the clan bard stood forward. After Lachlan Mor MacMhuirich had recited the long genealogy of the MacDonald princes, tracing their ancestry back to the mythic Irish hero, Conn of the Hundred Battles, he spoke not of courage but of something else that made clansmen dangerous enemies.

Sons of Conn,
Remember!
Hardihood in times of strife.

Wearing only their bonnets, linen shirts and plaids, their feet protected by buckskin *brogan*, Montrose and Mac Colla's men tramped through snow and waded freezing, flooding burns filled with meltwater. *Brogan* has been anglicised as brogues and the modern design of these shoes remembers the Highlanders' marches. The tooling, especially in the toecaps, shows a pattern of small, indented holes. In the 17th century, *brogan* had real holes. No one expected their footwear to keep them dry. *Brogan* were worn to keep bare feet from being cut by sharp stones and the holes were there to let water out as the men marched on.

When Montrose's and Mac Colla's men met at Inveraray, there was great slaughter and terrible destruction. The town, the town-ships and farms around it were destroyed, fire scorching and black-ening the wooden buildings, leaving them smoking and stark against the snow. Mac Colla was feared as *fear thollaidh nan tighean*, 'the breaker of houses'. There was massacre. Any captured Campbell clansmen old enough to fight were killed and perhaps as many as 900 died, cut down by avenging MacDonald blades.

Laden with plunder, the army marched north to Stewart country, the mild coastal province of Appin, to rest and shelter. Montrose and Mac Colla could regroup and plan the next stage of their winter campaign as their men feasted and boasted. And many, clutching their plunder, slipped away in the night, back to the warmth of their home fires.

After little more than two weeks, the army marched once more. The attack on Inveraray had sparked the government into action and Covenanter forces were mustering in the Highlands. Montrose led his men into the Great Glen and they made their way up the road to Inverness. But, at the south-west end of Loch Ness, at the village of Cille Chuimein, later to become known as 'Fort Augustus', a visitor arrived to talk with the Marquis and Mac Colla. Iain Lom MacDonald, the great bard of Keppoch, had walked from his native country near Fort William to pass on urgent news. It was not good. A trap was being set. Montrose already knew that the Earl of Seaforth, chief of Clan Mackenzie, was waiting with an army, perhaps 3,000 strong, at Inverness. But Iain Lom told him that Sir Duncan Campbell had marched to Inverlochy Castle near Fort William with an even larger force, about 3,500 men. He was behind

Montrose and Mac Colla, bottling them up in the Great Glen. They would have to cut their way out.

Military logic and common sense dictated that the royalist army should continue north-east to Inverness. Seaforth's army was smaller and he was known to be an unenthusiastic Covenanter. Once more Mac Colla could not be persuaded. Hatred triumphed over every military argument. The bitter, blood enemies of Clan Donald lay to the south-west, at Inverlochy Castle, where the Campbells had camped. There would be no need to exhort his men to fight – ancient enmities would speed them into the charge.

But there were great difficulties to overcome. Montrose knew that Campbell of Auchinbreck would have set substantial pickets on the road from Cille Chuimein down to Fort William as well as sweeping the Great Glen with parties of scouts, probably mounted. He was a seasoned soldier who had fought in Ireland, where he had ravaged the lands of Alasdair Mac Colla's cousins in the Antrim Glens. Campbell's pickets and scouts would have been able to give him ample warning of any approach from the north-west. That mattered because it allowed the Covenanter general time to array his army on flat ground near the castle, where he could use his superior numbers to outflank Montrose, roll up his much smaller army and finally, decisively, defeat him.

Montrose decided that it would be him who would outflank Campbell. And he also decided to make his army disappear. As a graduate of St Andrews University, the King's Lieutenant may have remembered his classical authors, and especially the histories of Livy. He chronicled the extraordinary exploits of the great Carthaginian general, Hannibal, and his spectacular journey through the Alps in the depths of winter with his war elephants and the descent into unsuspecting Italy, as it were out of nowhere. The men of Clan Cameron knew of a high pass through the mountains to the south-east of the Great Glen, but it was only possible to traverse it in the good weather and long days of the summer. In the deep snows of late January and the numbing cold, the pass of the Allt na Larach, 'the Scar Burn', could not even be attempted. The land rose very

steeply, up to more than 2,000 feet at the summit, the drifts would
be deep, the snow shelved and piled, driven by the winds. The days
were short and, in the darkness, exhausted men would be lost. In
hidden crevasses, many would die of cold, suffer frostbite, their
plaids would freeze. The Cameron scouts shook their heads.

Montrose and Mac Colla were not listening.

Led by the reluctant Camerons, who had no doubt advised every
man to cut long rods to probe the drifts, the army began to disappear. From Cille Chuimein in the Great Glen, they marched south
in single file up Glen Tarff on a narrow path by the river. It was easier
going at first but, beyond Culachy, the Camerons turned towards
the west and led the army up a narrow valley. Druim Laragan, 'the
ridge of the larch trees', screened the march from the Great Glen
where Campbell's sharp-eyed scouts were patrolling. Having crossed
to Glen Buck, they followed the course of the Scar Burn up into the
high mountains and the deep snow. Darkness was falling but perhaps
there was a clear sky and a moon to light the way. The drifts must
have been deep and progress very, very slow, perhaps only half a mile
or so in an hour. They climbed between Carn na Larach and Carn
Dearg, both peaks of more than 2,000 feet. Towards dawn, the
scouts at last saw that the ground was beginning to fall away. The
army climbed down into Glen Turret and, from there, to the mouth
of Glen Roy. It had taken them thirty-six hours to march thirty-six
miles.

*

It was late summer when I walked down Glen Roy and through a
very different landscape. But there was still drama, some of it ancient.
The mountains at the head of the glen are majestic, their flanks
steep, grey and stony. But, as I made my way further down, trees
began to cluster along the banks of the river and there was good
grazing on the lower slopes. Even in the snow, the march through
the glen must have been much easier going for Montrose and Mac
Colla's Highlanders. I was following a fraying, single-track tarmac
road whose twists, turns and vertiginous blind summits suggested it

was the descendant of a much earlier track, perhaps one followed on 1 February 1645.

Above the road, there appeared to be three others, all of them thousands of years old. Along the flanks of Glen Roy, mystery ribbons through the landscape. Three precisely parallel tracks run for seven or eight miles from the head of the glen to its mouth. Each is about thirty-five feet wide and so perfectly level that, for centuries, it was believed they were man-made – or perhaps the work of giants or heroes like Finn McCool. Early Ordnance Survey maps showed them as tracks and local fables held that one was for walkers, another for carts and the third for livestock. Charles Darwin was so fascinated by them that he came north in 1838 to Glen Roy to examine these 'Parallel Roads', as they became known, but the great scientist could not unravel the mystery.

In 1840, the Swiss-American geologist, Louis Agassiz, travelled to Scotland. He was very interested in the Scottish geologist Hugh Miller's discoveries and collection of fossils and, when he saw the roads, he adopted the Cromarty man's dictum and 'made a right use of his eyes'. Agassiz quickly realised he knew exactly what he was looking at. These were not tracks at all but the remains of a series of prehistoric shorelines. Glen Roy had once been a huge loch.

Towards the end of the last ice age, a glacier known as 'the Lochaber Ice Lobe' had moved and effectively dammed the mouth of Glen Roy. Unable to drain into Loch Linnhe and the sea, the River Roy formed a loch and its shoreline created the lowest of the Parallel Roads, probably by a combination of regular, uniform wave action and intense frost. When the weather became even colder, the glacier grew and pushed the waters of the loch further into the mountains. It rose higher to form the second parallel road. And as temperatures dropped even lower, the level of the loch rose once more and created the highest of the three roads.

When the Earth at last began to warm, about 11,000 years ago, the ice dam made by the glacier suddenly broke down. Almost certainly in a matter of hours and with a deafening roar, a raging torrent of very cold water raced towards the Great Glen, carrying everything before it. The first dam-burst probably drained to the north-east, to Loch Ness, Inverness and into the sea at the Moray Firth. The highest of the Parallel Roads of Glen Roy remembers a cataclysm but also the moment when the ice age ended and life in the Highlands began.

On the switchback tarmac road, I came to a car park, a viewpoint with an information board. It described the geology I was looking at well but made no mention of Montrose's snow march. Looking at my Landranger map, I could see that the lowest of the three Parallel Roads ran only a few hundred feet above me. Scattering some well-washed ewes, I climbed up to discover that the road was not in fact a completely flat shelf. The ground was like a gently sloping window-sill, and I noticed that the sheep had cropped the grass close. Perhaps it drew nourishing minerals out of the shoreline of the ancient loch.

The glaciers left other deposits in Glen Roy. As they ground across the landscape, these slow-moving rivers of ice pushed along vast quantities of till or boulders, gravel, sand and clay. It acted like primeval sandpaper. When the glaciers melted, the till was eroded by streams and redeposited as what are known as 'fans', wide areas at the mouths of streams that feed into the River Roy. I could see that these are now very obvious, even at ground level, close to the road I was walking on.

Despite its mass and seeming solidity, the landscape left by the ice in Glen Roy can be unstable. When the glacial loch suddenly drained, it left steep sides where landslips are not uncommon. Eleven thousand years later, in the winter of 1989–90, the glaciers were still producing drama. At Brunachan in the glen, a huge landslip carried away part of the modern road and, according to an observer, the ancient deposit of mud and gravel moved downhill, 'flowing like porridge'.

Glen Roy is now a world-famous site for Earth scientists, one of the few places where the millennia of ice have left a graphic mark on the land. Few remember the hardy, intrepid men who marched down the glen in the winter of 1644–45 and now the signs on the A86 advertise an 'Ice-Age Landscape'.

*

Montrose's scouts almost blundered into a party of Campbells at the mouth of Glen Roy. In reprisal for the destruction around Inveraray, they were burning and looting farms along the banks of the River Roy. An encounter would have been disastrous, negating all of the benefits of the extraordinary march through the mountains. The Campbells would have raced back to Inverlochy to report what they had seen. Montrose quickly turned his army back up the glen and they were forced to make their way behind Maol Ruadh and through the hills north of Glen Spean.

An hour or two later, there was another encounter. Somewhere below Spean Bridge, perhaps on the edge of the Leanachan woods, the vanguard of the royalist army blundered into a small group of Campbell clansmen. There was a startled, sharp fight and many of them escaped, fleeing towards Inverlochy Castle, the headquarters of Sir Duncan Campbell of Auchinbreck. Montrose must have thought the game was up and, as the early dark descended, he led his army into the woodland on the western flanks of Ben Nevis. Whatever was going to happen would almost certainly happen at first light but, in fact, the flanking march was not detected or reported.

At Inverlochy the Campbell commanders continued to believe that Montrose and his army were still at Cille Chuimein thirty miles to the north-east. Scouts had reported no movement down the Great Glen. What Auchinbreck's men had run into was a raiding party, perhaps Keppoch MacDonalds or Camerons. It could not be Montrose.

In the darkness, on the steep flanks of Ben Nevis, exhausted men sank down wherever they could to rest and eat whatever scraps of cold food they had. No fires could be lit, no sign given of the presence of so many men. Inverlochy Castle and the Campbell camp were less than a mile away. As their officers gathered around Montrose and Mac Colla, they knew they had to wait. The long single-file line of stragglers from the snow march was still strung out on the track behind them. Meanwhile the royalist commanders counted the Campbell campfires in an attempt to estimate the size of Auchinbreck's army. There were many flickering points of light on the flat flood plain around the castle walls. Watching their enemies huddle around the warmth of the flames, the men crouching on the hillside shivered in the darkness. There was a half moon and, if the cloud cover was thin, it will have lit the camp, the towers of the castle and the waters of Loch Linnhe beyond them.

There seems to have been enough light to fight. On the lower slopes of Ben Nevis, Campbell pickets began to skirmish with the parties of men they found lurking in the woods. Musket shot rang out and some soldiers called to each other in the darkness. Who were they? Where were they? How many? But all the Campbells could see were shadows moving through the trees. Even though Auchinbreck still believed Montrose to be at Cille Chuimein on the shore of Loch Ness, his chief, the Marquis of Argyll, boarded a birlinn and had his men row out to the midstream of the River Lochy where they steadied the little ship against the current. Archibald Campbell was not fleeing, as he had been forced to do at Inveraray. He had injured his arm in a fall from his horse and was leaving matters to his kinsman.

Just before dawn on 2 February, everything changed. The landscape suddenly came alive as an army emerged from the woodland to the north-east. Auchinbreck was shocked to hear a fanfare of trumpets ring out and see the royal standard raised above an army arrayed before him. Their pipers played the battle rant of Clan Cameron, 'Sons of dogs, come and I will give you flesh'. The standard signified the presence of the King's Lieutenant. Montrose had appeared out of nowhere, somehow outflanking the Campbell pickets and, if he had come, then Mac Colla, his MacDonalds and the Irish regiments were with him. These last were on the flanks, one commanded by Manus O'Cahan, the other by Alasdair Mhor himself. In the centre, Montrose was with the chiefs and their clansmen – Glengarry, Maclean, Keppoch, Glencoe, Atholl, Appin and Lochaber. Sir Thomas Ogilvy's small troop of cavalry, their horses exhausted by the snow march, were clustered around the royal standard.

Auchinbreck was forced to move quickly. Facing the royalists, he anchored his left wing on the massive walls and moat of Inverlochy Castle and set 200 musketeers on the battlements. In the centre were the Campbells, the core of the army, perhaps more than 1,000 men, many with a score to settle after Inveraray. On the flanks were eight companies, four on each, of Lowland infantry. Many were battle-hardened, experienced men, unlike at Tippermuir, and they had fought in England and Ireland.

As priests walked up and down the royalist battle lines, set only two men deep to counter any attempt to outflank them, and men knelt to pray and ask forgiveness, Montrose noticed Iain Lom MacDonald walking alone, away from the army.

'Will you desert us, Iain Lom?' he is said to have shouted.

'If I stay and fall in battle,' said the great bard, 'who will sing your praises tomorrow?'

MacDonald continued walking until he found a vantage point.

Auchinbreck knew what to expect. To break the engulfing fury of the charge that would surely come, he deployed a vanguard forward of the main line. When Montrose saw what was happening, he quickly sent a despatch to Manus O'Cahan. As the battle rants reached their crescendos, the Irishman gave the order to charge. His regiment raced forward, fired a single volley at close range, threw down their firearms, formed wedges and tore into the Campbell vanguard. As they drove them backwards, Alasdair Mac Colla and his men charged and then the whole line, led by Montrose, roared down the hillside. They had momentum – *an cothrom a' bhraighe*, 'the advantage of the brae'. The ranks of Campbell's Lowland companies disintegrated, their discipline collapsing in chaos, and they turned and ran into the ranks behind them, overrunning their own comrades.

But in the centre it was different. Under Auchinbreck's command, the Campbell regiments fought like furies. They may have been surrounded and doomed but they were determined to sell their lives dearly. Sir Thomas Ogilvy's small troop of royalist cavalry had cut off the possibility of retreat into the safety of the castle and its garrison surrendered without a fight. Finally, the Campbell standard fell, their clansmen fled and, as ever, hundreds were cut down as they ran or were driven into the river or the loch to drown.

Others were pursued for miles, some of them into the hills. Royalist casualties were negligible but more than 1,500 of the Campbell army were killed. Victory was complete and Auchinbreck was taken prisoner.

What followed on the afternoon of 2 February 1645, the day of Candlemas, probably took place inside Inverlochy Castle and it was salutary, a reminder. The romance was always with the royalists and dashing, brilliant, charismatic commanders such as Montrose in part because history tells us that they ultimately lost to the dour, plain, severe Covenanters and the Roundheads. Almost from the first, the Jacobite cause was an engine that generated sentimentality as the long end of an old song echoed across the centuries. Clan Donald, the Lords of the Isles, the title itself is the stuff of poetry and even wistful nostalgia, whereas Clan Campbell's dogged, pragmatic pursuit of power is the stuff of prose.

At the time, these sentiments were much qualified and, lest we see Montrose, Mac Colla, Lord George Murray, Prince Charles and the Jacobite pantheon as the valiant, gallant heroes of a sad but noble story, we should remember the fate of Sir Duncan Campbell of Auchinbreck and the poetry of Iain Lom MacDonald after Inverlochy.

Presumably in the hall of the captured castle, Alasdair Mac Colla had Sir Duncan brought before him. Campbells had burned, looted and ravaged the Antrim lands of his cousins, and Auchinbreck must have known he would get no mercy from MacDonalds. Two choices were offered by Mac Colla. Campbell could decide to be made longer, that is strung up and hanged by the neck to choke to death, urine running down his leg, his bowels voiding, his face turning purple. Or he could be made shorter, by decapitation.

'*Da dhiu gun aon roghain*,' said Sir Duncan with admirable sangfroid. 'Two terrible things with nothing to choose between them' was the sense of his reply.

Without any hesitation, Mac Colla unsheathed his great two-handed claymore. Auchinbreck was almost certainly bound and made to kneel and Alasdair swung his blade. But in his bloodthirsty fury, he almost missed his mark, cleaving off the top of Sir Duncan's head above the ears, scattering his bloody brains over the flagstones of the castle hall.

Standing on his vantage point on the lower slopes of Ben Nevis, Iain Lom was exultant as he watched his MacDonald kinsmen tear into the ranks of the Campbells on the flat ground around the castle. His praise poem gloats and glories in the blood spilled and the fate of families who had lost fathers, brothers and sons.

> Early on Sunday morning I climbed the brae above
> the castle of Inverlochy.
> I saw the army arrayed for battle,
> And victory in the field was with Clan Donald . . .

> You remember the place called the Tawny Field.
> It was manured not with the dung of sheep or goats,
> But by the blood of Campbells, well congealed.
> To Hell with you if I feel pity for your plight,
> And I listen to the distress of your children,
> Lamenting the band that went into battle,
> The wailing of the women of Argyll.

Iain Lom's rage was matched by Sir Duncan Campbell's sister who wrote:

> Were I at Inverlochy with a two-edged sword in my hand,
> And all the strength and skill I could desire,
> I would draw blood there,
> And I would tear asunder the MacLeans and the MacDonalds.
> The Irish would be without life.
> And I would bring the Campbells back to life.

The lyrics of the song of Alasdair Mac Colla played in my head as I drove around Fort William looking for Inverlochy Castle. Karen Matheson's beautiful, clear voice and the insistent beat of the music described a year of slaughter and bloodshed as well as extraordinary prowess, the generalship of Montrose and the perfection of the Highland charge by Mac Colla.

When I finally found the castle, down a bumpy, potholed road that might once have led to an industrial site, now demolished, close to the railway line, I drove across a narrow bridge to find it closed to the public. Large rectangular wire barriers were linked together around its surprisingly intact walls. An information board told me that it had been built in 1280 by the once-powerful Comyn family, the rivals of Robert Bruce, and that it was largely unchanged. Its deep moat had been filled in but the walls still rose to an impressive height. Apparently, Queen Victoria was unimpressed, having visited in 1873. 'There is so little to see,' she said, oddly.

What disappointed me was that there was no mention of the battle of 1645. It was difficult to picture how events unfolded. Behind me a burn ran into the River Lochy and to the east a soap factory and shop had been built on the open ground where the Highlanders probably charged. If Sir Duncan had anchored his left wing on the walls of the castle, that had to be where the battle was fought. Beyond the soap factory was a wide park much used by dog walkers, some of whom were picking up poop in little plastic bags. The site of the battle and the castle are sandwiched between the 19th and the 20th centuries. The railway bridge that carries trains to the west, to the Glenfinnan Viaduct, to Mallaig and the Skye ferries, runs close to the castle, and the new road to Inverness rumbles to the south past petrol stations and a retail park. All the spirits of the place seemed to me to have fled.

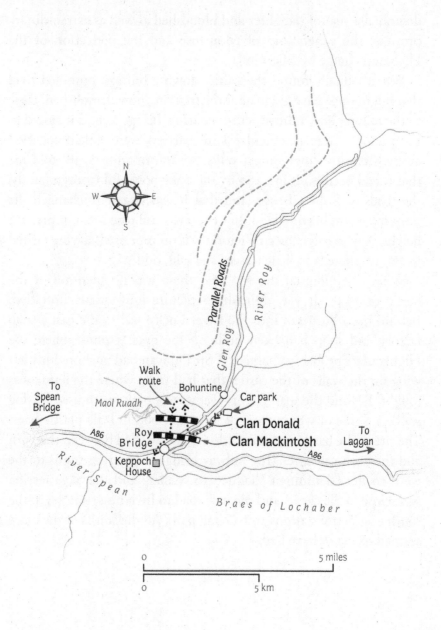

5

The Perfect Ground

Mulroy, 6 August 1688

In 1723, Sileas of Keppoch – or, in Gaelic, Sileas na Ceapaich – composed a lament for Alasdair Dubh, Black Alasdair, the 11th Chief of the MacDonnells of Glengarry. A loyal Jacobite and a famous warrior, he was mourned by her in the language of trees, attributing their virtues to him. Yews were long-lived, their wood hard and, unusually, new growth forms inside the old, a symbol of constant renewal. Oak is associated with strength, resilience and confidence while holly was thought protective, its sprigs often attached to doorways or doors, much like holly wreaths at Christmas are now. Apple trees were fruitful and the long slender thorns of the blackthorn could inflict deep wounds. By contrast, the alder was sometimes thought to be evil or secretive, the aspen had links with the otherworld and the lime was understood as feminine. In his magisterial elegy about the deserted township of Hallaig on Raasay, Sorley Maclean used similar analogies – images of birch trees, hazels and rowans. Here is an English translation of the original Gaelic of Sileas of Keppoch's lament for Alasdair Dubh – Black Alasdair of Glengarry. Inevitably, its mouth-filling fluidity is somewhat lost but the sentiment is clear:

> You were the yew above every forest,
> You were the strong, steadfast oak,
> You were the holly and the blackthorn,
> You were the apple tree, rough-barked and many-flowered.

You had no kinship with the aspen,
Owed no bonds to the alder;
There was none of the lime tree in you;
You were the darling of beautiful women.

Although born and raised in Keppoch, a lovely, leafy series of intertwining glens in Lochaber, where the rivers Spean, Roy and Lochy thread their way through the mountains, Sileas spent much of her life in the east. She married Alexander Gordon, the Duke of Gordon's factor, and they lived on his estates in Banffshire. But Sileas never forgot her heritage or the glens of the western Highlands, writing poems in praise of the Jacobite cause as well as laments for those who were killed fighting for the restoration of the Stuarts. Keppoch and Clan Donald never wavered in their loyalty and its intensity formed part of the clan's cultural fabric.

Older than Sileas but broadly contemporary was Iain Lom MacDonald, another gifted bard whose work was highly political and partial. But, unlike many artists who observe life and events from the margins, Iain took an active part, famously in Montrose and Mac Colla's campaign of 1644 and 1645. The feral power of his hatred for Clan Campbell after their defeat at Inverlochy leaps off the page.

What the work of these two Keppoch bards and that of Alasdair Mac Mhaighstir Alasdair shows is something counter-intuitive, something unique to Highland society and crucial to understanding it. The raw courage of the clans and their chiefs as the wedges formed in the gun smoke and they drove into the ranks of their enemies, the savagery of the swordplay at Prestonpans and the merciless slaughter of fleeing Covenanters at Tippermuir – all of these exploits were praised and memorialised in elegantly composed poetry. And, in the case of Iain Lom and Alasdair Mac Mhaighstir Alasdair, it was poetry made by brilliantly gifted men who could stab with dirks and slash with the razor-sharp blades of their swords, maiming, killing, fighting hand-to-hand, the blood of their enemies spattering over them as they fought like furies.

What this seeming contradiction tells us is that, whatever it was and however its enemies saw it, clan society could be savage but it was not primitive. Because men fought principally with bladed weapons, confronting their enemies face to face, as soldiers had since the Greek hoplites and the Roman legionaries and long before, that does not mean that the society that fostered such elemental courage and the other martial virtues was itself backward, an isolated pocket of ancient atavism in the north of Scotland. Even though there was little material wealth amongst those who were not chiefs or related to chiefs and they worked hard and ceaselessly to wring a living out of what was often an unforgiving landscape, this was a society with a rich cultural life.

Much of it has vanished. Sileas of Keppoch, Iain Lom and Alasdair Mac Mhaighstir Alasdair were exceptional because they were literate and wrote down some of what they composed. Many bards did not. Memory mattered much more in Highland culture and had done for millennia. There were many bards, many musicians and many story-tellers who wrote down nothing and whose work has disappeared into the darkness of the past as communities were fractured and the chains of cultural transmission were broken. Memory fades and can quickly be lost. The legacy of these three poets is almost certainly only a tiny fraction of what was recited, sung and celebrated around countless circles of firelight in the glens and on the islands.

Sileas of Keppoch's brother, Coll MacDonald, matriculated at St Andrews University in 1682. He was about eighteen years old and his family clearly believed that his future demanded a decent education. At that time, the university was small with only a few hundred students, most of them studying divinity at St Mary's College in order to qualify as Church of Scotland ministers. Like his family and his clan, Coll had remained a Catholic and it's probable that he went to lectures in history or perhaps Latin and Greek. There were other disciplines taught by distinguished men. A descendant of Clan Gregor whose persistent lawlessness saw them banned from using their name, James Gregory was Professor of Mathematics and a brilliant man.

In 1662, he published the *'Optica Promota'*, a paper that set down the theoretical and practical principles for constructing the world's first reflecting telescope. Much admired by Isaac Newton, Gregory also produced the first proof of the fundamental theorem of calculus. And, for the entertainment of his students, he used a feather to show how sunlight split into its spectrum of component colours. It was in this intellectual, innovative atmosphere that Coll MacDonald found himself and perhaps he was aware that the mathematical genius Gregory, who taught at St Andrews until the late 1680s, was the very recent descendant of clansmen.

But Coll's university education was cut short. A year after he matriculated, his father died and the nineteen-year-old was forced to return to Keppoch to become clan chief. There were immediate difficulties. It appears that Clan Mackintosh, based on the Moray coast and its hinterland, had rights over land in Keppoch and the chief, Lachlan Mackintosh, had Coll arrested and imprisoned at Inverness for the non-payment of rent. Released on bail, the young man was nevertheless furious, insulted and determined to have redress. Using what he had learned at university to good effect, Coll personally petitioned the Scottish Privy Council to settle matters by a 'legal decision or amicable determination' and he offered to plead the case himself. And he might well have succeeded. Colonel John Hill, the commander of the government garrison at Fort William, wrote that Coll 'speaks better than any Highlander I know, and is a pretty fellow'. In the event, there was no resolution and the dispute was allowed to fester.

By 1688, Lachlan Mackintosh had persuaded the Privy Council to grant him a 'Commission of Fire and Sword' against the MacDonalds of Keppoch. Essentially this gave Mackintosh a completely free hand, draconian powers to capture, destroy and kill without reference to the law or central government. A small army began to muster in the east. Despite the refusal of Clan Grant and Clan Fraser to join him, Lachlan Mackintosh could put 1,000 of his own men in the field and they were reinforced by government troops, one of the independent Highland companies. It was commanded by Kenneth Mackenzie of Suddie and its role was to help keep order in the Highlands.

In early August 1688, Mackintosh led his men deep into Keppoch and they camped at Roy Bridge, on the northern bank of the Spean. Coll MacDonald was waiting for them. When dawn broke on 4 August and Mackintosh looked north, up at the slopes of Maol Ruadh, he saw arrayed on its summit the men of Clan Donald. And with them were the MacDonalds of Glencoe, the MacDonnells of Glengarry and the MacMartins, a sept of Clan Cameron.

*

It was a morning of meteorology for children. I drove north over the splendid new bridge over the Firth of Forth in brilliant sunshine and saw the autumn russets, yellows and deep browns glow on the trees of Perthshire. But, the moment the A9 began to climb into the mountains, the skies immediately darkened and the rain began to bounce off the road in front of me. In my rear-view mirror I could see the sunlit Lowlands receding. I was on my way to Roy Bridge, to the site of what was probably the last clan battle in British history.

As it was between Clan Donald and Clan Campbell forty years before at Inverlochy, there could be fierce, long-running internecine enmity in the Highlands that could erupt into bloodshed at any time. After the disintegration of the Lordship of the Isles at the end of the 15th century, decades of disorder ensued. *An Linn nan Creach*, 'the Age of the Forays', it saw clans almost continually fighting amongst themselves, with land and its associated rights almost always the issue. Bloody, full-scale battles were joined. In July 1544, Clanranald, led by its chief, John of Moidart, attacked Clan Fraser on the flat flood plain between Loch Lochy and Loch Oich near the foot of the Great Glen. It was such a warm day that men stripped and fought only in their shirts, giving the battle its name, *Blar na Leine*, 'the Field of the Shirts'. Hundreds were killed as the clansmen hacked at each other and, after the slaughter, Clanranald could only claim victory because more of their exhausted warriors were left standing.

The rain stopped suddenly when I turned off the A9 at Dalwhinnie to drive west past Loch Laggan and the sun sparkled on the water with a tinsel glint. I was moving through the high heart of the Highland massif, much of it dun-coloured moorland, some of it spectacular, like the great mountain of *Creag Meagaidh* and the peaks around it. At the western end of the loch, Glen Spean begins and, as I made my way along the tree-lined road and passed well-drained fields, I realised I was in Keppoch at last, the area also marked on the map as the Braes of Lochaber. In Gaelic, *ceapach* means 'a plot or area of good ground, land that could be tilled and sown with barley and other crops'. The Highland economy has long been predominantly pastoral, with cattle, sheep and goats grazing the lush, rain-fed high pasture in summer while crops ripened down in the glens. These were for human consumption only and oats made oatmeal that made oatcakes and porridge. The ancient journey of trans-humance brought the herdsmen and their animals down into the harvested fields so they could get some meagre grass before the privations of winter, and fertilise the ground with their muck. I could see that Keppoch was perfectly suited to this annual rotation. It was a place worth fighting for.

In the tiny village of Roy Bridge, I turned sharp right and immediately found myself following an old road. Single track, winding around rocks, hummocks and field ends, it ran along a shelf above the rushing River Roy. The sound of cascading water was constant, although I couldn't see the river through the dense stands of trees on the steep slope below where I parked. There was a small cairn by the roadside that remembered the Battle of Mulroy and it told me that 'the hill opposite' was where it was fought.

Maps are the language of the Earth and I love them. I can fritter away too many hours looking at them spread out on my desk, comparing them to my recollection of places and how they relate to other features or imagining other locations I haven't ever seen. For use in the landscape, there will never again be any maps as good as the Ordnance Survey Pathfinder Series. Small, manageable in a wind and richly detailed, they were an adornment to life in Britain and are, tragically, no longer published. Of their successors, the Explorer Series are simply absurd. At sixteen square feet – and sometimes double sided! – they are huge and impossible to manage out of doors. When folded to show the section you need, they are too bulky to fit into any sensible pocket. Once, in a rage, I simply tore out the part I needed. And as for those who walk in the countryside and are guided by their mobile phones, there are no words.

Second-hand Pathfinders are hard to come by and so I was forced to buy some of the Landranger series for this trip. At less than nine square feet, they can be manageably folded and don't turn into kites in a breeze. And they are not double sided. On the Ben Nevis map, number forty-one in the series, I found Maol Ruadh easily enough and at 256 metres above sea level – not very far away at Fort William – it looked an easy, steady climb.

As I walked down the rain-washed road towards a field gate, high-altitude winds sent the clouds scudding eastwards and Maol Ruadh was bathed in autumn sunshine. An arrowhead of geese, honking, bickering it sounded like, flew suddenly out of the blue sky over the summit like a squadron of fighters. But everywhere there was peace. As I clanked open the metal gate, the hill looked like its name. *Maol* can mean 'bald' in Gaelic and it became shorthand for tonsured monks, giving many modern men a Christian name in all senses. Malcolm is from *Maol Chaluim*, 'the monk or the follower of St Columba'. But on the map, *maol* is 'a rounded, bare hill' and that's precisely what I was beginning to climb. *Ruadh* is often translated as 'red' but 'russet' is better – a more appropriately autumnal gloss. On the slopes near the summit, I could see that the withering, die-back grasses were taking on a rich brown.

Beyond the gate, an old metalled road led straight up a gentle incline, leading to a stand of hardwoods with more rich russets at their foot, an undergrowth of toffee-coloured tangled bracken and ferns. Turning to the right towards more mature trees, oaks and chestnuts with leaves only beginning to lose their shades of green, the road crossed a burn. Hidden in a deep declivity, it made its way diagonally across the face of the hill. It wasn't wide but might have been a surprise to anyone who did not know the ground. As I walked on, it occurred to me that Coll MacDonald and his captains did know the ground and that Lachlan Mackintosh and Kenneth Mackenzie did not. This must have influenced the conduct and outcome of the battle that took place on this wide, open and apparently unbroken hillside pasture. It faces south and catches the sun from early morning until it slips behind the mountains to the west. Anyone looking up from the road will not have seen the deep ditch through which the burn runs.

This Lochaber brae of Maol Ruadh was fenced only at the road and at the summit, where I could make out a row of posts silhouetted against the blue horizon, probably with stock and barbed wire strung between them. But to the east and west I couldn't see any other boundary except distant shelter belts of what might have been commercial forestry. This was a very wide area, most of it unimpeded, a good place to fight – if you knew the ground. At Tippermuir, more than 5,000 men faced each other but here the numbers were much smaller – perhaps fewer than 2,000 in all. I wondered about tactics. There was no cavalry and so events would move only as fast as men could run. Did either the MacDonalds or the Mackintoshes worry about outflanking when they arrayed their men? Did either of them have the numbers to do that? And, in any case, these two small armies were both made up of clansmen, including Kenneth Mackenzie's Highland company, and they would fight hand-to-hand as tradition and experience had taught them rather than present a battle line as the Covenanters had done outside Perth forty years before.

Beyond the diagonal burn and scattered, small stands of more hardwoods, I came to a series of sheep lawns, wide areas where the grass had been cropped close and was still a vivid green, like billiard table baize. Even though this southern slope of Maol Ruadh was fenced to the north and the south, it looked to me that the sheep had been hefted. Shepherds with flocks on open hill pasture – and there would have been no fences in 1688 – try to keep them in one place, using their dogs, where their grazing creates lawns that encourage them to stay there. With their sharp teeth, sheep crop constantly and, in so doing, make the grass sweeter as new growth comes up from the shoots, like a vast version of pruning. Ewes pass on the heft to their lambs who will also graze the same hillside down the generations. And as they do so, they muck and fertilise the grass, further encouraging the cycle of renewal. Hefting makes the sheep much more manageable and easier to protect. The lawns on Maol Ruadh were also close to trees, places of shelter when the scourging winter winds whip down off the flanks of Ben Nevis and across the brae.

About halfway up the slope I came to a shelf, a wide area of well-cropped grass that seemed to run across the face of the brae like a road. From there I could see all the way down to the foot of the hill and the course of the River Roy below it. I wondered if this was where Coll MacDonald drew up his clansmen, where Lachlan Mackintosh saw them when he looked up from his camp on the morning of 4 August 1688.

Out to the west, the massive, glowering, brooding bulwark of Ben Nevis began to disappear, engulfed by cloud rolling off the ocean and up the Firth of Lorne. When I felt the first spots of rain, I put on my hat and pulled up the hood of my waterproof over it as a pleasant, easy climb turned into a plodding uphill tramp. I discovered that the ground changed abruptly. Above another diagonal burn, one that ran so straight I wondered if it had been dug as a drainage ditch, there was platchy, peaty bog. Trickles were everywhere and, as the rain sheeted down out of the west, the damp ground seemed to quake under my tread. On the morning of 4 August, Mackintosh had been hampered by the effect of 'extraordinary rains' and both the rivers Spean and Roy had been in spate the week before, making crossing impossible. There seems little doubt that on the day of the battle the ground was very wet indeed, much more boggy than the clatch I was tramping through. And the burn near the foot of the slope will have run much deeper.

The Battle of Mulroy was well recorded but, very unusually, by the losers. When Lachlan Mackintosh arrived in Keppoch, he ordered the building of a fort near the confluence of the Roy and the Spean, near where Keppoch House had been built. I'd driven down its sternly signposted 'PRIVATE ROAD' and rung doorbells both front and back but no one had answered even though the back door was ajar and there were lights on. I looked below the house at the flat ground by the rivers, but I could see nothing that suggested a fortress. The Landranger plotted a motte in that olde-worlde font the OS uses to signify antiquities, in this case a medieval motte and bailey castle, but I could see no sign of that either.

It seems that the bad weather in August frustrated and surprised Mackintosh, a man from the Moray coast where it rained less. Here is a letter – with the text rendered in modern spelling but the sense unchanged – he sent to the Earl of Perth, a member of the Privy Council that had granted his Commission of Fire and Sword:

> My friends and I are making up a little fort, in which we are to leave some men for securing me in my possessions, this being the only, most probable means for reducing the rebels, and if it had not been for this, we had been at them by now. Besides that, the spates are impassable, but as soon as the waters fall, we hope to make an account of them.

The incessant rain made a waiting game inevitable. Coll MacDonald was quietly mustering his forces and, as Captain Mackenzie of Suddie made clear in a letter to General Douglas, the officer commanding the king's forces in Scotland, they were aware of enemy activity around them.

> May it please your Excellency. According to your order, I joined Mackintosh at this place on Saturday last. In which time we have always extraordinary rains. The first two or three days we could see none of the rebels, but now that the waters are not passable for their greatness and there being no bridges . . . There appear to be about two hundred of them on the other side of the water about half a mile from us, and we have intelligence that there are

presently the like number, if not greater, not far off here. By this we conjecture that their friends from all places run to them, for all that tribe of the MacDonalds on [Mackintosh's] land will not exceed two hundred men.

Amongst the written sources there is a deal of confusion as to what happened next. It may be that Coll MacDonald led his men up the source of a burn, the *Allt Bo Loin*, that flows into the River Roy at Bohuntine. The name means something like the 'Burn of the Cattle Glade' and there may have been a track. This approach will have screened the MacDonald forces and allowed them to advance from the north to the summit of Maol Ruadh unseen by the Mackintosh army. At dawn, they may have moved downhill, to below the boggy ground, to the much better drained shelf of flattish ground I'd come across. Coll MacDonald and his captains will have known this area and its contours very well. From there the ground below was good, perfect for the charge.

Most sources agree that, when Mackintosh had arrayed his forces on the lower slopes, the chief of the MacDonalds ordered the charge. His men fired a single volley from muskets and pistols, drew their swords and dirks, formed wedges and tore into their enemies. But all agree that the fighting lasted for about an hour. The Mackintoshes did not immediately break and flee. They were Highlanders, they knew what to expect and stood their ground – at first.

There exists an account of the battle from someone who was probably too young to have been there but later became an experienced soldier. Brigadier William Mackintosh of Borlum fought with distinction in the 1715 rebellion – indeed, many said he should have led it rather than the Earl of Mar. But he was only nine or ten years old when his clansmen faced the MacDonalds at Mulroy. His original sources, men who told him what happened, will almost certainly have had first-hand knowledge of events.

Borlum later claimed that, instead of a classic general charge, Coll MacDonald first mounted an attack on the left wing of the Mackintosh army 'to pass by us to Keppoch and there seize

Mackintosh, his Lady, and all our baggage, horses and spoil at the old fort at Keppoch'. But Captain Mackenzie and his Highland company stood fast and appear to have repelled the charge. MacDonald then pulled back and moved the point of attack to the right wing before ordering a charge on the whole line. According to Borlum, that succeeded:

> Their whole body immediately rushed furiously over a strip that runs between them and us (all naked except their shirts) and forced a detached party that stood in defence of that pass opposite to Mackintosh and his colours, to retire hastily to their own body.

It seems that, at that moment, the Mackintosh line finally broke.

> Our own body . . . gave ground at first, and then immediately, shamefully, began to run disorderly towards the scounce [probably a reference to the River Roy] notwithstanding all of the strokes and threats of their officers to the contrary.

On the right of the Mackintosh line stood a young soldier who had enlisted in the Highland company and, much later, he described the MacDonald attack in vivid, honest detail. His account smacks of authenticity and is very unusual since it comes not from a general or a leader who might have been tempted to be partial, even self-justifying, in what he recorded. Here is what Donald McBane remembered of Mulroy, beginning with the march to the battleground:

> The two clans were both on foot, and our company was still with Mackintosh, who marched towards MacDonald and his clan, until we came in sight of them. Then both parties ordered their men to march up the hill. A company being in the front, we drew up in a line of battle as we could, our company being on the right. We were no sooner in order but there appears double the number of the MacDonalds, which made us then to fear the worst, at least for my part. I repeated my former wish [not to be there], I never

having seen the like. The MacDonalds came down the hill upon us without either shoe, stocking or bonnet on their head. They gave a shout and then the fire began on both sides, and continued a hot dispute for an hour. Then they broke in upon us with sword and targe, and Lochaber axes, which obliged us to give way. Seeing my captain sore wounded, and a great many more with heads lying cloven on every side, I was sadly affrighted, never having seen the like before. A Highlander attacked me with sword and targe and cut my wooden-handled bayonet out of the muzzle of my gun. I then clubbed my gun and gave him a stroke with it, which made the butt-end fly off. Seeing the Highland men come fast upon me, I took to my heels and ran thirty miles before I looked behind me. Every person I saw or met, I took for my enemy.

Private Donald McBane was born in Inverness in 1665 and apprenticed to a tobacco spinner. Bored and hankering after the excitement of a soldier's life, he ran away in 1687 and enlisted in a Highland company of the British army commanded by Colonel Grant. McBane's recollections are very valuable, unique and they have the unmistakable whiff of authenticity about what it was like to face the Highland charge.

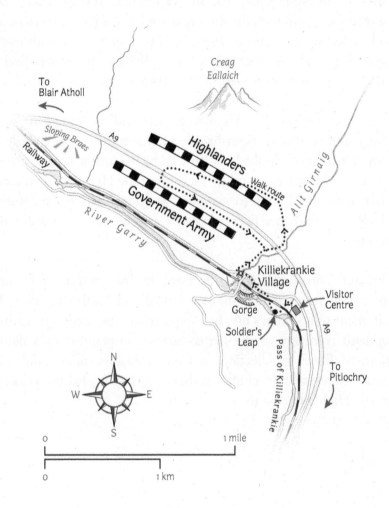

To Blair Atholl

Creag Eallaich

Sloping Braes

A9

Railway

Highlanders

Walk route

Government Army

Allt Girnaig

River Garry

Killiekrankie Village

Visitor Centre

Gorge

Soldier's Leap

A9

Pass of Killiekrankie

To Pitlochry

N
W   E
S

0   1 mile

0   1 km

6

A' Dol Sios

Killiecrankie, 27 July 1689

On the evening of 11 December 1688, four men slipped quietly out of the sprawling Palace of Whitehall in London. In the winter dark, torches lit the way to the stables where saddled horses were waiting, their snorted breath pluming in the cold night air. Sir Edward Hales was a Privy Councillor and with him were Obadiah Walker, Ralph Shales and a servant. Once mounted, the party trotted under an archway into a narrow lane. After making sure they were not followed, Hales led his men down Millbank to the horse ferry for crossing the Thames. They had been waiting all day for dead low water, the hour or so when the tide was out, when the great river was still and could be safely forded.

After Sir Edward had handed over some silver coins, his men dismounted and coaxed their horses out onto the flat raft, their weight making it tilt and bob until all were aboard, settled and made to stand still. When the ferrymen at last cast off, torches flaring in the chill of the December night, they pushed hard down on their poles and began to punt across to the lights of the Lambeth shore. Sir Edward's servant waited until the raft had reached midstream, well beyond the mudflats on either bank. Then he opened a leather satchel, drew out the Great Seal of England by its golden chain and dropped it into the river.

Disguised in a short black wig and wearing dark clothes, Sir Edward's servant was in fact his master, King James II of England, Ireland and France and James VII of Scotland.

A month before the night ferry across the Thames, William, Prince of Orange, had landed with a 14,000-strong Dutch army at Brixham in Devon. Blown along the Channel by a 'Protestant wind', he had come to remove from the throne a Catholic autocrat who threatened not only the stability of his own realms but also the Protestant states established all over northern Europe at the cost of much blood and pain. Married to James II's daughter, William had a proxy claim to the thrones of England, Scotland and Ireland as her consort but, in reality, he was a usurper and one who had widespread support.

Despite the fact that only a tiny minority of the population of his three kingdoms were Catholics, James had begun to install his co-religionists in powerful positions as judges, in his government and his personal household and he also set about repealing legislation that discriminated against them. Parliament was ignored and the aristocracy became largely disaffected. Europe was recovering from the appalling slaughter of the Thirty Years' War, the conflict between Protestant and Catholic states, and no one wished to see religious issues flaring into hostility in Britain and Ireland. But, in the beginning, James II's excesses were tolerated as a temporary aberration, one that would cease with his death. The queen, Mary of Modena, had suffered the terrible grief and pain of losing ten children either at birth or in infancy. James's heir, and very likely to succeed, was his fiercely Protestant daughter, Mary, the wife of William of Orange. So it was only a matter of time.

On 10 June 1688, everything changed. A healthy son was born to the king and queen, a Catholic heir to the three kingdoms. The Stuart dynasty would now continue on into what would become an increasingly fractious future.

Letters were sent immediately across the North Sea to William of Orange from prominent English politicians and aristocrats. They told him that people 'were dissatisfied with the present conduct of government' and wanted change. If Prince William were to invade England, he would find support from 'much the greater part of the nobility and gentry'.

James II panicked as rumours began to swirl around the Palace of Whitehall, courtiers whispering behind their hands, and he frantically began to reverse the pro-Catholic policies and practices that had alienated almost all of his subjects. The king quickly had more ships fitted out to defend against a sea-borne invasion, new regiments were recruited for the army and others brought back from Ireland. But it was all too late and too little. Authority and credibility had drifted away from him. The wheels of change had begun to grind.

After William landed at Brixham on 5 November and made surprisingly slow, cautious progress towards London, James found he had time to regroup and take a grip of the situation. He joined his army at Salisbury but soon realised that morale was low and many of his officers deeply disaffected. At that point, the king appears to have had a breakdown. Terrible nosebleeds kept him from sleeping at night and he began to panic, shaking and weeping. Officers openly deserted to William of Orange and towns such as Nottingham, York, Leicester, Gloucester and Carlisle declared for 'the Protestant religion and liberty'.

Unable to trust his general staff, James decided to retreat to London, in effect surrendering the south of England to William without a fight. When he arrived at the ant-heap of the Palace of Whitehall and its 1,500 rooms and countless courtyards, the king found it almost deserted, most of his court having apparently abandoned him and his cause. Even Anne, his younger daughter and destined eventually to be the last Stuart monarch, had defected to William. One of the few courtiers who remained noted 'the king is much out of order, looks yellow and takes no natural rest'. By which he meant that James could not sleep without the aid of opiates.

On 9 December 1688, matters came to a head. Queen Mary disguised herself as a laundress and left Whitehall with her five-month-old baby son and escaped across the Channel to Calais. Two days later James threw the Great Seal of England into the dark waters of the Thames, believing that William would find it difficult to summon parliament or enact legislation without it.

And so it began, more than fifty years of intermittent Jacobite rebellion, warfare in Scotland and Ireland and ultimate, crushing and final defeat. None shed more blood in the Stuart cause than the Highland clans and none suffered worse after the final catastrophe at Culloden.

When news of James VII's flight to France reached Edinburgh, crowds spilled on to the High Street. More than 25,000 citizens crowded into the tottering tenements between the Netherbow Port and the gates of the castle and, in moments, a mob had formed, chanting anti-Catholic slogans, no doubt spoiling for a fight. Except there was no one to fight. Instead, their numbers were swollen by the Trained Bands, an early version of the city's police force, and they sallied out of the Netherbow Port, drums beating. Having marched down the Canongate, the mob swept aside any who might have been guarding the precinct around the royal palace at Holyroodhouse. Meeting little resistance, they broke into the Chapel Royal. James VII had had the old abbey church of Holyrood fitted out for the celebration of the mass. The mob tore the interior apart, smashing the stained-glass windows, pulling down what they saw as idolatrous sculpture, desecrating the royal tombs and rejoicing at the fall of a Catholic king.

But, in fact, James VII was still King of Scotland. After he dropped the Great Seal of England into the Thames and ultimately fled to France, William of Orange and his supporters could argue that, in effect, he had abdicated. No such argument could be made in Scotland. Instead, the Convention of the Scottish Estates was summoned to convene in Edinburgh at Parliament Hall. The matter of the kingdom of Scotland would be decided in Scotland and not in London.

On the morning of 16 March 1689, the barons, the bishops who governed the Church of Scotland at that time and the burgesses from all the major towns were not only forced to run the gauntlet of the jeering mob, they also had to pass by James VII's brother. An equestrian statue of Charles II had been recently raised on a high plinth in the cobbled street between the High Kirk of St Giles and the law courts. By the end of the day, it would become a monument – all that remained of the deposed Stuart dynasty.

The symbolic and residual powers of the Stuarts were never far from the thoughts of the commissioners or the mob that waited outside Parliament Hall, their chants ringing through its high windows. The Duke of Gordon stubbornly held Edinburgh Castle for the deposed king and reports were filtering south that many of the chiefs of the Highland clans were minded to rise in rebellion. And what made the atmosphere in Edinburgh even more febrile was urgent and disturbing news of James VII. Four days before the Convention met, he had landed in Ireland with French troops at his back and, to make matters worse, the Irish Parliament had declared that James was the rightful king and William a usurper, and it passed bills attacking those who had supported the Dutch prince. Dynastic, religious and military battle lines were quickly being drawn.

John Graham of Claverhouse had been created the 1st Viscount Dundee by James VII in 1688 but he chose to attend the convention in Edinburgh despite the hostile crowds. An experienced, battle-hardened soldier, he may have taken the precaution of bringing fifty dragoons with him as a bodyguard. Claverhouse had seen active military service in the Franco–Dutch War of 1672–78 before return-ing to Scotland to command one of the Highland companies. Their mission was to suppress the field services, the conventicles, of the Covenanters, a fundamentalist Presbyterian movement outlawed by the governments of the Stuart kings, and take more severe measures if needed. He had fought at a minor battle at Drumclog against a force of Covenanters and his efforts at suppression earned him the nickname of 'Bluidy Clavers'. In 1688, Viscount Dundee was given command of all the king's forces in Scotland, such as they were.

High up on the massive western walls of Edinburgh Castle there is a black, cast-iron grille, a small postern gate that witnessed a secret conference in March 1688. It became quickly clear to Dundee that the Scottish Convention – the Convention of the Three Estates, the bishops, barons and burghs – would be implacable in its support of William and Mary. With his fifty dragoons, he rode through the

Grassmarket and out of the West Port but then dismounted and climbed the steep castle rock to the postern gate. Talking to him through the cast-iron grille, Dundee encouraged the Duke of Gordon to stand firm, to hold Edinburgh Castle for the king, while he rode north to raise the Highland clans.

Sir Ewen Cameron of Lochiel, Chief of the Name, had been a witness to history as he marched south with General George Monck in 1660 to attend the parliament that restored the Stuarts to the throne after the convulsions of Cromwell's Commonwealth and the bloody Wars of the Three Kingdoms. Appalled at the deposition of James VII and II only twenty-eight years later, he mustered about 1,800 clansmen at Glen Roy, not far from Fort William, and Dundee joined him there on 18 May.

There exists a remarkable and little-known account of Dundee's campaign, written not in Gaelic or in English but in Latin. Dr James Philip of Almerieclose, near Arbroath, composed *The Grameid: An Heroic Poem Descriptive of the Campaign of Viscount Dundee in 1689*. A self-conscious, flowery pastiche of Virgil's *Aeneid*, it is frequently excruciating and always contrived as it talks of William of Orange as the 'Batavian Tyrant', using the Roman name for part of the Low Countries, and the Highlanders as 'the many-hued plaided tribes of Caledonia'. But Dr Philip was there, was an eyewitness to history in Glen Roy when the clans mustered, and his unique account does contain colourful nuggets.

As the chiefs gathered in Lochaber, each brought not only their fighting men but also a retinue – a piper, a bard, a *seanachie* or historian, a bannerman, a sword-bearer and so on. Even as late as the 17th century, these trappings of ancient power and status were still very much in evidence. The chiefs dressed and rode in some splendour. Sir John Maclean of Duart and his brother were on 'pure white horses', wore scarlet tunics that were 'scaly with gold' (gold lace), while on their shoulders 'floated a flowing plaid with yellow stripe'. This was no fanciful invention by Philip, for the modern Maclean tartan does indeed have such a stripe through it. Cameron of Lochiel wore 'a tri-coloured tunic' trimmed with gold lace, a kilt and, under it, tartan hose, while McNeill of Barra had 'as many colours woven into his plaid as the rainbow in the clouds shows in the sunlight'. Coll MacDonald of Keppoch came wrapped in a great tartan plaid and a targe studded with brass on his arm. And his neighbour and ally, Black Alasdair of Glengarry, the warrior whose death was mourned so eloquently by Sileas na Ceapaich, was also richly clad in bright tartan, his plaid fastened by a brooch made from 'the grinning head of some wild animal'.

In the late 17th and early 18th centuries, tartan was more than gloriously colourful – it also came to be seen as a political statement, something approaching a uniform worn by enemies of the British state. But all of those early connotations and connections were brought to an end forever in a matter of days, in an extraordinary incident in Scotland's cultural history. In 1822, only seventy-six years after the last Jacobites were hanged at Carlisle and their captured leaders executed at the Tower of London, kilts and plaids abruptly ceased to be the garb of war, sedition and savagery and, instead, became the costumes of farce – an epoch-changing farce written by the Wizard of the North, Walter Scott.

Old, ill and daft, George III had at last died in 1820 and, after nine years of regency, his son succeeded as George IV. Anxious about unrest in the north and keen to establish the new king as ruler of all of Britain, courtiers and ministers advised him to visit Scotland. No reigning monarch since Charles II in 1650 had done so and, after initial reluctance, George IV agreed. Walter Scott had persuaded him not only that was he a descendant of the House of Stuart – almost true – but also that he would receive a very warm reception in Edinburgh – possibly true, if it was well stage managed – especially if the king would embrace the outward show of Highland culture – risky. After the unprecedented success of his historical novels, the first true bestsellers, and especially *Waverley*, with its storyline woven around the 1745 rebellion, Scott's instinct was to clothe the royal visit in tartan – what he called, strangely, 'the garb of Old Gaul'. And, as a Stuart prince and therefore with a claim to be a Jacobite Highlander, George IV should allow himself to be swathed in the stuff.

There were difficulties but none of them arising from considerations of spectacular historical irony or a 19th-century version of cultural appropriation, although both were unmistakable. On the Saturday afternoon of 15 August 1822, the king attended a levee at the Palace of Holyroodhouse in full Highland fig. The difficulties were more physical than metaphorical or symbolic. At five foot, two inches, George IV was tiny but his waist was vast at fifty-one inches, only eleven inches less than his height. It was reckoned that he weighed more than twenty stone. Contemporary cartoonists were merciless. When the double doors were opened, a fanfare sounded and the king entered the levee, there must have been stifled gasps for he wore pink tights to conceal his varicose veins but it seems that they hid little else. Even though his belly was restrained by wide belts above a dangling sporran, the king's valets had hitched up his kilt far too far above the knee, so much so that Lady Hamilton-Dalrymple was moved to remark, 'Since he is to be among us for such a short time, the more we see of him the better.'

Despite these elements of farce – or perhaps because of them – Scott's wizardry had the effect of rendering the kilt and tartan harmless as symbols. At the same time, he persuaded the rest of Scotland to adopt all things Highland in large part because the monarchy were then the setters of trends followed by the rest of society or at least those who could afford them. They were also making a political statement, asserting themselves as monarchs of the glens and lochs as well as the rest of Britain. Queen Victoria's enthusiasm for Highland Scotland was both genuine and infectious. It was a remarkable cultural reversal.

During the late 17th and 18th centuries, tartan, plaids, kilts and the knitted blue bonnet were all closely associated with the Stuart cause, with rebellion and the removal of the Hanoverian dynasty. The great MacDonald bard, Iain Lom, went as far as criticising his kinsman, Lord MacDonald, for his over-frequent visits to London and its corrupting influences:

You seem to me to be a long time in England, being ruined by
    gaming.
I would more prefer you in a coat and plaid
Than a cloak which fastens
And that you should walk in a sprightly manner in trews made
    of tartan cloth.

In other words, 'Dress like a Highlander – like a man!'

When the Earl of Mar raised the standard of rebellion in 1715,
tartan was understood almost as a uniform. Lowland lairds who
joined him took plaids with them to show their allegiance. Particular
setts or patterns began to be associated with different clans, septs
and individual lairds. The MacDonalds who followed Dundee may
have worn tartan with a great deal of red through it and, in the
Grameid, James Philip wrote of the Glengarry men 'all clothed in
garments interwoven with the red stripe'. In 1704, the Grants of
Badenoch and Strathspey wore 'tartan of red and green sett, broad
springed', meaning a pattern of wide squares. In addition to natural
colours from roots, lichen and berries, bright imported dyestuffs
were widely available in the Highlands and Philip's florid descrip-
tions of the muster of Dundee's army may have been only a little
embellished

The Highlanders of the late 17th century also looked different in
other ways. Lowlanders and Englishmen were generally clean-shaven
and wore their hair short. Those who could afford them had wigs.
By contrast, the clans traditionally had their hair long and, before
battle, Philip watched Dundee himself, who had clearly imitated his
men, as he 'pressed his long hair up under a gleaming helmet'. The
clansmen probably used their knitted blue bonnets in the same way,
to keep their hair from getting in their faces. Many also wore full
beards. As the clans formed up, Philip noted that Cameron of
Lochiel's moustache was 'curled as the moon's horn' and that
MacDonald of Glencoe was 'rolling his wild eyes, the horns of his
twisted [braided] beard curled backwards'. To the Lowlanders and
Englishmen who faced them, the clans must have seemed like

savages from another world, another age, from the wild, primitive, atavistic past.

Show of all sorts mattered to leaders in the 18th century even though fine clothes and weaponry marked them out as targets. But this was less important in an era when battles were joined as men fought hand to hand with bladed weapons and not at a distance with guns and artillery. Dr Philip reserved his most florid language for Dundee himself. '*Clara viri sic fama valet pro mille maniplis,*' he wrote. 'Thus the bright flame of a hero is worth a thousand swords.' What happened soon after the muster shows that that judgement was something more than empty, rhetorical hyperbole.

Some reinforcements arrived as the clans were gathering at Glen Roy. A brigade of 300 Irish soldiers landed at Castle Duart on Mull under the command of Alexander Cannon. While James VII and II built up an army in Ireland, he could spare no more than token support. But he did want to see rebellion flaring in Scotland, a war against the usurper, William, fought on two fronts. By the beginning of July, Dundee had marshalled his Highlanders and finally led the small Jacobite army south to Blair Atholl.

General Hugh Mackay commanded a government force of about 3,500 men and they moved north from Perth to prevent Dundee's Highlanders from breaking out into Lowland Scotland. The armies met on 27 July 1689 near the Pass of Killiecrankie.

*

The 21st century thunders through the midst of history at Killiecrankie. The battlefield is brutally bisected by the line of the A9, the arterial road that runs from Edinburgh into the heart of the Highlands to Inverness and beyond. On the sloping braes to the south of the great road, General Hugh Mackay drew up the ranks of his government army while, to the north where the undulating meadow begins to climb steeply towards Creag Eallich, John Graham of Claverhouse, the man who came to be known as 'Bonnie Dundee', rode up and down the lines of clansmen, shouting words of encouragement over the summer breeze.

I wanted to see them there, in the empty fields, picture in my mind's eye the clan regiments arrayed on the hillside, wrapped in all the colours of their plaids, their banners fluttering, the pipers skirling out the battle rants, their weapons glinting silver in the sunshine, their shouts echoing down the brae. I wanted to imagine what General Mackay's men, many of them inexperienced recruits, saw once they had marched through the Pass of Killiecrankie and turned to face their enemy.

I'd come north to walk over the battlefield not on the anniversary in July, when re-enactors and spectators would attempt to bring history back to life in their own way, but on a cold January morning. Having visited Killiecrankie once before in summer, the densely wooded, steep slopes of the pass had made it difficult to see how geography had affected events. Spectacular views had occasionally opened up but the lush canopy of the trees had hidden a great deal and I found it difficult to read the landscape, to see how an army had moved through it. The winter wood would show me more.

In Gaelic, the original name of Killiecrankie is *Coille Chnagaidh* in one version. My knowledge of the language is now sadly very patchy and my listening comprehension very poor but I did immediately recognise the first element. *Coille* means 'a wood' but for the second I relied on my well-thumbed copy of Edward Dwelly's magisterial dictionary. At the back is a definitive list of the Gaelic equivalents of Scottish placenames and, for Killiecrankie, unusually, he offers two renderings. *Coille Chnagaidh* means 'the bunchy wood, the dense wood', while *Coille Chreithnich* is 'the aspen wood'. It may be that the first name refers to the pass and the second to the little village at its western mouth. These glosses are not footling, lexical details. They matter because the Gaelic names describe history, how people saw places in the past, what they looked like, how they understood them. And, of course, places have changed radically over time.

Having parked at the Killiecrankie Visitor Centre and paid £3 – surprising but a comfort that all proceeds go to Historic Scotland (now known as Historic Environment Scotland). I was given a map of the walks in the pass and the battlefield beyond it. Once I had worked out compass directions on my phone, I made my way into the Bunchy Wood and down the diagonal paths on the steep slope of the gorge. I couldn't see any aspen; instead, oaks clung to the slopes, their russet leaves everywhere a carpet, a memory of summers past. Sometimes at the turns, the vistas down the pass opened to reveal how narrow and precipitous it is as the River Garry rushes down to join the Tummel and then the Tay. But, because Killiecrankie is a gateway through the encircling mountains, four roads are forced through the narrow defile, each one jostling for space with the other.

I'd driven up from Edinburgh on the A9 and above me I could see the tall piers of the concrete viaduct that carried its humming traffic along the flanks of the gorge. It looked like an Italian autostrada in the Apennines. Below it runs the old A9 and down near the bottom of the steep slope was the railway line. A spectacular feat of engineering, it clings on to a narrow shelf at the foot of the gorge and, where it becomes impassable, a tunnel was dug through the rock in 1863. Long before the advent of mechanical diggers and excavators, the stones and the earth were moved by hand with pick, barrow and shovel and with the aid of explosives. And finally, below the railway tracks was the path above the River Garry that had been used for millennia, the route General Mackay's men had taken before the battle.

On my way down through the Bunchy Wood, I met no one, another good reason for a winter trip. What I wanted to do was follow in the footsteps of the government army and understand events from their point of view but that seemed impossible. My map told me that a path led back through the pass, east and away from the battlefield, but I could see no safe way in the opposite direction or any means of getting down to a path that might or might not be there. I felt I had no option but to climb up out of the oak wood, cross the old A9 and walk towards Killiecrankie village.

*

Very early on the morning of 27 July 1689, Lieutenant Colonel George Lauder rode at the head of 200 fusiliers. They had left their

camp at Dunkeld at 4 a.m., just as a clear day was dawning behind
the hills that rise to the east of the town, and begun a sixteen-mile
march to the pass. Lauder's commander, General Hugh Mackay, was
well aware of the strategic importance of Killiecrankie and how vital
it was to secure it. If Dundee's Highland army could break out into
the Lowlands beyond Dunkeld, it may well have ignited a more
widespread rebellion, with the Jacobites of Perthshire and Angus
swelling the ranks of his army. Many clans and their chiefs were
hedging their bets, waiting to see what happened, and few were
more cautious than the Murrays of Atholl. Mackay left a memoir
and an account of the battle and here is an extract:

> I marched to Dunkeld, where I was informed that my Lord
> Murray had retired from before the castle of Blair, my Lord
> Marquis of Atholl's [his father] house: upon which I presently
> judged that Dundee was marching into the country, which
> thoughts were confirmed by a letter from the said Lord Murray,
> who wrote that according to my desire he had secured a pass with
> 80 men which I should pass conveniently with baggage and horse,
> but since they were but countrymen and volunteers, he was not
> sure they should stay there long: whereupon I sent Lt Col. Lauder
> with 200 chosen fusiliers of the whole army, to keep the said pass
> till I should come up. About ten of the clock I arrived at the said
> pass, and having met with my Lord Murray, he told me that the
> most part of his men were gone from him to save their cattle from
> the Highlanders; with all that he thought he should get them kept
> from joining Dundee so long as he should stay upon their head,
> but that by no means they would join me.

*

Twisting and turning with the contours at the mouth of the pass, the
old A9 leads through Killiecrankie village, where the traffic is still
well policed. I had to look twice at a life-size cardboard cut-out of a
policewoman holding a speed camera that had been set up outside
one of the houses on the road. There was no doubt that the

unconventional idea worked – the sight of a policewoman brandishing a speed camera would cause any speeding motorist to hit the brake before they had time to work out that she was not moving.

Before the River Garry rushes down into the gorge, it is joined by another torrent, the Allt Girnaig. My map directed me across a bridge over it and then up a road to the right on the far bank of the little river. At last I was walking with the ghosts of Hugh Mackay and his soldiers. He had secured the pass and brought his army through it but what might have proved to be a Highland Thermopylae cost him many men. It was a process that must have taken several hours since the narrow track only allowed three men abreast and the baggage train of packhorses will have needed careful handling, but soon the general found himself in much more open country.

After passing between two comfortable-looking houses, one of them a small version of the Victorian Highland lodge, complete with corner turret and splendid views across Blair Atholl, I began to see what Mackay saw and realised when he rode out of the pass. Dundee had also been moving. It had never been his intention to hold the pass, even though it could have easily been done with only a few resolute men. That would have been a defensive tactic. Dundee wanted to bring the government army to battle, defeat them and then march south into Lowland Scotland. I found myself walking up the steep slope that Mackay had spurred his horse up and his memoir continues:

> I discovered the Highlanders approaching and gaining the heights, and pretty near before I could get my men to the ground which I judged by their motion they would be at. So changing my march and facing with every battalion as it stood by a *quart de conversion* [a wheel through ninety degrees] to the right, having viewed the ground where I judged apropos to range them, I made every regiment march straight before its face up a steep brae, above which there was a plain capable to contain more troops than I had, and above that plain the matter of a musket-shot [75 to 100 metres at

most], a rising of a hill above which and betwixt it and a great hill at his back Dundee had place enough to range [array in battle order] his men.

Once at the top of the steep brae, the battlefield opened before me, like a parting curtain revealing the stage. Blotting out the rumble of the A9, I could see that Dundee had chosen his ground carefully – an absolutely vital consideration for a clan army that relied on the charge as its only tactic. And he had moved quickly enough to force Mackay to array his troops below him, where the river was at their back, the narrow pass their only escape to the east. Dundee had them exactly where he wanted them.

The clansmen were outnumbered and he knew he needed every advantage. The government army was significantly larger at around 3,500 and facing them were about 2,300 Highlanders. These are rough estimates for, in war, exaggeration is not unknown. When I walked up to Dundee's position, I noticed that the bouldered gorge of the Allt Girnaig formed an emphatic barrier to the east, further confining Mackay's men and leaving little room for manoeuvre. Also between the two armies there were several deep dips where men would have been out of sight and, therefore, out of musket shot, certainly from a position below them. But what surprised me – and Mackay – was the scale. The Gaelic name for the location of the battle of Killiecrankie is Raon Rhuaridh, 'Rory's meadow', and he could have pastured many animals on what I estimated was at least 150, maybe 200 acres. It was a wide area where nearly 6,000 men had come to kill each other.

I followed a path above the gorge of the Allt Girnaig to where I reckoned from his memoir the government general had ranged his ranks. In the broad meadow, Mackay was worried about being 'outwinged' or outflanked. For what would be an infantry battle, this was crucial. Unusually, the government army had very little cavalry, only about 100 troopers, and Dundee had even fewer. If the Highlanders, who could move fast even over rough ground, were able to get around his flanks, they could have rolled up the government army, encircled it and there would have been no escape from the claymores and the Lochaber axes.

Mackay's account is unclear but it seems from other sources that he arrayed his army in three ranks. As I looked out to the west, below the A9, I could see that the sloping ground had few undulations and, as each regiment dressed its lines, allowing approximately a metre for each soldier, I estimated that Mackay's forces extended for more than 1,000 metres. It was a long ribbon of bright scarlet stretching across the green meadow. The government musketeers wore knee-length red coats with broad yellow cuffs and black-brimmed hats. Hanging from their cross belts were small leather pouches that held powder charges for their muskets, and some had a sword belt buckled at their waist. Officers wore red sashes and perhaps a feather in their hats.

Although they looked splendid in the July sunshine, most of Mackay's men had never faced the brunt of battle before, the shock and clash of the charge, the vicious hand-to-hand fighting. As they looked up the slope to Dundee's Highlanders, some will have been sick with fear, unable to prevent the shame of vomiting, trembling, a few soiling themselves as the pipers on the slopes above them played their war music and the clansmen, exhorted by Cameron of Lochiel, howled down at them like wolves slavering after their prey.

'Look to your fronts!' roared the sergeants and officers of each regiment. 'Stand your ground!' The government ranks had been stiffened by experienced regulars who had fought in European wars with Mackay and they will have tried to encourage the younger men, and not because they felt sorry for them. In battle, a line was only as strong as each and every man who stood in it. If it broke, all were in mortal danger.

In his memoir, Mackay made it clear that, at the bottom of a slope, with a river at his back and the sole means of retreat through a narrow pass, he was in no position to attack. He and his men would have to endure the agonies and uncertainties of waiting and, after a sixteen-mile march, this waiting, knowing they could face the charge at any moment, must have been draining, the courage of many already hanging by a thread.

The path uphill ducked under the thunder of the A9 at the bridge over the Allt Girnaig. Beyond it were runs of drystane dykes roughly built with large, lichen-covered boulders cleared off the meadow, the deposit of years of back-breaking work. They seemed old to me, probably in place when the clans marched on to Raon Rhuaridh. Along the line of where I imagined the Highlanders were arrayed was an oak tree with more huge boulders piled around its bole. It looked familiar. On the southern boundary of my farm there stands a mighty oak, its thick trunk studded with burrs covering the wounds of limbs lost long ago. An old forester told me my tree was about 400 years old, 'getting near its prime'. In Rory's meadow, I found myself looking at a very similar ancient oak, its grey trunk thick, squat and burred, its branches twisted, short, zigzagged against the winds of the same 400 winters.

Wednesday, 27 July 1689, was a bright sunny day and perhaps Dundee, Cameron of Lochiel, Maclean of Duart and the other chiefs met under its shade to discuss tactics. In the event of disagreements – and it seems that some of the clans wanted to attack immediately – these would ultimately be decided by their general. No Highland chief would suffer another chief to lead the army. That had to be done by an outsider, a neutral, and, in the shape of Dundee, an experienced and charismatic soldier.

When I reached the top of the meadow, another old dyke ran east to west and beyond it horses and ponies were nibbling at the bitter winter grass, their coats shaggy against the chill winds that blew down off the mountains. I estimated that I was standing about 350 metres uphill from the government lines and remembered that Dundee was said to have been troubled by the sun. As it moved around to the west, above Blair Atholl, it was shining directly in the eyes of the Highlanders. He would wait. It would be a long day of high summer. The weather was good, no rain clouds gathered over the dark heads of the mountains and the sun would not set until after 9.30 p.m. and, at least an hour before then, it would dip behind Creag Eallaich. It would be an evening battle. Below where he rode up and down the lines of clansmen, the red-coated ranks would also have to stand and wait. Dundee had fought in many engagements and he knew that, as the sun moved slowly around, the resolve of Mackay's men would drain as they looked anxiously up the hill, shading their eyes as they squinted, looking for signs of movement, straining to see what was happening, constantly alert.

As afternoon wore on into early evening, Mackay ordered his artillery to begin firing. With only three small cannon, all he could hope to do was provoke Dundee into attacking. From where I stood in the shade of the old oak, I judged that their range might have been enough to reach the Jacobite lines. There then followed a sharp skirmish when Mackay sent a detachment of musketeers to dislodge enemy snipers who had found cover at some cottages that stood further down the sloping meadow. It seems that, at that moment, Dundee finally gave the *claideamh mor*, order to attack, and the clan regiments threw off their plaids. Dr Philip noticed that 'they cast their brogues of bull hide and made a pile of their plaids and then stripped, prepared for battle'. Once all were ready, barefoot and wearing only their linen sarks knotted between their legs, the Highlanders picked up their weapons and began to move downhill.

What was about to happen at Killiecrankie would have surprised the ancestors of Dundee's clansmen. By the second half of the 17th century, it seemed that the military history of the Highlands and Islands had turned full circle.

In the Middle Ages, during the pomp of the Lordship of the Isles, disorder was kept to a minimum by exporting its potential, by encouraging a tradition of mercenary soldiering in Ireland's interminable internecine wars and their attempts to resist English invasion. Each spring and early summer, bands of young warriors sailed the North Channel to fight for money, land and other rewards. They were known as Gallowglasses and had a fearsome reputation. The term derives from the Irish Gaelic *gall-oglaigh* and it means 'young foreign warriors'. The sharper definition has earlier history attached. When Norse settlers colonised the Hebrides and parts of the mainland, they became known as *Gall-Gaidheal*, 'the Stranger-Gaels'. The Outer Hebrides are still called Na Innse Gall, 'the Islands of the Strangers', and sometimes known as Tir nan Gaisgeach, 'the Land of the Warriors'. The names of the Norse clans remember the Vikings: MacAskills were originally 'the children or people of Asgeir'; MacAulay is from Mac Olaf; and MacIver from Mac Ivar. Some of the most famous and feared companies of Gallowglasses were MacSweens, 'the sons of Svein', and many of them settled permanently in Ireland, their surname changing a little to become MacSweeney.

Irish kings valued these mercenaries very highly because their discipline and fighting techniques were effective in repelling English settlers who had begun to arrive in the 12th century. Norman noblemen like Strongbow – Richard de Clare, Earl of Pembroke – used armoured cavalry and Welsh archers to devastating effect against native Irish levies. Formations of Gallowglasses were much more successful because they possessed the confidence and iron discipline to stand their ground – what General Hugh Mackay prayed his ranks of redcoats would do at Killiecrankie. Bristling with pikes and Lochaber axes and two-handed broadswords, these mercenaries could turn a cavalry charge. Horses will instinctively wheel away from what they see as immovable, from men deployed in a well-organised line of battle. Gallowglasses fought for rewards and aimed to stay alive to collect them. That created a culture of iron, pitiless discipline. If only one or two men broke and fled, potentially fatal gaps would be left that could see formations disintegrate.

Good equipment was vital. Here is what the MacSweeneys insisted on when they fought in the service of Irish kings:

And Clan Sweeney say they are responsible for these as follows, that for each man equipped with a coat of mail and a breastplate, another should have a jack and a helmet: that there should be no forfeit for a helmet deficient except the Gallowglass' brain (dashed out for the want of it).

A jack was a long, padded leather tunic worn by men who could not afford chainmail. Below this they wore protective, knee-length boots, known as 'jackboots', and a shorter padded tunic for those few who fought on horseback was a jacket. Good equipment and good discipline meant that these mercenaries were more likely to collect their pay and, if they could turn a battle, then there was also the opportunity for loot. In the early 16th century, English observer Sir Anthony St Leger admired their fighting qualities: 'These sort of men are those that do not lightly abandon the field, but bide the brunt to the death.'

By the 16th and 17th centuries, new military technology was beginning to render the techniques of the Gallowglasses obsolete. More manoeuvrable and more accurate artillery and more widely available muskets made their static formations into densely packed targets. The Highlanders were forced to develop a different way of fighting and it was in war-torn Ireland that this first developed. By the time of Tippermuir in 1644, Alasdair Mac Colla had imported and improved the Highland charge, combining speed of movement with musket fire and devastating swordsmanship. All that remained from the time of the Gallowglasses was their physical courage.

When Montrose met Mac Colla at Blair, by no means all clansmen owned firearms but, after victories, they could loot those belonging to their enemies. In the 17th century, there were two sorts of musket. Matchlocks were fired by the smouldering end of a thin rope which ignited a prime charge of gunpowder in the small metal pan, which in turn set off the main charge that propelled a lead ball along the barrel. The action did not always work and the phrase 'a flash in the pan' comes from that. For obvious reasons connected with a damp climate, flintlocks were preferred in Scotland. These ignited the powder with a shower of sparks produced when a flint struck a frizzen, a small curved plate of hardened steel. Dr Philip's florid prose described what happened next: 'The muskets thunder and discharge their balls of livid lead.' Some of General Hugh Mackay's soldiers will have carried lead balls in their mouths. To make reloading faster, an absolutely crucial factor, they spat the next ball down the barrel of their still smoking muskets.

Before Killiecrankie, Viscount Dundee fretted about gunpowder. In a letter, he noted:

> When we came first out, I had but fifty pounds of powder, more I could not get; all the great towns and seaports were in rebellion [i.e. anti-royalist], and had seized the powder, and would sell none. But I had one advantage, the Highlanders will not fire above once, and then take to the broad-sword.

Once the clansmen had fired their single volley at close range, they dropped their muskets, drew their swords with one hand and gripped their dirks and targes with the other before charging out of the smoke. The two-handed claymores used by the Gallowglasses were obsolete by 1689 and most men carried a basket-hilted sword. Almost all blades came from Spain and Germany and, before battle, men used whetstones to give them razor sharpness so that they sliced easily through flesh. Basket hilts were forged and attached to the imported blades by Scottish armourers, many of them based in Stirling or the Ayrshire town of Kilmaurs. Iain Lom, the MacDonald bard, admired these weapons and the men who wielded them: 'Beloved by me is the young heir-apparent with his sharp Spanish blade smoking in his hand; he was no poltroon behind a shield.'

While swords slashed and parried, dirks were used for close-quarter stabbing. In the early 18th century, the English traveller and diarist, Edmund Burt, wrote that 'the blade is straight and generally not above a foot long . . . in a close encounter there is no defence'. Targes were strapped to the forearm above the hand that gripped the dirk and its blade extended just below the rim. At between eighteen and twenty-one inches in diameter these shields were small and generally made of wood covered by tough cowhide, or were iron-plated. Sometimes they were decorated with studs or even a projecting iron spike set at the centre, the boss. William Lindsay, a shield-wright working in Perth, made hundreds of targes for the army of Prince Charles in 1745. He offered two grades – ordinary and an 'officer's targe'. These were not protective shields of the sort carried by Roman legionaries but were designed to be light enough to parry bayonet or sword thrusts and protect the heads of clansmen as they charged.

After the disastrous defeat at Culloden in 1746, the Disarming Acts banned Highlanders from using all of these weapons and many were confiscated. The ban included one other item, something much less obvious. Bagpipes were considered a weapon of war and playing them was against the law. Before the order to charge, pipers played the battle rants of the clans and these were believed to inspire men to acts of bravery. And amidst the clash and din of the fighting, commanders used the pipers like buglers, issuing orders, moving men around.

The pipes were still inspiring soldiers in the wars of the 20th century. On 25 September 1915, the Kings Own Scottish Borderers were ordered to go over the top, climb out of their trenches and charge across no-man's land at the Battle of Loos. But their morale was at a low ebb, the German bombardment was heavy and there had been gas attacks. Perhaps there was a danger of mutiny. A regimental piper, Daniel Laidlaw, blew air into his instrument, climbed up the ladder to the parapet and, at great risk of being shot by snipers, he marched up and down playing 'All the Blue Bonnets Are Over the Border'. He was awarded the Victoria Cross.

On 22 October 1943, the companies of the 51st Highland Division were ordered to march through the night in the Second Battle of El Alamein. They were led by the skirl of the pipes, each piper playing the company march. The companies stayed together in the darkness and the attack was successful but many of the pipers were killed. After El Alamein, they were not allowed on the front line.

After the battle of Culloden, James Reid was captured by the Duke of Cumberland's men and put on trial for treason. Arguing that he was innocent because he carried neither musket nor sword, Reid said that all he did on that fateful day was play his instrument. After conferring, the judges decreed that since no Highland clan would march to war without a piper at their head, Reid was indeed guilty of treason and the pipes were therefore a weapon of war. He suffered the hideous death of being hanged, drawn and quartered.

Two hundred and fifty years later tragedy became part of a farce. In 1996 local residents complained about the dreadful sound of the bagpipes. A Mr Brooks had taken to playing on Hampstead Heath, marching up and down to keep his rhythm and these ignorant, uncultured Londoners did not enjoy it. A Victorian by-law banning the playing of musical instruments in public places was invoked. In court, Brooks pleaded not guilty on the basis that the pipes were not a musical instrument but a weapon of war. The case of James Reid was cited as evidence. But Brooks lost the case and the glories of the pipes were banned once more.

Watching the Highlanders advance, listening to the pipes skirl out the battle rants, standing in the ranks near the centre of the government lines at Killiecrankie was an unlikely chronicler of the drama that was about to burst over the meadow. In the summer of 1689, Private Donald McBane's company marched with the army from Dunkeld to Killiecrankie and, as he waited for battle to be joined, he knew what was coming. Forty years later, in a memoir entitled *The Expert Sword Man's Companion*, Private McBane set down what he saw on the braes of Killiecrankie and what he had first experienced at Mulroy. 'We gave them a shout,' wrote McBane, 'daring them as it were to advance, which they quickly did to our great loss.'

When the charging Highlanders ran within range, perhaps 50–70 metres, 'we could only fire three shots apiece' but, nevertheless, these volleys did great damage. Around 600 clansmen were killed or wounded in the charge. But the musket fire did not check them. McBane remembered why they came on when they did: 'The sun going down caused the Highlandmen to advance on us like mad men, without shoe or stocking, covering themselves from our fire with their targes . . . they drew their broad swords, advanced furiously upon us, and were in the middle of us.'

In his memoir, Ewen Cameron of Lochiel wrote of a strange, eerie pause when his men 'fell in pell-mell among the thick of them with the broadswords. After this, the noise seemed hushed; and the firing ceasing on both sides, nothing was heard for some moments but the sullen and hollow clashes of broadswords with the dismal groans and cries of dying and wounded men.' That was an atmosphere and a set of sounds and images that would have been recognisable to soldiers who had fixed bayonets in Afghanistan more than three centuries later.

In the centre and on the government army's right wing, the Camerons, often said to be the bravest of the clans, smashed into the redcoat lines with the Glengarry MacDonalds charging beside them. There was not only honour amongst these warriors but also rivalry between the clans, and none would take a backward step. They met resistance but it did not last long. The left of Mackay's line collapsed almost immediately and, according to their general, who rode about the meadow trying to rally his men, many 'fled without any firing'. The battle may have lasted less than fifteen minutes before it turned into a murderous rout. But, in that moment of triumph, it became clear that Killiecrankie was an expensive victory for the Jacobite cause.

Having read most of the eye-witness accounts, I judged that the hand-to-hand fighting took place on the part of the meadow that lay below the A9 and towards the east and the gorge of the Allt Girnaig. The battle had largely been fought and decided where Mackay had arrayed his troops.

I crossed the main road and, momentarily dragged back into the 21st century, I was appalled at the amount of litter on the verges. The louts who had thrown drinks cans and food wrappers out of the windows of their cars and lorries can have had no idea they were in a place where more than 2,000 men had died – no idea how much disrespect their behaviour showed – but it still made me shake my head to see the brainless mess they had made in that place.

When I climbed the fence on the south side of the A9, I found myself suddenly confined. Instead of being able to walk across the battlefield, I had to make my way along a very narrow fenced corridor. Below it was farmland, pasture that would be grazed in the spring and summer, and I understood why visitors would need to be kept out. Cows with calves at foot can be dangerous. But the walkway was so narrow and on such steeply sloping ground that I had to give all my attention to making my way along it safely and none to what had happened in the fields below it.

In the frantic minutes after the Highland charge had slammed into the government lines and broken through, Dundee was leading part of his small troop of cavalry into the smoke-filled melee, probably intending to mop up resistance. Sources suggest that he became detached from the other troopers as he rode over to the Highlanders' left wing. The MacDonalds of Sleat had charged the government ranks and, unlike the rest of Mackay's army, his right wing had offered some resistance. It was the only part of the battlefield where intense fighting was still going on.

Somewhere near the old road, well behind where Mackay's line had been swept away, the Jacobite general was shot out of the saddle, a musket ball striking him under the arm, perhaps when he had raised his sword. 'Shot under his armour into the belly and be-twixt his eye brows' was how an officer from a government battalion described Dundee's death in a letter sent from Perth two weeks after the battle. The second wound may have been a coup de grâce from a government soldier.

The florid line from Dr Philip's *Grameid* came to have real historical significance, 'Thus the bright flame of a hero is worth a thousand swords'. As the government soldiers frantically fled the field, Ewen Cameron and the other chiefs knew that they had won a hollow and expensive victory. After the death of Dundee, those clans who had hesitated, waiting to see what happened at Killiecrankie, would now stay at home and continue to wait upon events.

All that Private Donald McBane knew was that he needed to save his own skin:

I fled to the baggage [train] and took a horse, in order to ride the water. There followed me a Highlandman with sword and targe, in order to take the horse and kill myself, you'd laugh to see how he and I scampered about; I kept always the horse between him and me. At length he drew his pistol and I fled, he fired after me; I went above the pass, where I met with another water [the River Garry as opposed to the Allt Girnaig], very deep, it was about eighteen feet over betwixt two rocks, I resolved to jump it, so I laid down my gun and hat, and jumped and lost one of my shoes on the jump . . . The enemy pursuing hard I made the best of my way to Dunkeld, where I stayed till what of our men was left came up.

I walked back to the visitor centre and made my way down the path where the little robin had sung to me. It leads to a viewpoint directly above what is now known as 'the Soldier's Leap'. In the peace of a January afternoon when the sun that had troubled Dundee was setting behind the mountains, I looked back up the Bunchy Wood to the braes above. I heard the distant echoes of battle, the fading war cries of the clans, the screams of the dying and wounded and, looking at how the white torrent of the Garry rushed between the rocks, I reflected that a badly frightened man, running to save his life, could do extraordinary things.

7

The Godly Commonwealth

Dunkeld, 21 August 1689

Upon Mount Zion, God had caused the Israelites to build His temple in the city of David. When his son, Solomon, placed the Ark of the Covenant in the Holy of Holies, the Word of God, written on tablets of stone, was enshrined inside it. God had chosen the Israelites and given His laws to Moses on Mount Sinai, and down the ages His prophets would proclaim His will and His will would be done.

On 1 June 1679, God's Covenant with Scotland was celebrated below Loudon Hill. Rising dramatically out of the rolling hill country of the River Irvine, its sheer cliffs and grassy summit commanded wide views over eastern Ayrshire, as far as the sea, the Firth of Clyde and beyond to the island of Arran. On top of the hill men might raise their faces heavenwards, their hands clasped in prayer, but more likely the soldiers posted as lookouts shaded their eyes on this Scottish Zion to search the horizon for the approach of an enemy. Below them there was piety, a profound and passionate belief that needed armed protection. Many hundreds had walked to the braes below Loudon Hill for a field conventicle, a form of outdoor worship led on that sunny morning by the Reverend Thomas Douglas. As praise and the psalms rose up into the clean summer air, many felt the spirit of the Lord descend as they remembered Zion.

These devout and determined men and women were Covenanters, true believers, as they saw themselves, in the purity of the original reformation of the Church in Scotland. After the convulsions of 1560, led by John Knox, the Lutheran principle of the priesthood

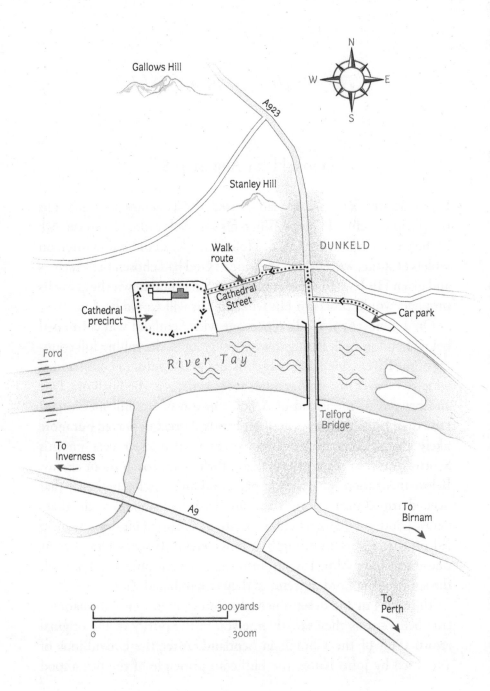

Gallows Hill

A923

N
W · E
S

Stanley Hill

DUNKELD

Walk
route

Cathedral Street

Cathedral
precinct

Car park

Ford

River Tay

Telford
Bridge

To
Inverness

A9

To
Birnam

To
Perth

0   300 yards

0   300m

of all believers had taken a strong hold as almost every vestige of Catholicism was swept away. In essence, the reformed Church adopted the doctrine that each Christian was responsible for his or her own salvation and that they could pray, sing and communicate directly with God without the intercession – or, indeed, the interference – of a priest. Mass literacy was essential so that everyone could read the sacred Word of God for themselves and that was an early and laudable goal for the reformers. Out of this religious and civic ferment developed the notions of the Godly Commonwealth of Scotland and Christ's Kingdom of Scotland. Like the Israelites, the Scots came to believe that they too were God's chosen people. This inevitably gave rise to conflict with the secular state and eventually the shedding of the blood of martyrs on both sides. In a famous encounter with James VI at Falkland Palace, the reformer Andrew Melville took the king by the sleeve and explained his status before God: 'Thair is twa Kings and twa Kingdomes in Scotland. Thair is Chryst Jesus the King, and his Kingdome the Kirk, whase subject James the Saxt is, and of whose kingdome nocht a king, nor a lord, or a heid, bot a member!'

This was a doctrine destined not to last and, when the Stuarts became kings of England and Ireland as well as Scotland, it would be hotly contested. By 1679 and the restored reign of Charles II – James VI and I's grandson – the Covenanters had been savagely persecuted and many ministers turned out of their manses and churches. Congregations followed them and, because they were excluded from worship under the roof of a church, Covenanters took to the open air and their ministers preached at field conventicles sometimes attended by thousands. Government forces patrolled the countryside to disperse these services forcibly and arrest itinerant ministers. That is why armed Covenanters climbed Loudon Hill to keep lookout and many more armed men guarded the worshippers on the braes beneath them.

William Cleland was a poet, a graduate of the University of St Andrews, a passionate Covenanter and a surprising product of the Scottish Reformation. The son of Thomas Cleland, gamekeeper to the Marquis of Douglas, his humble background did not prevent him from going to university. Perhaps he was the beneficiary of a good parish education in the Douglas village school – an early example of that peculiarly Scottish educational phenomenon, the 'lad o' pairts'. He was certainly the beneficiary of the doctrine of the priesthood of all believers and the mass literacy that flowed from it.

Probably after he had graduated from St Andrews, Cleland used his poetic gifts, such as they were, to compose 'On the Expedition of the Highland Host who came to destroy the western shires in winter 1678'. Written in English rather than Scots, it recounts the government's posting of about 6,000 Highlanders in south-west Scotland, what was seen as the cradle of the Covenant. They harried the local population, stealing, burning and killing as they roamed the countryside, suppressing conventicles and attacking known Covenanters. It was that paradox, organised anarchy, deliberately brought about by the government in a crude and cheap attempt to suppress dissent. Crucially, it also set one part of Scotland against another – yet another example of Lowlander against Highlander. These clansmen were not paid and plunder was what they sought. Few will have understood much English or Scots and they left a bitter legacy of resentment, especially in the south-west of Scotland. William Cleland's view of Highlanders was shaped by what he saw of these roaming bands of clansmen and how they terrorised the people chosen by God. He saw them as subhuman. He called them 'monkeys'.

On the morning of Sunday 1 June, the young man rode to Loudon Hill, well armed and ready to protect the pious who had gathered on the braes. It seems likely that he took his place amongst the cavalrymen in the cordon of soldiers posted around the field conventicle.

When the prayers and psalms were suddenly interrupted by shouts from the lookouts at the top of the hill, William Cleland's moment had come, although he could not have known it. A force of government dragoons had been seen to the east, moving down the valley of the River Irvine towards Loudon Hill. Someone may have informed, betrayed fellow Covenanters, told their commander what was happening and where. When the Reverend Thomas Douglas was warned of the imminent threat, he blessed and dispersed the congregation and turned to their protectors, roaring a grim exhortation: 'Ye have got the theory, now for the practice!'

More than 200 Covenanters, some armed with muskets, others with pikes and pitchforks, marched up the track by the river to engage the government force. They had about forty cavalry trotting beside them, including young Cleland. Led by Robert Hamilton, a graduate of Glasgow University, these soldiers of Christ took up a position near the village of Drumclog. In front of their lines was a stank, an area of boggy ground that had not dried out in the summer, and this made it very difficult for the government dragoons to engage. All they could do was exchange musket fire.

William Cleland appears to have then taken the initiative and, spurring his horse into a gallop, he led the Covenanter cavalry around the end of the stank and, despite murderous, close-range musket fire, they attacked the dragoons in the flank. The charge scattered them, killing thirty-six and wounding more. It was a rout, a triumph for the Army of the Covenant and a victory for Christ's Kingdom of Scotland that resonated through the south-west. The hero of Drumclog, William Cleland, was only eighteen years old. And although he did not know it at the time, he had defeated a man whose ghost would come to seek revenge ten years later – John Graham of Claverhouse, the future Viscount Dundee.

Glory was transient. Three weeks after what in reality was little more than a skirmish, a full-scale battle was fought at Bothwell Bridge in South Lanarkshire. Much buoyed by the victory at Drumclog, the Army of the Covenant had swollen to between 5,000 and 6,000, outnumbering the government forces led by James, Duke of Monmouth, the illegitimate son of Charles II, and John Graham of Claverhouse. But numerical superiority meant little as dissent and bickering splintered the command of the Covenanters. Robert Hamilton, nominally the victor of Drumclog was their general but he seemed much more interested in theological dispute than military matters. As the armies arrayed themselves on opposite banks of the Clyde, Hamilton busied himself supervising the building of a huge wooden gibbet and piling ropes around it to intimidate the dragoons and the militia men who watched from the far side of the river.

The narrow bridge at Bothwell was strategically crucial and, under the command of David Hackston, a detachment of Covenanters rushed forward to block it. They held out for two hours before running out of ammunition. For reasons no one understood at the time, Robert Hamilton seemed unwilling to reinforce or supply them. When Hackston's men were finally forced to retreat, the battle was essentially decided. Hamilton seems to have fled, 'leaving the world to debate whether he acted more like a traitor, coward or a fool'. When Monmouth and Claverhouse led the government army across the bridge, they quickly outflanked and overwhelmed the leaderless Covenanters. Many were killed and about 1,200 were taken prisoner and marched to Edinburgh to be temporarily imprisoned in a camp near Greyfriars Kirkyard. They were then taken down to the port of Leith before being transported to the colonies in North America as indentured servants, a form of slavery. No doubt some Covenanters were consoled by biblical comparisons with the captivity of the Israelites by the waters of Babylon. And far across the Atlantic, exiled from Christ's Kingdom of Scotland, they would have wept and remembered Zion.

William Cleland escaped with David Hackston from the chaos at Bothwell Bridge and both of them soon joined a charismatic young minister called Richard Cameron. Having been ordained in exile in Holland, he returned to Scotland in the late summer of 1679, Cameron was to become the 'Lion of the Covenant', its most famous martyr, a fate he seems to have embraced from the outset. After preaching at the last field conventicles of the year – these large outdoor services were rarely held in winter – he met David Hackston and probably William Cleland. On 22 June 1680, Cameron rode with twenty followers into Sanquhar in Upper Nithsdale, the heartland of the Covenant. After they had sung a psalm at the Mercat Cross, his brother, Michael, read out what became known as 'the Sanquhar Declaration'. It was, in effect, a declaration of war on the British state as it denounced Charles II as a tyrant and demanded that his openly Catholic brother, James, be excluded from the succession.

Reaction was immediate, blunt and effective. The Privy Council placed a huge bounty of 5,000 merks on Richard Cameron's head and, despite having sixty armed men as an escort, he was hunted down three weeks later. At Airds Moss, a blanket bog between Muirkirk and Cumnock in Ayrshire, Cameron was killed on 22 July and his head and hands were cut off for public display on the Netherbow Port in Edinburgh. When they were shown to his father, who was imprisoned in the Tolbooth, Alan Cameron was asked if he recognised them. He kissed his son's head and said, 'I know them. I know them. They are my son's, my own dear son's. It is the Lord. Good is the will of the Lord, who cannot wrong me or mine, but has made goodness and mercy to follow us all of our days.'

Nine years later, on 14 May 1689, a regiment was raised at Douglas in south Lanarkshire by the Earl of Angus and it was known as the Cameronians in honour and in memory of the Lion of the Covenant. Its first commanding officer was Lieutenant Colonel William Cleland. It was at Douglas Church that the first muster took place and this remarkable declaration was read out to the recruits. It spoke of faith as much as military service:

All shall be well affected, of approved fidelity and of a sober conversation. The cause they are called to appear for is the service of the King's Majesty and the defence of the nation, recovery and preservation of the Protestant Religion; and in particular the work of reformation in Scotland, in opposition to Popery, prelacy and arbitrary power in all its branches and steps, until the Government of Church and State be brought back to that lustre and integrity which it had in the best times.

The recruits listening to this clearly needed none of the sabre-rattling and tub-thumping of a recruiting sergeant that were usually used to inspire and induce men to join the ranks. As much a congregation as a regiment, each company of sixty men had an elder as well as an officer and all were issued with a copy of the bible. It became a Cameronian tradition to post sentries at church parades long after the persecution of Covenanters ceased and the sermon could not commence until an officer reported to the minister and the congregation that 'the pickets are posted, there are no enemy in sight'.

On 14 May 1968, 279 years later, within a mile of where it was raised, history had turned full circle. The 1st Battalion Cameronians (Scottish Rifles) held a field conventicle and lowered the regimental flag to mark its disbandment. Such was the power of their unique traditions, steeped in the bleak piety of the Covenanters, that they had refused to merge with another Lowland regiment. In a sombre ceremony held on a windy, showery day, the battalion marched at their unique, very brisk pace and formed up around a flagpole – and a communion table. Many hundreds of veterans attended this last conventicle but, before the psalms, prayers and speeches could begin, pickets, facing outwards over the Douglas Valley, were posted at each of the cardinal points of the compass. Flares were sent up to signal all was well, the presiding minister was quietly spoken to and only then could the sermon begin.

Various generals and dignitaries made brief speeches but the ceremony was dominated by history, by the Covenanting origins of the Cameronians and the ghosts of the past. Wearing a Geneva cap of the sort favoured by John Knox, the Reverend Donald MacDonald, a former chaplain of the regiment, walked slowly to the communion table. Without a note and in a clear ringing voice that was carried on the wind, he recounted the Christian values of the Cameronians and raised his arms in a silent, clearly emotional, blessing. When the regimental flag was at last taken down, it was placed on the communion table under a cross. Beside it was the sword of William Cleland.

Two months after they were first mustered at Douglas in 1689, the Cameronians were called into action. On Saturday 17 August, they marched into Dunkeld to defend the town from a possible attack by the victors of Killiecrankie.

*

About ten miles north of Perth the Highlands begin. The forests close in and the pine trees loom up tall and dense, like regiments of guardsmen on either side of the A9. Gradients begin as the road swoops and sweeps around the foothills and the steep sides of the valley of the Tay. Horizons appear at many corners. Framed by the forests, snow-capped mountains rise in the far distance. Instead of the homely geometry of the fields and farms of lowland Perthshire, a wilderness waits in the north.

I had driven up the A9 countless times, cursing the fact that such a vital artery, Scotland's longest trunk road, had not been completely converted to dual carriageway decades ago. But at least I wasn't going far – not up and into the heart of the mountains. Dunkeld stands close to the Tay, where it begins to break out of the Highland passes and meander over the Perthshire plain. The placename derives from the Gaelic *Dun Chaillean*, 'the Fort of the Caledonians', and the implication is that the people to the south, in the flat, fertile farmlands, were not Caledonians, not Highlanders. Dunkeld may be seen as a frontier town.

I turned right off the A9 and crossed the magnificent bridge over the Tay designed by Thomas Telford, the great and energetic engineer from the Borders whose skills improved communications in the north enormously in the early 19th century. He was known as 'the Colossus of Roads'. Having found a car park by the river, I walked down to its bank to admire the elegant arches of the bridge. I'm old enough to remember when the A9 crossed it, having run through the narrow streets of the little town behind me.

Dunkeld seemed hemmed in by geography as well as history, bunched like the Bunchy Wood fifteen miles to the north at Killiecrankie. Behind the car park I couldn't miss a very steep little hill, one that needed a wooden staircase to climb. There were attractive houses perched on shelves that had been cut into its western flank. The Tay marks a formidable southern boundary, for there was no bridge in 1689. To the north I could see the wooded top of a small hill and a fringe of higher hills beyond it. Another hill rose to the west. Within minutes of arriving and getting my bearings, I understood that what happened on 21 August 1689 took place in a very small area compared to the wide acres of the braes of Killiecrankie.

Having read several accounts of what is known as the Battle of Dunkeld – it was really a siege – my interpretation of how events played out was brought sharply into focus when I saw the scale of the place. That is the great value of getting out from behind a desk, from shutting the lid of a laptop, putting on a pair of boots, taking a phone camera, a notebook and pen and going to the places where history happened even if they have radically changed in the interim. I immediately understood that the small, very restricted scale of Dunkeld was the most decisive factor in determining what happened on that remarkable day.

The architecture of the narrow main street where buses and lorries used to squeeze through to reach Telford's bridge had changed little in the forty or so years since my last visit. But its atmosphere was wholly different. Niche food shops and delicatessens were interspersed with cafes – at least one vegan establishment, of course – restaurants and gastropubs, each one of which seemed busy even though it was not yet mid-morning. My habit when I visit places I want to understand better is to walk around, map in hand, taking photographs and notes, sniffing like an inquisitive collie dog. When every nook, cranny and corner has been investigated, most of them leading nowhere in particular, I try to find somewhere to sit down and write down my impressions, such as they are. After seeing how busy Dunkeld was, I suspected I might be doing that in my car with a sandwich.

At a crossroads in the main street, I looked east to the very steep slopes of the hill by the car park before turning west to walk down to the market cross. As often happened in old towns, the street was left deliberately wide so that stalls could be set up on market days. As usual, rows of parked cars made the space seem smaller and more restricted. Through a gateway in a high stone wall to the right of the cross, there was a grassy park and only a few yards away another small but steep hill. A sign told me this was Stanley Hill. That had confused me when I looked at maps and read accounts of the siege.

Sources from 1689 and soon after spoke of Shochies Hill and, at first, I didn't realise it was an older name for Stanley Hill. From Gaelic, it means 'Fairy Hill'.

To the left of the market cross runs Cathedral Street, a lane with white-painted houses on either side and whose narrow width suggested it was old. When I came to the gates of the cathedral precinct, blue plaques on the walls told me that at least three of these houses had been standing in August 1689. Neil Gow, the great fiddler and a famous son of Dunkeld, had joined Robert Burns – the maker of the plaque had spelled his name as Robbie for some benighted reason – to entertain audiences in The Old Rectory. It stands close to the gates into the precinct. Bright sunlight reflected off the white walls but tall trees cast shade over the entrance. Though the town had been busy, I could see no one in the precinct. I looked down to my left along a narrow lane to the Tay and wondered if the high stone wall had been standing when the Highlanders charged up Cathedral Street, roaring their war cries. Where I stood, in this narrow street little more than twenty feet across, the fighting had been fierce, but all I could hear was a summer breeze soughing through the ancient yew trees, their branches dappling the sunlight.

Dunkeld Cathedral lasted only sixty years. Built on the site of an ancient Celtic monastery that once housed the relics of St Columba, construction of the medieval church began in 1260 but was not completed until 1501. The fury of the reformers and especially their rejection of what they saw as the idolatrous nature of relics meant that Dunkeld was attacked and partially destroyed after 1560, losing its roof. Much later, the choir was restored and now serves as the parish church. I could see that the nave and its towers remained a substantial ruin.

What surprised me once again was how small the precinct was. An oval shape, it was bounded by walls on the east, the Tay to the south, a wood to the west and a row of well-trimmed yew bushes to the north. It might have been the size of two rugby pitches. I had been told that I'd be able to make out holes in the walls of the cathedral made by musket balls but I could see nothing that didn't look like ageing, spalling stonework. Many years ago, I went to Berlin to give a lecture and I remember walking down Unter den Linden and seeing thousands of bullet holes on several buildings and on the fluted columns of the Brandenburg Gate. But those were made by powerful 20th-century weapons and not muskets firing soft lead balls. Still, I was disappointed. As would be clear in moments, an atmosphere of love and peace, not war, floated around the old cathedral.

When I had walked around the margins of the small precinct and was making for the gateway, I was passed by a happy couple followed by a dog-collared minister and a group of chattering, excited friends. I guessed that a wedding was about to be rehearsed in the church.

*

When William Cleland rode into Dunkeld on 17 August 1689, at the head of the Cameronians, he saw a very different little town. Rather than lying to the east of the cathedral, the lanes and streets were clustered around it. From the market cross Cathedral Street led much as it does now to the gates of the precinct. But, in the open ground to the north, there stood a mansion belonging to the Marquis of Atholl and behind it were the houses of the cathedral canons and beyond them was Scots Raw, a lane that dog-legged south at its western end to enclose the precinct on that side. Perhaps the name was an old reference to the houses of people who were not Highlanders, who had come from the south. Dunkeld was probably a bilingual frontier town where business was done in both Scots and Gaelic. In the south, on the banks of the Tay, were more canons' houses. The engraving made by John Slezer, published as part of his *Theatrum Scotiae* in 1693 but almost certainly drawn before 1689, shows Atholl House as grand and large with many windows on the two facades visible. At that time, the cathedral precinct was surrounded by buildings, their yards, lanes and streets. It could not be approached over open ground on any side. It is very different now.

Lieutenant Colonel Cleland was not happy when he reached the town and nor were his men. There were no town walls he could defend and the fighting strength of his regiment had shrunk from 1,200 to 700 men. There is some evidence to suggest that several companies of the Cameronians had been posted to Argyll to deal with unrest in the west but it is also highly likely that there had been a good deal of desertion. The soldiers were said to be unhappy with Cleland and his second-in-command, Major Henderson. They had imposed experienced, professional officers on them but these men were not Covenanters and they were much given to blasphemy and the use of profanities. Cleland had also sent away men from the ranks he deemed fanatics – 'madd men not to be Governed'. The soldiers suspected their commanding officer of embezzling their pay and failing to buy sufficient provisions. They also had no uniforms. What had happened to the money for those? When the Cameronians reached Dunkeld, many argued that they had been betrayed and demanded to retreat immediately back to Perth. Clearly, the independence of mind and spirit of the Covenanters did not lend itself to unquestioning acceptance of military discipline but there are more than hints that Cleland's character was not as principled, pious and selfless as is often portrayed. It was with some difficulty that the officers prevented simmering resentment from exploding into mutiny.

Cleland had been told that the Highland Army, as they now called themselves, had been pursued after Killiecrankie as far north as Aberdeenshire by General Mackay and a much-reinforced government army. Alexander Cannon, the commander of the Irish troops sent from the army of James II and VII earlier that summer, had taken over leadership after Dundee's death. What Cleland did not know was that Cannon had outwitted and outmanoeuvred Mackay, given him the slip and was moving quickly south towards Dunkeld.

After a rapid reconnaissance in the fading evening light of the first day, Cleland posted sentries around the margins of the little town and the regiment bivouacked amongst the tombstones in the cathedral precinct. Even though the following day was the Sabbath, the

Cameronians began the urgent work of fortifying Dunkeld as best they could. Where possible, they dug ditches in front of the walls of the precinct to make them higher and harder to scale and repaired breaches with whatever came to hand – loose stones and tree branches. Cleland sent a detachment to climb the cathedral's towers to act as lookouts while others built up the dykes around the yards behind Atholl House. At the market cross, a barricade was improvised with carts and barrels to prevent access to the narrow lane of Cathedral Street.

In the middle of the afternoon of the second day, the lookouts shouted down to Cleland. They could see small groups of Highlanders moving through the trees on the slopes of the hills to the north of the town. At about 4 p.m., a large company of several hundred had managed to get much closer undetected for they emerged like phantoms from the dense woodland on Stanley Hill only a short distance from Atholl House. Orders were immediately shouted and the Cameronians stood to on the walls, their muskets primed. But then a messenger approached carrying a halberd with a white cloth attached to its point. He solemnly handed Lieutenant Colonel Cleland a letter. It was an ultimatum. 'We the gentlemen assembled, being informed that you intend to burn the town, desire [to know] whether you come for peace or war, and to certify that if you burn one house, we will destroy you.'

The men who emerged from the trees on Stanley Hill turned out to be a local militia who believed that the Cameronians had come to destroy the town rather than defend it. Cleland attempted to allay their fears by reading out the articles of an Act of Indemnity issued by William III's parliament pardoning those who had opposed him. But, since some of his men had already plundered houses in the town, this attempt at conciliation foundered. Cleland went on to say that he would not retreat. But as soon as he returned to the cathedral precinct, he ordered that a galloper should be got away to Perth as soon as possible to seek immediate reinforcements. It was only fifteen miles to the south. Cleland hoped that word would come back soon and it would be followed by troops of soldiers.

Dhu and Roy Campbell, two Gaelic-speaking officers in the regiment, had been gathering intelligence and it appeared that the clansmen in the surrounding area were prepared to join a relieving Highland army if and when it arrived so that they could protect the town. As late as the evening of the second day, no one yet knew where Alexander Cannon and the Jacobites were. In fact, they had made their way quickly south through the mountain passes and more clans were marching to join them.

On the morning of 19 August, the lookouts in the cathedral towers called down the welcome news that they could see cavalry moving quickly up the road from Perth. Thanks be to God, Lord Cardross had come with five troops of dragoons, about 500 well-armed men.

Later the same day, Alexander Steuart, a Tayside laird, led a substantial force of Atholl men to attack the town and its garrison. There were between 600 and 1,000, it was difficult to tell exactly in the wooded terrain. The lookouts saw them moving through the trees on the hills to the north. At the same time, Cardross received orders from Colonel Ramsay, the officer commanding the Perth garrison, that he should return immediately. A devout Covenanter who had accompanied William of Orange when he had landed at Brixham a year before, Cardross, Henry Erskine, had been made a Privy Councillor and was a man of independent mind. He had also fought in Mackay's army at Killiecrankie and perhaps he sought some redress after that murderous debacle. In any event, he ignored Ramsay's letter and attacked the Atholl men, driving them back north into the mountains above Strathtay. Probably believing Dunkeld to have been relieved, Cardross then ordered his dragoons to cross the river and ride with him back to Perth.

It may be that it was at this moment the Cameronians threatened mutiny once more. News came from the north that the Highland Army had reached Blair Atholl, their ranks swollen to about 5,000 men, more than double the number who had fought and won at Killiecrankie. The Cameronians declared that they would wade across the Tay and follow the dragoons to the safety of Perth rather than be butchered 'in an open and useless place'. Cleland considered that he had been betrayed by Cardross and 'charged those returning [to Perth] dragoons with the loss and blood of their regiment'. The Cameronians were not popular in the army and its generals and colonels worried about their fanaticism and what they saw as indiscipline. The Duke of Hamilton, who had presided over the Scottish Convention of the Three Estates in Edinburgh, wanted the Cameronians disbanded because they were in the habit of 'silencing' Episcopalian ministers. And yet, despite these suspicions of betrayal, Cleland and his brother officers made a dramatic gesture. They told the mutineers that they would stay and fight and shoot their own horses to prove their resolve.

It was enough and, as their enemies began to approach the town, the 700 Cameronians settled down for the night behind the walls of the cathedral precinct. Sentries were posted and the lookouts in the towers peered into the darkness for signs of movement and listened for the whispers of the advance parties of the Highland Army.

Early the following morning, 21 August, after about 4 a.m., the lookouts watched the eastern sky begin to glow with the coming dawn. In the half-light, they were certain they could make out movement in the wooded hills to the north and they alerted Lieutenant Colonel Cleland. As the sun began to climb, it quickly became clear that the Highland Army had indeed come. Perhaps 5,000 clansmen and at least four troops of cavalry were deploying around Dunkeld. Sheltering behind their makeshift defences, watching the clan regiments emerge from the trees, their banners flying, pipers playing the battle rants and their cavalry riding around the edge of the town, the Cameronians realised that they were outnumbered at least seven to one, maybe more – impossible odds. If ever there was a time for prayer, it was then.

No retreat would be possible. Colonel Cannon had sent two troops of his cavalry to guard the fords across the Tay to the west of the precinct and two more to block escape to the east. On Gallows

Hill, to the north of Stanley Hill, four cannon that had been captured at Killiecrankie were emplaced and the Appin Stewarts were sent to circle round the town to the south, to occupy the ground behind the canons' houses by the river.

By 7 a.m., all were in position and orders came from Cannon for the pipers to skirl out the *claideamh mor*, the order to begin the attack. The clans moved downhill out of the trees and across the fields towards the town. According to a defender, they were 'like a living tide'. Led by Sir Alexander Maclean, 100 of his clansmen had put on steel helmets and upper body armour and, carrying targes and broadswords, they charged the Cameronian outpost on Stanley Hill. Captain Hay, one of Cleland's officers, and his men stood fast, firing their muskets in volley order from behind the rows of dykes on the flanks of the little hill. But the Macleans kept coming, more and more of them.

With the steep hill overhanging it, the east end of the town was indefensible and Cleland ordered only token resistance. As they retreated, the Cameronians burned houses and soon the smoke of war swirled in the air above Dunkeld, confirming the fears of Alexander Steuart and his Atholl men. The government soldier, Lieutenant Stewart, shouted for his troops to run down the street to the market cross while the men behind the barricade of upended carts and barrels gave them covering fire.

Cleland feared that the momentum of the Highland charge would breach his defences at weak points. The dykes around the precinct had gaps and some had been filled with benches from the parish church. Others around Atholl House were even more fragile – 'and all their defence was but low garden-walls, in most places not above four feet high' is how a contemporary source described them.

Stewart's men were holding the barricade at the market cross, repelling each charge with volley fire and their long pikes. But, on Stanley Hill, Captain Hay was being slowly forced backwards by the Macleans and, at around 8 a.m., he led his men in a fighting retreat back to the thick walls of Atholl House even though his leg had been broken by a Highland broadsword.

All round the cathedral, the defences were beginning to buckle as wave after wave of clansmen attacked. When Lieutenant Stewart could hold the barricade no longer, the Cameronians turned and retreated towards the precinct gates at the top of Cathedral Street, running up the narrow lane as fast as they could. The men on the walls attempted to give covering fire but muskets are not effective over the 120 yards the defenders had to run. In the desperate sprint back to safety, Stewart was cut down and killed. To the south of the street, at the same time, the Appin Stewarts were attacking through the gardens of the canons' houses and approaching very close to the precinct wall. In the west, all of the defenders and some of the towns-people who had been caught up in the fighting had been forced to seek refuge inside the perimeter. When the Appin Stewarts had stormed all the houses to the south, they mounted a furious attack on the walls but were much hampered by the lack of scaling ladders. Cleland ran over with reinforcements and the attack was repelled.

Assaulted on all sides, the Cameronians had no option but to fall back. After an hour of desperate hand-to-hand fighting, all their outposts had been overrun and they only held the precinct, Atholl House and three of the canons' houses beyond it. Having taken all of the other houses around the walls, the clan chiefs sent snipers to their upper floors or onto the roofs. It turned out to be an effective tactic.

Sometime after 8 a.m., William Cleland was picked out near Atholl House by snipers and mortally wounded, hit by two musket balls. It was said that before he died, he dragged himself out of sight of his men so as not to discourage continued resistance. Soon afterwards the snipers brought down Major Henderson, the second-in-command, and Captain Munro took over. The Cameronians had stripped lead off the roofs of the cathedral and Atholl House to make more ammunition but it was not enough. As fast as they could be plunged into cold water, musket balls were being fired. Ammunition was running dangerously low and the snipers had killed another captain and a lieutenant and wounded three more officers, clearly targeting the leaders of the Cameronians.

A radical change of tactics was urgently needed. Munro ordered parties to sally out of the precinct with burning faggots on the points of their pikes. They set fire to the thatched houses taken over by the Highland snipers. As those trapped inside burned and choked, their screaming rent the smoke-filled air. In his *History of the Highlands*, first published in 1834, James Browne appears to have recorded a genuine inherited memory of those moments in the siege:

The whole town was in a conflagration, and the scene which it now presented was one of the most heart-rending description. The din of war was no longer heard but a more terrific [terrifying] sound had succeeded, from the wild shrieks and accents of despair which issued from the dense mass of smoke and flame which enveloped the unfortunate sufferers. The pikemen had locked the doors of such of the houses as had keys standing in them and the unhappy intruders, being thus cut off from escape, perished in the flames. No less than sixteen Highlanders were burned to death in one house. With the exception of three houses, possessed by the Cameronians, the whole town was consumed.

The streets and lanes were becoming choked with bodies of dead and dying men and it became clear that the Highland charge was being badly impeded and not only by the narrow streets. Repeated and very costly charges had not yet overcome the defences but it was a finely balanced business. Munro knew that the resistance of the Cameronians might quickly and fatally weaken. Not only were supplies of musket balls very low but the defenders were also almost out of gunpowder. Soon their muskets, which had no bayonets, would be little better than clubs. In that event, only the pikemen could mount any effective resistance and there were too few of them. Only officers had swords. Munro quickly made plans for a last stand, a suicidal defence of Atholl House where the remaining soldiers would trust in God's mercy as they sold their lives dearly in His service.

But then suddenly everything changed. As the smoke cleared from the burning houses, Munro could see that only the dead remained in the streets and lanes. Lookouts climbed the towers once more and shouted that the Highland Army appeared to have moved out of the town and retreated to the hills in the north. The stunned silence around the cathedral as men looked at each other was only broken by spontaneous piety, the sound of devotion, when the exhausted Cameronians began to sing psalms and give thanks to God for their deliverance. An hour or so later, the lookouts called down with more welcome news. Lord Cardross and his cavalry were riding hard up the Perth road. When the government dragoons crossed the fords, the Highland Army melted back into the hills and retreated towards Blair Atholl where their baggage train and all their plunder waited.

With God's grace, the Cameronians believed they had achieved an extraordinary victory against overwhelming odds. The failure of the siege at Dunkeld effectively ended the first Jacobite rising as Colonel Cannon was forced to allow the clansmen to return home to the glens and straths to bring in the harvest.

The contrast with Killiecrankie only three weeks before could not have been starker. A much smaller Highland Army had swept Mackay's men off the field, but the sole tactic of the charge was wholly inappropriate in the streets of a town. A Glencoe bard, Aonghus Mac Alastair wrote: 'They were not accustomed to stand against a wall for protection, as was done at Dunkeld. The stalwart young men fell . . . felled by bullets fired by cowherds.'

Like most generals, Alexander Cannon had directed his army from the rear where he could see more clearly how the battle was unfolding. The clans were used to being led from the front by their chiefs and the Irishman was seen as 'a devil of a commander who was out of sight of his enemies'. Cannon later claimed that he had been forced to order a retreat because his men had run out of ammunition but, in fact, the resolve of the Cameronians, compared to those like Donald McBane who had fled the field at Killiecrankie, was crucial, perhaps the deciding factor. The Highlanders saw them as 'mad and desperate men' and called them 'devils'.

As they unfurled their colours and raised their exultant voices in a psalm of thanksgiving, the Cameronians believed that God had given them victory. Richard Cameron's martyrdom had not been in vain and the Standard of the Gospel was raised once more in triumph in Christ's Kingdom of Scotland. It was also long overdue vengeance for the excesses of the Highland Host ten years before as they ravaged the south-west. But, sadly for him, William Cleland did not live to see it.

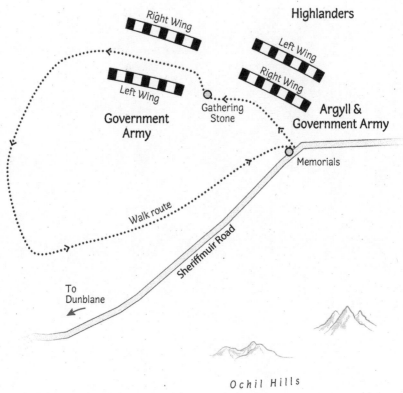

Highlanders

Right Wing

Highlanders

Left Wing

Right Wing

Left Wing

Government
Army

Gathering
Stone

Argyll &
Government Army

Memorials

Walk route

Sheriffmuir Road

To
Dunblane

Ochil Hills

0   1/2 mile

0   1 km

8

Blaeberries

Sheriffmuir, 13 November 1715

By the side of the road, looking over the wind-blown wastes of high moorland and with dark and dense ranks of Sitka spruce behind, the monument glowered at me. Blunt, built out of grey boulders that might have been picked up from the banks of burns or pulled out of the peaty earth, it rises like a tapering cairn defended by iron railings. Set into the roadside face is an inscription in Gaelic:

CLAN MACRAE
MAR CHUIMHNEACHAN AIR CLANN MHIC-RATH A
  THUIT
AN CATH BLAIR AN T-SIORAIMH AIR AN TREAS LA
  DEUG
DE CHEUD MHIOS A GHEAMHRAIDH 1715 NUAIR BHA
IAD DION TIGHE RIOGHAIL NAN STIUBHARTACH
BHA BUIDHIONNAN NAN TAILECH AGUS NAN
  AILSEACH
AN ORDUGH CATAH AIR SGIATH CHLI AN FHEACHD
GHAIDHEALAICH, AGUS DE NA SEOID SO BHA A
  MHOR
CHUID LE AN CINN RE LAR AIR CRIOTH AN LATHA
THA AN CARN-CUIMHNEACHAN SO AIR A THOGAL LE
COMUNN CLANN MHICRATH AIR AN TREUS LA
  DEUG
DE CHEUD MHIOS A GHEAMHRAIDH, 1915

THE CLAN MACRAE
IN MEMORY OF THE MACRAES KILLED AT
SHERIFFMUIR 13TH NOVEMBER, 1715, WHEN
DEFENDING THE ROYAL HOUSE OF STUART
THE KINTAIL AND LOCHALSH COMPANIES
FORMED PART OF THE LEFT WING OF
THE HIGHLAND ARMY, AND FELL
ALMOST TO A MAN
ERECTED AT THE INSTANCE OF
THE CLAN MACRAE SOCIETY
13TH NOVEMBER 1915.

On the flat face of a heart-shaped stone above the inscription, two more words are carved in a more informal but more emphatic style. *SGUR URAN!* was the war cry of Clan MacRae, the name of one of their places, what they were fighting for at the Battle of Sheriffmuir in the early winter of 1715, exactly 200 years before their monument was built. Sgurr Fhuaran is one of the Five Sisters of Kintail, a dramatic range of mountains at the head of Loch Duich in Lochalsh. The name means 'the mountain of the rushing spring' and it watered the lands of Clan MacRae, their native, ancestral home-place, what brought them to the windy moor between Perth and Stirling, what gave them courage in battle and what they died to protect. But it turned out not to be their courage that failed and destroyed the MacRae companies. They were the victims of hesitation and catastrophic indecision.

*

To be a Tory was to be insulted. The term derives from the Irish Gaelic *Toruidhe* and it originally referred to native Irish people who were dispossessed by English settlers and forced to take to the woods and wild places. Over time *Toruidhe* refined its meaning and came to be attached to outlaws or papists or robbers or those who were seen as all three. By the middle of the 17th century and the Wars of the Three Kingdoms, the insulting label was attached to the royalist party and later to those who opposed the Whigs and their control of parliament after the accession of the Protestant William of Orange.

John Erskine, Earl of Mar, wasn't sure what he was. At the beginning of the 18th century, he was appointed one of the commissioners for the union of the parliaments leading up to the Bill's enactment in 1707 and was later made a Secretary of State under Queen Anne, the last of the Stuarts. Mar had inherited an earldom in the north-east of Scotland that groaned under the weight of great debt and he was, therefore, particularly interested in the calculation and distribution of the Equivalent. A huge sum for the times, more than £400,000, this was in essence a bribe paid by the English parliament to buy influential support for the union. Amongst the Edinburgh mob and elsewhere in Scotland, the proposed abolition of the Scottish Parliament was deeply unpopular but the English MPs and Queen Anne's government were very anxious to avoid any possibility of the return of the Catholic Stuarts to Scotland after her death and they were willing to pay a fancy price to avoid that. Mar and others understood that the cash would be paid in coin but, not only was it late, most of it was in Exchequer bills – English Exchequer bills. Paper money was still a novelty north of the Border and the idea that English promises to pay had any value in Scotland was still shaky. A nervous Mar flirted with changing his allegiance from the Tory faction in parliament to the Whigs and the nickname 'Bobbing John' was coined. It stuck and was applied to more than political allegiance.

After no fewer than seventeen pregnancies, Queen Anne had to endure the heartbreaking death of the only child to survive infancy or miscarriage, her son, the Duke of Gloucester, at the age of eleven. When she died in 1714 without an heir, George I, the first Hanoverian, was crowned and everything changed. Mar rushed to assure the new king of his undying loyalty, pledging his support in Scotland, promising to maintain stability and support for the union. But the political weather was febrile, even fevered. When George I was proclaimed at the market cross in Inverness, the ritual rehearsed cheers of 'God save the King!' were drowned out by 'God damn them and their King!' But, despite all the fawning assurances and promises, the new king sacked Mar anyway. Across Britain, Tories who were suspected of supporting the exiled James III and VIII were bundled out of office and some were even taken into custody. Robert Harley, Earl of Oxford and Queen Anne's Lord High Treasurer, was arrested, imprisoned, impeached and accused of treason. For some time, his fate hung in the balance as the hideous death of a traitor loomed. The Earl of Mar moved quickly to avoid a similar fate and instead went off in a mighty huff.

Between promising his loyalty to George I and being sacked, Bobbing John did not elect to bide his time and work his way back into royal favour, as others did. Instead, he secretly took ship for Scotland, buying a passage on a collier, a coal ship. On 27 August 1715, he summoned a council of war at Braemar. Many clan chiefs and powerful noblemen attended. On 6 September, he raised the royal standard and summoned those loyal to the house of Stuart to join him in rebellion. All of which came as something of a surprise to James III and VIII. The exiled king knew that the accession of George I and the unrest it aroused presented a genuine opportunity. He had written seeking support from the Pope and also sent a letter to his half-brother, the Duke of Berwick saying, 'I think it is now more than ever. Now or Never!'

It seems likely that Mar had raised the royal standard without telling King James anything of his plans beforehand. Unlike Montrose or Dundee, he had no royal commission at all, neither a letter nor an understanding, nothing from the Stuart court in France to allow him to do that. When word of the rebellion reached the king, he had no choice but to fall in with the enterprise and make plans. He would land in the south-west of England where loyal supporters and those who were unhappy with the new German king would rally to him. But there had been a change of regime in France. Louis XIV had died and the regent, the Duke of Orleans, was much less supportive, not at all enthusiastic about a rebellion in Britain. No material assistance was to be given. And French troops were vital to any chance of success.

Nevertheless, Mar pressed on regardless and met with some initial success. Thousands had come to the muster on the Braes of Braemar, and Inverness, Aberdeen and Perth had all fallen to the Jacobites. The north of Scotland quickly came under Mar's control. They did less well in Edinburgh. The government had laid up a huge store of arms and ammunition in Edinburgh Castle, enough for 10,000 soldiers, a great prize for the rebels. With eighty men, Lord James Drummond planned to scale the walls under cover of darkness. But they stayed too long in the tavern where they had agreed to meet, the sentries they had bribed went off duty and the rope ladder they had brought was too short. Four of Drummond's men were arrested after falling off the castle's walls while the others fled into the darkness, some of them no doubt floundering in the boggy Nor' Loch, probably the worse for drink.

Meanwhile, Mar marched south to Perth with a huge army, perhaps as many as 12.000. Rebellion had also flared in the north of England and a force of 4,000 had rallied to the royal standard. But, when Mar reached Perth, he seemed to freeze, waiting for reinforcements he didn't need and who never came and, crucially, not moving rapidly south to unite with the English Jacobites. John Campbell, the Duke of Argyll, was quickly in the field but with a much smaller government army, perhaps fewer than 4,000. Finally, by 10 November, before more of them deserted, Mar was persuaded to lead his men south out of Perth. Even though he was outnumbered by three to one, Argyll responded and moved up from Stirling to Dunblane, only two miles from Sheriffmuir.

*

About twenty yards along the road from the grey mass of the MacRae monument is another, more modest marker. A small, rubble-built stone cylinder carries a commemorative message noting the date and place of battle. It's much easier to read than the weather-worn Gaelic and its English translation on the big cairn. Despite, or perhaps because of, its scale the little monument seemed to me to have dignity, something that matters in a place where many men were killed more than 300 years ago.

On the southern side of the minor road that had led me out of Dunblane was open moorland that gradually climbed up to the green flanks of the Ochill Hills. To the north lay the site of the battle, where most but by no means all of the fighting took place. The Ordnance Survey had told me that Sheriffmuir was carpeted with many acres of commercial forestry and, as I walked up a good, well-made path, I didn't expect to see much. But, almost immediately, I found myself confronted with surprising memories of the battle. A signpost offered the Argyll Trail to Dunblane (3.9 km) or the Mar Trail to the Gathering Stone (0.6km). I opted for the latter. On the other side of the path stood a rickety notice board with sheets of paper encased in plastic pinned to it. They were pages from *A True and Particular Account of the Battle at Sheriff-Muir &c.* They appeared to be from a near-contemporary publication of an eyewitness account of what happened around where I was walking. As at Tippermuir, an arterial road was important. On the northern edge of the moor, down in Strathallan, was the road from Perth to Stirling and it seems that, at first, Mar disposed his army on one side of it after they had mustered and orders were issued.

I had decided on the Mar Trail because it would lead me to the Gathering Stone, the place where some of the events of 13 November 1715 had unfolded. Almost immediately, expectations were happily confounded. Instead of being hemmed in by towering ranks of dense commercial forestry, I could see long vistas on every side. Large tracts of the great wood had been recently clear felled and to the north, across Strathallan and Strathearn, there were the mountains, the ramparts of the southern Highlands, the Gaidhealtachd, the country of the clans. On the flanks of the nearer ridge was a small wind farm, the elegant turbines turning slowly. Sheriffmuir is a high plateau and, in 1715, the views would have been even wider.

Turning away from the raw landscape of the felled plantation, I found myself in a wide, heather-covered clearing. It was a still morning and a gossamer sun gently lit the rich purple blossom and picked out all of the small glories of open moorland on the edge of the Highlands. I found little bushes of sweet blaeberries growing out of the peat with yellow trefoils and other flowers I didn't know growing in clumps between them. In this rich natural carpet, miniature oak saplings had somehow survived the browsing deer and the clustered crimson berries of rowans glistened in the sunshine. And everywhere were the gentle colours of Scotland – the hundred shades of green, the bracken turning brown, the purple heather blossom, the chocolate peat banks and the oatmeal stalks of die-back long grass. Amongst the little plants and flowers, I could find no tree stumps at all. Perhaps some of the clearing had never been planted.

A butterfly that might have been a red admiral fluttered up as I approached an open area with a bench and an information board. Beside them was a strange object. Shaped like the ribs of an upturned boat, an iron grille had been set over a collapsed and broken stone – probably a prehistoric standing stone. In 1715, it had been intact and upright and had acted as a mustering point for the Earl of Mar's army at some point in the battle. The very well laid out and well written information board told me that, in 1848, when a railway was being built down in Strathallan to link Stirling and Perth, the English navvies, men who did the back-breaking earth moving with pick, shovel and barrow, had argued with their Scots and Irish counterparts. In revenge for perceived, almost certainly anti-English slights, they had come up to Sheriffmuir on a Sunday and 'got their own back' by smashing and knocking down the Gathering Stone with their mallets and picks. The landowner, the Laird of Kippendavie, had the grille made by a blacksmith to protect this piece of history from more acts of vengeance.

Taking off my backpack, I sat down on the bench and looked around the wide clearing. The morning seemed to settle and, instead of listening for the echoes of battle, the roar of war cries in a thousand throats, the clash of sword on shield and the *brosnachadh*, the songs inciting men to battle, perhaps a memory of Alasdair Mac Colla, I heard birdsong and silence. Behind me was a majestic stand of tall Scots pines, apparently a remnant of some early 19th-century planting. Amongst the clumps of vivid, blooming heather, some self-seeded birches, rowans and thorns punctuated the skyline, their limbs and leaves silhouetted by the blue behind them. More than 300 years ago, thousands of soldiers had massed around the old stone and their chiefs and captains had exhorted them to battle. Only a few yards away that battle had raged as men fought hand-to-hand, as horrific wounds were inflicted, limbs severed and heads cleaved open. Hundreds of men from Clan MacRae had been slaughtered. But I could hear none of them.

The landscape seemed to me to be at peace, to have healed and in three centuries covered over the horrors of war with the precious, delicate beauty of the heather, the blaeberries and the fragile, tissue-like peeling bark of the silver birches. At Prestonpans, roads, railways, pylons and houses had been built over all that ancient violence but here Mother Nature had dressed the wounds of warfare and given the men who died a soft and beautiful grave, changing colour as the seasons turned and the years wore on, covering them with sweetness and flowers, remembering them with the incense of pines and the music of the birds. Against the azure sky, a buzzard floated, calling out *piou-piou* on the wind.

Whoever raised the standing stone smashed by the English navvies knew that this was a sacred place thousands of years ago, a high plateau where the sky gods were close and spirits flew in the pure upland air. And, on that sun-bathed, fresh morning, alone in the clearing, I felt their presence and also the wraiths of the MacRae dead and the other clansmen who fell. That's not a sentence I'm embarrassed to write. Not everything can be explained. A sense of history is not always rational, a matter of ascertaining the facts, getting them in the right order and applying a little analysis. Understanding the past is more complicated, more spiritual. Even the recent past. I have a friend who is devoted to the stirring history of the Lancaster bombers of the Second World War. There are now very few left and she often goes to air shows to see the last of these huge aircraft. When the pilots fire up the engines and she stands close to their roar and shudder, feeling the power vibrate through her, something more is intuited. While she knows everything there is to know about these magnificent aeroplanes and the brave men who flew them, she feels rather than understands their history at that moment.

More unexpected glories waited at Sheriffmuir. Beyond the clearing, a wide path led downhill to younger plantations of Sitka spruce. Stacks of cut logs lined it, waiting to go to the sawmills and it seemed that foresters had been thinning the wood. The scent of pine was everywhere, hanging in the woodland air. Under the branches were green velvet carpets of moss lit by the dappled, ancient light of the forest. It lay over large stones and climbed up the boles of trees. It was as though a bolt of cloth had been thrown over the floor of the wood. I walked downhill and another signpost told me that the Mar Trail had run into the Argyll Trail.

*

Even allowing for the fact that the landscape looked very different, much more open in 1715, it is difficult to understand why a battle should have been fought at Sheriffmuir. If the ground was as uneven, tussocky and riven with small streams and pools as I had found it to be in the large clearing around the Gathering Stone, it would not have suited the Highlanders well. I visited the site in August, in the midst of the driest summer on record, and the battle was fought in November when the moor must have been much wetter. Above all, the clans needed ground they could move quickly over, and, if possible, have *an cothrom a' bhraighe*, 'the advantage of the brae'. There seemed to me to be neither on the high moor. A few days after I came back from Sheriffmuir, I met a retired regular soldier and he told me that now, three centuries after the Earl of Mar led his men, the ground is still the first and principal tactical concern when an attack is planned.

In fact, it was always so. Before the coming of mechanised warfare, when feet and horses brought combatants together, battles were sometimes fought at agreed places, or somewhere convenient, reachable by both sides. Fords over rivers were commonly near battle sites. Killiecrankie was at the mouth of a strategically important pass that led from the Highlands to the Lowlands, and the siege of Dunkeld was important for the same reason. At Prestonpans, Lord George Murray wanted to prevent Sir John Cope's forces from reaching Edinburgh. But Sheriffmuir seemed to me a particularly inconvenient place and one certainly not suitable for the Highland charge, Mar's greatest weapon.

Contemporary accounts of the battle also mention 'a morass', an area of treacherous, boggy ground near the centre of the moor. November frosts had apparently made some of it passable for infantry, if not cavalry. But who would trust the thickness of ice unless they were forced to? And it would not be easy or quick to traverse. Some men will have ended up on their backsides or worse. With a much superior force of at least 7,000 men and probably more, the Earl of Mar could and should have overwhelmed the Duke of Argyll's army of 3,000 or 4,000 on decent ground. Or he could have forced his way around them and reached Stirling, the gateway to the Lowlands and to the Jacobites who had risen in the north of England. But, instead, he chose to risk battle up on the moor.

There was also very little daylight. On 13 November 1715, the sun rose at about 8 a.m. and set at 4 p.m. No reports of the weather on that day have survived but, if it was cloudy or wet, even less time would have been available. There appears to have been poor visibility – or perhaps it was just incompetence – because reconnaissance reports were either incomplete or inaccurate on both sides. There was more than one surprise after battle was joined.

Early in the morning, as soon as there was enough light, Mar gave orders for his army to form up at the northern foot of Sheriffmuir, just off the road that led from Perth down to Dunblane. Between large squadrons of cavalry on each flank, he set the Highland clans in the centre and, to their left, the Lowland levies from Perthshire and Forfar. Behind them was a second line of infantry with the Seaforths, men commanded by Lord Huntly, the Earl of Panmure and the Marquess of Tullibardine. It was a classic deployment but one that would quickly unravel as events began to accelerate.

Lookouts saw what they did not realise was a small troop of cavalry up on the high ground on the western edge of Sheriffmuir. Was it Argyll's army? Had they claimed the high ground? The sighting seemed to induce something close to panic, certainly some hasty decision making. Mar called a council of war in front of the cavalry squadrons on the right of his line. It was decided to move the army uphill without delay and attack. But no sooner had the Jacobites begun to march than Argyll's men disappeared. There then followed confusion compounded by poor leadership.

The left wing of Mar's army formed up into columns so that they could climb up the tracks that led to the high ground. But suddenly, near the top, they were confronted by troops of enemy dragoons, the Scots Greys and other seasoned units commanded by the Duke of Argyll himself. He was a very experienced soldier, unlike Mar, and had fought under John Churchill, the first Duke of Marlborough, in Europe at famous victories at Ramillies, Malplaquet and Oudenarde. Seeing that the Jacobites were surprised and seizing his chance, Argyll ordered an all-out attack. Frantically trying to form line out of their marching columns, the left wing of Mar's army was in no position to return fire with any effect. 'They fell into some confusion,' said a contemporary account, 'in forming and some of the second line of foot jumbled into the first, on or near the left and some of horse formed near the centre' – where they were of no use. It was chaos and, when the Perthshire and Forfar levies came under sustained fire followed by an attack, they turned and fled downhill. In their panic, they swept the Camerons, a reliably brave and ferocious clan, along with them. But there must have been some resistance. The MacRae memorial lamented the fall of companies from Kintail and Lochalsh 'to a man'. Perhaps this was a dark moment in the clan's history remembered only by their kinsfolk. The accounts I read made no mention of it and the losses sustained by the whole army were not great. Argyll's cavalry and infantry charged on and pursued the left wing of Mar's army down to the road and the Allan Water where some drowned in an effort to escape.

The Jacobite army seemed to break in half. In the clearing around the Gathering Stone, where the right wing may have been brought together, the clans executed a classic Highland charge across the heathery moorland. Another account reported that they 'made a most furious attack, so that in seven or eight minutes we could neither perceive the form of a squadron or battalion of the enemy before us. We drove the main body and left of the enemy in this manner for about half a mile, killing and taking prisoners, all that we could undertake.'

In essence, the right wing of each army defeated and scattered the left wing of the other. Two battles were fought on Sheriffmuir and at some distance from each other. But perhaps because the light was fading, the Earl of Mar converted a draw into a defeat. He did not press home any advantage or commit all of his forces and, instead, allowed the Duke of Argyll to withdraw towards Dunblane. And rather than pressing on to take Stirling and its strategically vital bridge over the River Forth, Mar retreated back to Perth. A traditional song reflected the confusion if not the conclusion:

> There's some say that we wan and some say that they wan,
> And some say that nane wan at a', man,
> But one thing is sure that at Sheriff Muir
> A battle was fought on that day, man,
> And we ran and they ran and they ran and we ran,
> And we ran and they ran awa', man.

But the reality was not in dispute. Mar's retreat to Perth decided the outcome of the 1715 rebellion. Clansmen and Lowland levies began to drift away and, when James III and VIII finally managed to land in Scotland at Peterhead on 23 December, it was all but over. The morale of the army was shredded, the presence of the king doing little to raise spirits. When Argyll advanced to Perth with reinforcements, the Jacobites retreated northwards and the army disbanded. Mar and James both took ship for France, never to return.

The '15 was, without doubt, the most likely of all the Jacobite rebellions to succeed. Mar had recruited a large army, rebels rose in England and, in Scotland, the Union of the Parliaments was deeply unpopular. But not even the courage of the clans and their devastating charge could save the House of Stuart from incompetent leadership and chronic hesitation.

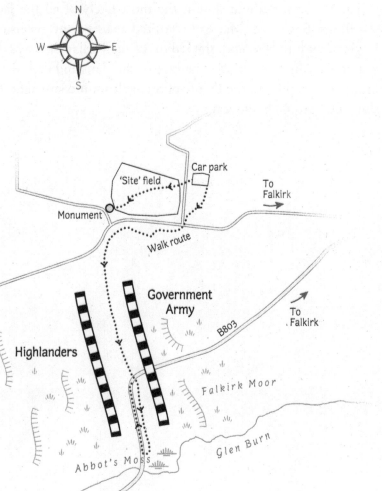

N
W E
S

'Site' field

Car park

To
Falkirk

Monument

Walk route

Government
Army

To
Falkirk

B803

Highlanders

Falkirk Moor

Glen Burn

Abbot's Moss

0   500 yards

0   500m

9

Rain, Sleet and Speed

Falkirk, 17 January 1746

On 3 December 1745, the market town of Derby witnessed remarkable events. Word came that the huge Jacobite army was closing fast, between 9,000 and 10,000 men, most of them the savage, ravening beasts who had cut a government army to pieces at Prestonpans only a few months before. The Duke of Devonshire had raised a new regiment, the Devonshire Blues, and he quickly decided to flee, retreating more than fifty miles to take refuge at Retford, leaving the town at the mercy of monsters.

But what the quaking townspeople saw was something quite different. Lord George Murray, easily the most capable Jacobite general, knew that desertions had badly thinned the ranks of the army, despite the recruitment of the Manchester Regiment, and he wanted to give the appearance that there were indeed 9,000 to 10,000 men marching into the heart of England. Derby is only 125 miles from London, no more than five or six days away for the fast-moving Highlanders.

At 11 a.m. on 4 December, packs of howling wolves intent on pillage, rape and plunder did not descend. Instead, a Jacobite vanguard of thirty cavalry troopers clattered under the arch of the northern gate, rode down Friar Gate and ordered the town council to arrange quarters and provision for at least 9,000 men. Later in the afternoon, Prince Charles and his mounted lifeguards in their royal blue uniforms arrived with most of his senior officers and the clan chiefs. No doubt their brightly coloured plaids and trews looked alien to the townspeople of Derby but there seemed to be no threat – at least, not yet. As it grew darker in the late afternoon, the main body of the army entered the town. Murray had ordered them to march in separate regimental detachments so that, in the winter gloom, all observers could see was more and more Highlanders arriving. Maybe there were more than 9,000? Maybe English Jacobites had joined the rebels? As Lord George knew it would, word quickly reached London and the city began to boil with panic, people withdrew cash from banks and many who had somewhere else to go made preparations to leave.

They need not have worried. To encourage his officers and men, Prince Charles had assured them that they would be met in Derby by Sir Watkin Williams-Wynn, a prominent and influential sympa-thiser and member of the Tory Party. No doubt he would bring news of French help, perhaps help to raise more recruits. The Duke of Beaufort was on the point of taking Bristol. The French would arrive in strength in the south of England at any moment. None of these things happened. And worse, there were three government armies in the field – one defending London and two to the north of the Jacobite army.

Exeter House used to stand in the centre of Derby until its demo-lition in the middle of the 19th century. A solid, brick-built mansion, it would become the setting for a historical turning point in all senses. Prince Charles established his headquarters there and, on the evening of 5 December, he called a council of war for the following morning.

On the same evening, Captain Dudley Bradstreet rode into Derby, where he was challenged by a Jacobite sentry. He recorded his response in his memoir: 'I told the fellow that I was a man of quality come to serve the Prince Regent, and would be followed by all my friends if my usage was good, and desired to be brought to the Prince's quarters directly. I heard them whisper that an English lord was come to join them.'

In fact, he was nothing of the kind. An Irish adventurer and conman, Bradstreet had offered his services to the government minister, the Duke of Newcastle, when Prince Charles' army marched into England. Quickly fixing him up with a credible back story, including a few days in prison with captured Jacobites, Newcastle arranged for the Irishman to be given £100, a set of good clothes and an alias. Oliver Williams was sent north to Lichfield, about twenty-five miles south-west of Derby, where he met the Duke of Cumberland. He was camped at the town with his army. The duke supplied him with 'a fine gelding, arms and furniture [tack]'.

At the council of war on the morning of 6 December, held in the oak-panelled dining room of Exeter House, Lord George Murray argued forcefully that the army should retreat. They could easily make themselves masters of Scotland again. They could carry on the war there 'for several years', forcing the London government to negotiate. War in Europe between Britain and France meant that troops were desperately needed elsewhere. It might be possible to restore the Stuarts to the throne of Scotland and end the hated union with England. In addition, despite the prince's assurances, no substantial help from the French had materialised even though the rebellion had been a spectacular success, and recruitment in England had been disappointing. Only the Manchester Regiment had come forward and there were just 200 of them. Even if the prince's army defeated one of the circling government armies, it would be in no condition to beat a second or third. Retreat to Scotland, overwinter and regroup – that was the sensible strategy – the only strategy. Many heads nodded in agreement.

The prince would have none of it and Cameron of Lochiel and Colonel O'Sullivan supported him. The army was undefeated. Morale was high and the clansmen who had come all that way, deep into alien territory, wanted to fight. The morning session of the council broke up in disagreement.

All was settled in the afternoon. Dudley Bradstreet had been talking, probably to staff officers, telling them that the Jacobites' situation was perilous, if not hopeless. Exaggerating the size of the three government armies closing in on Derby – and one of them, under

Cumberland, was only twenty-five miles away at Lichfield with 9,000 men – and adding a fictitious fourth at Northampton, he warned that, if Prince Charles led his men to London, they would be cut off and cut to pieces. When Bradstreet was brought into the council of war to repeat what he had said to the prince, Murray and the chiefs, that settled the matter. And, if Cumberland was close, there could be no delay. On the evening of 6 December, as the winter dark descended on Derby, the Jacobites formed up, left the town and turned back north, back to the safety of Scotland.

Lord George Murray conducted a brilliant fighting retreat, the fast-moving clansmen outpacing government pursuit as they reached Manchester, Preston and began to climb up into the foothills of the western Pennines. Only at Clifton Moor near Penrith was there any serious fighting. Taking command of the rearguard, Murray sent Prince Charles ahead with the bulk of the army. With Glengarry's MacDonald regiment, the Appin Stewarts, the MacPhersons and the Edinburgh Regiment, he turned to face the pursuing dragoons. The ground was good, the conditions were right and so Murray dismounted, placed himself at the head of the MacPhersons, drew his sword and roared the *claideamh mor*. The Highland charge was once more devastating as the dragoons broke and fled back to the larger force behind them. It was under the command of the Duke of Cumberland.

Stirling was a hinge in history, the great castle on its spectacular rock commanding the only road from the Lowlands to the Highlands and the fertile plains of Fife and the north-east. For many centuries, the castle had guarded the bridge over the Forth. If Prince Charles were once more to make himself the master of Scotland, his army needed to take the formidable fortress. And it was by no means impossible. Some help had at last arrived from France. Lord John Drummond, the brother of the Duke of Perth, had set sail from Dunkirk in late November with his regiment, the Royal Scots and part of the Irish Brigade, both units having served in the French army. The Royal Navy blockade intercepted most of the small fleet but Drummond's ship and three others slipped through and made their way up the North Sea coast. Drummond landed at the Jacobite-held port of Montrose and the others reached Stonehaven and Peterhead. With him he had money, weapons and cannon but only 150 soldiers had evaded capture by the navy. At least they were experienced, hardened in battle in Europe.

Ignoring Prince Charles's orders to join him and the main body of the army and claiming he had instructions from the French to secure Scotland, Drummond sent some of his men to Lord Lewis Gordon, a Jacobite nobleman from the north-east. In one of the forgotten battles of the rising, he led almost 1,000 men against a force of loyalist troops commanded by Norman Macleod, chief of Clan Macleod. Several other significant clans opposed Prince Charles – the Munros, Grants, Mackenzies and Mackays amongst them. Known as the Highland Companies, they had occupied the Aberdeenshire town of Inverurie. Gordon led his men out of Aberdeen but appears to have entrusted operational command to Major Cuthbert, an experienced officer from Drummond's Royal Scots. On 23 December, the regular soldiers from the French army attacked defenders to the south-east of the town, near the ford over the River Don, and they took casualties, making little headway. But Lewis Gordon mounted a surprise attack from the north and drove the Macleods and others out of Inverurie. As at Dunkeld, the charge was not possible in the streets of the town and most of the fighting was done with muskets. Nevertheless, the victory gave the Jacobites control of the north-east and Lord John Drummond led his men south. The two armies came together on 4 January, swelling the prince's forces to more than 9,000. He had never commanded more and, despite campaigning in the depths of winter, morale was high.

By 8 January, the town of Stirling had fallen and, with the artillery supplied by Drummond, the Jacobites laid siege to the castle. The prince set up his headquarters at Bannockburn House.

General Henry Hawley had been appointed commander-in-chief of government forces in Scotland. A professional soldier of long standing, he had a ferocious reputation as a strict disciplinarian, not hesitating to have men flogged or hanged for disobedience or cowardice. Hawley had fought at Sheriffmuir as a young soldier and had seen the Highland charge for himself. He left a very precise description of what it was like to face it:

> When the Highlanders come within musket shot of the enemy, they fire a volley, then they immediately throw down their muskets and charge with their swords and targes. As they charge they try to instill panic by their loud battle cries; and as they approach the enemy, they change formation. Having originally been drawn up in lines, as they come forward, they gather into groups or clusters. In these clusters or wedges, the Highlanders attempt to pierce the enemy lines in many places. The charge can be easily defeated if officers have their men hold their fire until the Highlanders are close. But if the fire is given at a distance, you probably will be broke for you never get time to load a second cartridge, and if you give way, you may give your foot [soldiers] for dead, for they [the Highlanders] being without a firelock or any load, no man with his arms, accoutrements etc can escape them, and they give no quarter.

Hawley had seen the charge again at Clifton Moor but seemed unworried when he heard of the siege of Stirling and the size of the Jacobite army. By that time he was based in Edinburgh and, on 13 January, he ordered his deputy, Major-General John Huske, a very capable commander, to lead out 4,000 troops to relieve the town. It may be that Hawley's experience of the confusion at Sheriffmuir, when he rode with the squadrons of dragoons that scattered the Highlanders under the Duke of Argyll had led him to overestimate their effectiveness. And despite his vivid description of the charge and the consequences of not standing against it, he seems to have underestimated the elan and the ferocious fighting qualities of the clans. All of which may have led to an extraordinary sequence of events.

Having followed in Huske's wake and advanced west from Edinburgh with 3,000 men, Hawley reached Falkirk on 15 January.

The general set up his headquarters and billeted himself at Callendar House while his men camped outside the town. Lady Anne Kilmarnock was Hawley's host and she is said to have wined and dined – and detained – the old man. He was sixty in 1745, old for the time. He ate and drank so well that it appears he did not take the Jacobite threat seriously, unwilling to believe that they would dare to attack. What he did not know, not until a scout reported it to him, was that, on the afternoon of 17 January, Lady Anne's husband, Lord Kilmarnock was less than a mile away.

Kilmarnock was a cavalry commander in Prince Charles's army. Lord George Murray had led the bulk of his forces up to the high ground above the government camp, to what was known as 'the Falkirk Burgh Muir'. It was a position, he later said, that 'had all the advantages nature or art could give them'. In other words, it was good ground and the clans had *cothrom a' bhraighe*, 'the advantage of the brae'.

When he was told of the Jacobite advance at 2.30 in the afternoon, Henry Hawley tore out of the dining room at Callendar House, mounted his horse and galloped with his staff officers towards the government camp. Remembering Sheriffmuir, he ordered the dragoons to lead the advance to the high ground where the Highlanders were forming their battle lines. Cantering to keep their horses in formation, the squadrons of dragoons reached the top of the rise well before the infantry following behind them.

There then followed a series of events that no one could have predicted. The ensuing battle lasted no more than half an hour. It was watched by a local man who had climbed a nearby church steeple and timed it with his pocket watch, beginning with 'the first puffs of white smoke' from musket fire. What was happening was the chaos and confusion of Sheriffmuir, except in reverse.

To the appalled astonishment of their colonel, Francis Ligonier, Hawley ordered the dragoons to attack immediately. They had mostly formed up on the high ground opposite the Jacobite right wing, the MacDonald regiments, the Camerons and the Frasers, all commanded by Lord George Murray. When he saw what was about to happen, Murray dismounted, stood out in front of the line with his musket and shouted that only when he fired should the frontline fire. The order was repeated along the line. The general waited and waited and, when the dragoons had kicked their horses into a gallop and were coming on fast, only twenty or thirty yards away, he fired a single shot. Instantly volleys rang out, rippling along the lines from the MacDonalds on the left to the Camerons, MacPhersons, Frasers and others beside them.

The effect was devastating and instantaneous. Many fell as 'daylight could be seen' in the government ranks. Those horses and dragoons not hit by musket balls were forced to swerve aside as the animals spooked at the crack of firing and the dense clouds of gun smoke that temporarily blinded them. Hundreds turned back and ploughed through the infantry that had come up behind them, stampeding, mowing down men, creating complete confusion. Amidst the din of wounded horses screaming, men shouting and the snap of musket volleys, some government infantry shot at their own dragoons. But one troop did not waver and did break through the Highland line. Cobham's 10th Dragoons were a well-seasoned group who had fought in Europe under the command of the Duke of Cumberland and, when Cobham's men smashed into the Clanranald regiment, it did not hold its ground and lost its leadership. The chief, John of Invercauld, was trapped under a dead horse and had to be pulled free. Others fell on their backs in the melee and stabbed upwards at the horses' bellies with dirks and swords. But the gap was widening and Cobham's troopers had routed Lord Ogilvy's men in the second line. Quickly seeing the danger, the Farquharson chief roared for his men to form a wedge with himself at its point. They fought their way through the ruck of horses and dragoons and plugged the gap in the front line. 'Three men to carry the chief!' shouted one of his tacksmen as they rescued the badly wounded John of Invercauld.

But in moments more chaos engulfed the burgh muir. Seeing most of the dragoons turn and flee, the MacDonald regiments pursued them downhill towards the government camp and all its loot. The pipers threw down their instruments and went in with their claymores. Without them and their ability to signal, like buglers, Murray tried in vain to rally his soldiers, shouting above the din, riding around the moor – because suddenly the prince's army had begun to take heavy casualties.

Lord John Drummond had been given command of the Jacobite left wing but, when the battle began, he was absent. Despite George Murray's pleadings, the prince did not appoint a substitute. And so, when the bulk of the army surged over the hill, there was no one of sufficient overall authority to restrain them or their chiefs. This headlong rush exposed the left flank of the clan regiments and those government troops on their right wing who had stood firm began to pour volley after volley of musket fire into them. It was devastating, and hundreds were hit. The downhill charge halted and, as Colonel O'Sullivan watched, 'the cursed hollow square came up, took our left in flank and obliged them to retire in disorder. There was no remedy or succour to be given to them. The second line, that His Royal Highness counted on, went off, passed the river [Carron] and some of them even went to Bannockburn and Stirling, where they gave out that we lost the day.'

But at that moment, when it seemed that defeat for the Jacobites was imminent, the weather and the winter intervened. As the government army was re-forming and as Murray continued vainly to try to recall the MacDonalds from their plunder, a sudden, wild storm blew in from the west. Wind-driven rain and sleet stung the faces of the advancing government infantry. Lord John Drummond's Royal Scots and Irish troops, although very small in number, were still in formation at the top of the brae. But, as the dark thunder-head clouds massed over Falkirk moor, it quickly grew murky and visibility shrank dramatically. No one was sure what was happening and who was where. As the sleet blew horizontally, blinding many, Hawley's infantry suddenly broke, many of them fleeing downhill without firing a shot. It was growing darker by the minute. Hawley ordered his army to fall back and march to Linlithgow and on to Edinburgh and that allowed the prince to claim victory – just as

Mar's withdrawal from Sheriffmuir to Perth had allowed the Duke of Argyll to do the same thirty years before.

*

Driving up through the suburban sprawl of Falkirk, I was looking for another roadside monument to a battle. At Sheriffmuir there was only open moorland, a lonely road fringed by dense commercial forestry and so the boulder-built obelisk raised by Clan MacRae was easy to find. But my search for Lord George Murray's good ground was going nowhere quickly as I drove up and down bungalow-lined cul-de-sacs. What struck me was how consistently steep the slope was. I had passed Callendar House on the outskirts of the town, having driven along the Forth flood plain from the motorway. Once I turned south, looking for the railway line and the well-named Falkirk High Station, the road climbed quickly and the views to the Ochill Hills and the mountains beyond opened majestically over the firth to the north. It was an unusual mixture of the picturesque and the industrial. On the shores of the Forth, before the vista began to sweep up to the misty foothills, lies Grangemouth, its petrochemical plants with their tall, flaring chimneys glinting in the early morning light.

As I drove on, it struck me immediately how difficult it would have been for General Henry Hawley to get his army uphill quickly to meet the Jacobites on the high ground. When he ran out of Lady Anne's dining room on the afternoon of 17 January, he must have had to kick hard to get his horse into a gallop and both will have been breathless by the time they had found their way up to the burgh muir.

After leaving the bungalows behind, I found myself abruptly in another country. Over the hill from the sprawl, there was an open, rural landscape. Dense stands of mature hardwoods lined the road and through gaps I could see rolling, undulating farmland – what looked like very well managed pasture. And then, round a corner, there it was – a tall, grey, somewhat phallic monument to the Battle of Falkirk. Attached to the base of the shaft was a bronze plaque with a single sentence: 'The Battle of Falkirk was fought around here on 17 January 1746'.

The key word was 'around'. Before setting off for Falkirk, I had taken photographs of three online maps of the battle site with my phone. None of them agreed. Each told a different story. I'd set most store by the satellite image of a wide field to the north-east of the monument that was clearly marked as 'site'. Another laid out the disposition of each battle line, marking the clans with their names – MacDonalds, Camerons, Frasers and so on. Opposite them, on the government side, the regiments of Wolfe, Blakeney, Cobham, Ligonier and others were clearly labelled. But the plan was only loosely based on local geography and that seemed to be out of scale. The map on the Historic Environment Scotland website was taken from the Ordnance Survey and it plotted the battle lines well to the south of the 'site' on the satellite image. Baffling, especially since the land, with its woods, modern roads, pylons, gates and hedges obscured the 18th-century landscape, somewhere that looked very different before the improvements of the agricultural revolution.

I'd parked badly when I quickly stopped on the corner where the monument stands before walking into the field to the north-east, the so-called site. When I returned to move my car to a clearing I'd spotted that seemed to be reserved for dog walker parking, I noticed an information board. It added to my bewilderment: 'The small valley in front of you played a significant part in the events of 17 January, 1746'. All I could find was what looked like a drainage ditch in a long ribbon of hardwood trees whose roots wound around its banks. Neither deep nor wide, it was easy to hop across and I climbed up a shallow incline beyond it to the field highlighted on the satellite image. None the wiser. The board did at least give a clear description of the disposition of the two armies and added an important detail I hadn't been clear about. The MacDonald regiments had arrayed themselves on the right wing just above a bog known as the Abbot's Moss. Lord George Murray quickly realised that it would anchor their flank because no attack could come across the morass.

After re-parking my car, I noticed a signpost for the Battle of Falkirk Muir Trail with an identifying logo of two crossed flintlock pistols. Beside it was another information board with the eye-catching headline: 'It was the largest battle of the Jacobite Rising, with approximately 8,000 on either side'. That was a timely reminder. The well-written copy on the board went on to claim that, in addition, there were probably the same number of spectators. I frankly doubt that but the statistics made it clear that 16,000 soldiers needed a lot of room to kill each other. The 'site' field was far too small.

The trail led me across a road and back into the middle of the 18th century. It was an excellent route punctuated by unusually informative information boards at places where crucial moments in the battle happened. A well-made path took me through shelter belts of old woodland and past open farmland with wide fields of pasture on either side, its vivid lushness very striking after a summer of drought. Significant details were added to what I'd culled from my reading as the boards explained more about why the charge of the government dragoons had failed. The burgh muir was where the townspeople of Falkirk came to dig for peat for their fires and clay to daub on the walls of their houses. Consequently, Murray's good ground for the Highlanders was potentially very difficult for horses since the surface was 'riddled with holes'. It was something the sharp-eyed Jacobite general will have noticed. The copy on the boards also made the point that the land was so undulating that it would have been difficult for the clansmen not only to see all of the enemy lines but also those regiments who fought at their side. When the fighting began, General Hawley was with the infantry toiling up the hill and he could not see how the Jacobites had set out their line.

When George Murray stood forward of the MacDonalds with his musket, he could only make out the forward squadrons of the government dragoons and could not have known how large a force they were. Behind the shallow ridge they charged down, I noticed that there was a deep dip that would have screened others until the last moment. And, according to another information board further down the path, that moment really was the last. The writer of the excellent copy reckoned that Murray would have waited until the thundering cavalry charge was very close indeed – 'twenty yards, fifteen yards, thirteen yards – then just ten yards before Lord George levelled his musket. The crack of the lone shot rang out giving a hollow peal in the cold winter air. That was the signal. A devastating volley echoed along the Jacobite line with dramatic effect.'

Good writing, it brought the quiet fields alive and reminded me of Murray's tremendous physical courage and excellent soldiering. It was said after the rising that, if Prince Charles had fallen asleep for a year after the muster at Glenfinnan, he would have awakened with a crown on his head if all had been left to Lord George.

After the volley, the MacDonald regiments charged along the south side of the ridge, close to the Abbot's Moss. I could see that it had been well drained in the centuries after the battle and only patches of spiky marsh grass in the fields gave away its location. But, in the winter of 1745–46, it would have been a deep and treacherous bog. I noticed that the folds of the ground would have meant that the MacDonalds would have lost sight of the northern part of the Jacobite line as they rushed forward. As the January daylight faded, Murray would have had great trouble finding them, let alone trying to rally and re-form them. It seems that many saw a large group of spectators who had walked up from the town and the clansmen chased them, avid for plunder and worse.

As the path swung steeply downhill from the ridge, another board made an excellent point. Francis Ligonier's amazement at Hawley's order to the dragoons to charge without waiting for the infantry was understandable because '[t]his was the first time in history that a cavalry charge had preceded an infantry advance, but it was not to be the last. A century later exactly the same mistake was made in the Crimean War with the now infamous Charge of the Light Brigade.'

The Muir Trail runs across the battlefield, mostly keeping to the no-man's land between the armies, down towards the Abbot's Moss for about three quarters of a mile and I could see the extent of the undulating pasture on either side. It is a wide area and, oddly, fields with very little stock in them. The emptiness of it all recalled for me what a vast melee it would have been on that winter afternoon as 16,000 men and horses fought or fled for their lives. The clash and clamour of battle, the screams of the wounded and dying, the squeal of injured horses, the snap of musketry and the roar of war cries all filled the darkling air as mud was churned and blood spilled. When the storm suddenly broke from the west, the rain and sleet would have swept across that high and probably treeless plateau, swirling and eddying down in the dips, causing men to slip and horses to skid. The already dislocated chaos would have become a mud-spattered charnel house before the coming night stilled the fighting and persuaded Hawley to get his men off the field in as good order as possible. Some of his wounded who were left behind might have crawled to a hiding place, perhaps in the dark shadow by one of the dead horses, but most will have been ruthlessly put out of their misery by the dirks of the Highlanders and stripped of their clothes and possessions.

Walking back uphill to the monument, I noticed carpets of blaeberry plants on either side of the path through the woodland. It was too late in the autumn for the sweet little berries I'd found at Sheriffmuir and some of the leaves were already tinged with brown. From the ridge where the MacDonalds fired on the dragoons, there was a wide gap to the north-west and another echo of that battle fought thirty years before. Through it, I could see what the clansmen saw. Beyond the smoke and flares of the petrochemical plant at Grangemouth, there rose the dark heads of the distant mountains silhouetted against a clear pale blue sky. That glimpse was the reason the Highlanders had come to the burgh muir to fight – their places, their homes, the land where their ancestors had worked and walked their lives lay beyond those far mountains.

By that dark winter afternoon in 1746, the old life was beginning to fade. Never again would Highlanders be able to muster such a large army, never again would their military power threaten the British state. After Falkirk, there would follow a bitter legacy, centuries of repression and decline as the working landscape of the clan lands shrivelled into scenery, sheep pasture and shooting estates before disappearing into the cloying mists of romance and myth-making. The battle on the burgh muir saw the last of the raw, inde-pendent power of these warriors from the north, almost the last of their elemental courage as the Farquharson chief charged at the point of a wedge to seal the gap in the MacDonald lines. After night fell on Falkirk, there was only one more act in a century-long drama to be played out.

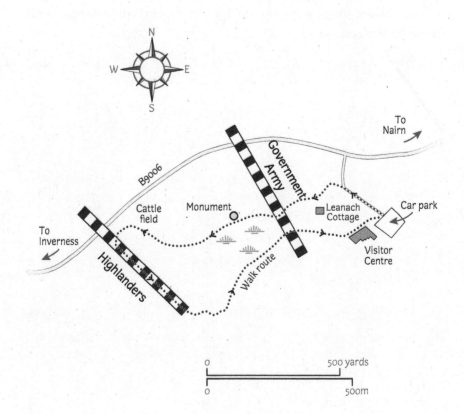

N
W E
S

To Nairn

B9006

Government Army

Cattle field

Monument

Leanach Cottage

Car park

To Inverness

Highlanders

Walk route

Visitor Centre

0   500 yards
0   500m

The Army of the Dead

Culloden Moor, 16 April 1746

Since the days shut down quickly and the light shrinks in late November, I decided to begin one of the last journeys, the long drive north, as early as possible. To avoid wasting time with breakfast, I made sandwiches, bought orange juice and stowed them in the car overnight so that I could get away at 5.30 a.m. The journey across the Lowlands of eastern Scotland, the Firth of Forth, west Fife, Lowland Perthshire and into the mountains would take four and a half hours. I wanted to spend as much time at Culloden Moor as I could.

But as soon as the car engine turned over, the beams of the head-lights diffused into thick fog – visibility no more than fifty yards. It shrouded the road all the way up Gala Water, cleared for a few minutes on Middleton Moor as a pale-yellow light glowed on the eastern horizon before the road disappeared again under the thick, grey blanket. The slow, halting drive would take much longer than four and a half hours.

Fortified by coffee bought north of Perth, I followed the A9 as it climbed into the mountains. The fog was patchy, thinning and thickening again in Strath Tay and masking that moment beyond Dunkeld when Lowland becomes Highland. Amidst all the majesty and magnificence of a landscape I'd seen often, watching it unfold on clear days as I travelled further and further north, I found that the world had shrunk and I drove very slowly while others raced past me. That encouraged even more caution as the possibility of suddenly braking when the wreckage of a collision reared up like a phantasm in front of me. After Killiecrankie, the battlefield invisible on either side of the road, the dark grey fog seemed to lighten, becoming more like gossamer mist along the Pass of Drumochter, the highest stretch of the A9. But all I could see to tell me where I was were roadside signs.

Suddenly, beyond Dalwhinnie, the fog cleared completely to reveal a landscape in sunshine, glowing in all its winter colours, the deep browns of died-back bracken, long yellow grasses and the dark evergreens that covered the lower flanks of the mountains. Their tops were brilliant with snow. More than a little disoriented, I couldn't tell which peaks I was looking at. And then, as quickly as they appeared, another grey curtain of fog closed down the splendour.

After a slow, slow drive, the road signs told me I'd reached Daviot, not far south of Inverness. And then, like clanking stage machinery working its magical illusions, the fog disappeared once more and below me, at the bottom of the long incline down to Inverness, I saw that the Moray Firth was filled with white, pillowy mist, like a gigantic bubble bath. Over to the east, where I knew the battlefield of Culloden lay, the land was bathed in brilliant sunlight.

It seemed that meteorology was playing a game of metaphors with history, hiding and revealing and then hiding again.

*

'I did not like the ground: there could never be more improper ground for Highlanders.' Lord George Murray's judgement on the suitability of Culloden Moor as a battlefield had the great benefit of hindsight but it may also have been prompted by a simmering enmity. Colonel John O'Sullivan had proposed the clans deploy across the road to Inverness between the walled enclosures around Culloden House in the north and the dykes of the farm at Culwhiniac to the south. Throughout the Jacobite campaign of 1745–46, Murray and O'Sullivan had frequently disagreed. But on this occasion, the Irishman seems to have been more clear-headed.

The Duke of Cumberland's government army had reached Nairn and it was vital to protect the Jacobite base at Inverness, where their provisions and other resources were stored. Murray thought the ground at Culloden was too flat. There was no advantageous brae down which the Highlanders could charge. Instead, he suggested a steep, sloping site near Daviot Castle. But that would have left the road to Inverness open, in effect surrendering the town. When Colonel Harry Ker of Graden, the brave and methodical officer who had looked so carefully at the ground at Prestonpans, rode over to see where Murray wanted to fight, he was not impressed. The ground at Daviot was overlooked and 'mossy and soft'. O'Sullivan's proposal was not perfect but the undefeated army of the clans would fight at Culloden.

Despite Ker's recommendations, Murray would not accept the consensus. He had a better idea – one that would settle any debate. The government army was camped at Nairn, about ten miles to the east. The Duke of Cumberland's twenty-fifth birthday fell on 15 April and there were reports that each of his regiments would be issued with two gallons of brandy to celebrate. Perhaps sentries might not be so vigilant. Murray proposed a daring night attack on the government camp and Prince Charles readily agreed.

It turned out to be a chaotic, exhausting shambles. When the Highland army arrived at Culloden, many men had not eaten that day. Supplies of oatmeal, cheese and other foodstuffs seem not to have come from Inverness. And so, in the afternoon, many men went foraging. By the time officers had rounded up their companies, it was late in the day and the march did not get underway until about 9 p.m. In order to avoid detection by lookouts in the crow's nests of the Royal Navy warships anchored in the Moray Firth or risk being seen by government patrols, the road from Inverness to Nairn was avoided. Instead, led by Lord George Murray and the Atholl Brigade, the army moved slowly through the countryside – very slowly, occasionally blundering about in the darkness, climbing dykes and crossing streams. They needed to reach the government camp and be in position by 2 a.m. But progress was halting, gaps appeared in the long column behind Murray and it became clear that the timetable was impossible.

Before dawn, before government patrols and sentries saw them, the army had to turn back. Hungry and very tired, many men simply sank down and slept in the lee of walls, in the cover of woodland or under bushes. As the darkness lifted, others simply drifted away to scour the countryside for food, but most trudged back to Culloden Moor. The audacious night march had been a disaster, a catastrophic miscalculation that decisively influenced the outcome of the battle without a shot having been fired or a sword thrust.

When dawn broke on 16 April, there was no battle line formed up on the moor. Instead, men had gathered around their clan standards, most of them hungry and exhausted, probably looking for a patch of dry ground where they might rest for an hour or two. Many men were still missing, still foraging, some had deserted and others were sound asleep in the open.

When the prince, O'Sullivan and Murray saw how sparse their line of battle was, they were forced to move it. It was a second negative consequence of the failed night march. O'Sullivan's preferred ground was a flat area of moorland a little to the east of where the battle was ultimately fought. With so few men, there was a real danger of being outflanked and so the army was re-deployed to a tighter, more restricted area, a place where the ground was more boggy and there was a scatter of small, brackish pools. The derivation of the Gaelic version, *Cuil Lodair*, described the ground. It means 'the corner of the little pools'. The moor was used as common grazing, a wide, unfenced area where surrounding farmers could pasture their beasts. By mid-April, new grass might have been flushing and the ground would have been cropped close by hungry cows, goats and sheep. On the northern and southern edges of the moor, there were drystane dykes that would anchor and protect the Jacobite flanks. According to Colonel Ker, the army formed up 'a mile westward' of O'Sullivan's original choice of a site. It was not the best ground for the charge but it would have to do.

After much discussion and some grumbling from Lord George Murray, the Highland army was finally arrayed in line of battle. On the right flank, hard up against the dykes of Culwhiniac, in the position of honour, was the Atholl Brigade, about 500 men commanded by Murray. To his left was Clan Cameron, 650 men led by their chief, Ewen Cameron of Lochiel. Beside him stood Charles Stewart of Ardshiel, a 'pretty man' accounted a great swordsman, and his 150 Appin Stewarts. Fraser of Inverallochy's 500 were in the line beyond them and their commander was looking to the north, towards the Inverness road. Another 500 Frasers were coming to fight, moving as fast as they could to join the prince's army. To their left was Clan Chattan, most of them Mackintoshes, about 500 men. They stood next to the Farquharsons, 150 clansmen from Deeside. Then there was a combined force of 280 Macleans, MacLachlans and Chisholms. Out on the left wing – and insulted to be there – were the three MacDonald regiments, 200 apiece from Keppoch and Clanranald and 500 under Glengarry. In all, about 3,600 men stood in the front line.

Behind them there was no formal second line but rather a series of companies who could act as a reserve and move to any point of need, where the line might be in danger of bulging or breaching. In the rear of the Atholl Brigade stood 350 Royal-Ecossais, regular troops commanded by Lord John Drummond. In the centre was Colonel John Roy Stuart with 200 of his own clansmen and commanding 500 from Aberdeenshire and another 500 from the Forfarshire Regiment. There were 200 of Lord Kilmarnock's Footguards. The same number were under John Gordon of Glenbuchat, one of the first to come to Glenfinnan. Now seventy years old, he was ready to plunge into battle if need be. Beside the old man was the Duke of Perth's regiment, about 300 of them.

In the rear were three small troops of cavalry and in the centre, flanked by his Lifeguards, was Prince Charles. His army nominally numbered almost 6,000 men but it is very likely that many were missing – asleep on the road from Nairn or foraging for food or long gone on the road home.

All of the men drawn up on Culloden Moor looked to the east, listening for the beat of drum and the coming of the enemy. And many of them pulled their plaids tight, for a keen wind was blowing sleet off the Moray Firth into the faces of the Highlanders.

*

Bathed in brilliant, chilly morning sunshine, the battlefield seemed to float, unmoored, with trenches of white mist on either side. To the north, the Moray Firth was invisible under thick, whipped egg-white clouds piled up on the water while, to the south, the valley of the River Nairn was hidden under long gossamer scarves.

I parked behind the visitor centre, a low building faced with neutral wood and stone with the long tail of a grassy bank on one side. It hid the moor more or less completely, like a stage curtain waiting to reveal the drama behind it. But I knew there was no drama, only memory and perhaps a fleeting, floating sense of atmosphere. On that chill November morning, there would only be silence behind the curtain – no echoes of cannon fire or of war pipes, the roared orders of sergeants major, the clash of steel or the screams of dying men.

At the top of the sloping grassy bank is a viewpoint over the battlefield, a wide, open area in front of a dense wood marking its western margins. Two rows of tall flags show where the lines of the opposing armies were – red for the Duke of Cumberland's position and blue for the Jacobites. Below me and to the right, I could see Leanach Cottage. Thatched, rubble-built, very tidy and with a garden bench by the low front door, it seemed to me to belong to a film set – *Brigadoon* perhaps. I made out a network of paths around the moor that run along the lines of flags and also link them. Walking down to the government position, I came across an etched metal diagram of the battlefield on a low stone plinth but it had become so badly weathered that it was illegible. What was also unclear was the full extent of the marked lines. It seemed to me that they covered only the southern part of the battlefield. It extended over the B9006, a busy road leading to Inverness. The starting positions of the

MacDonald regiments and the government troops opposite them were not represented.

There was no one to ask for the visitor centre was closed. But, on the inside of a window near the entrance, a member of its staff had helpfully Sellotaped a large map of the site. Or perhaps unhelpfully – the map had been reversed, showing the battle site to the east of the centre and its car park, with the Jacobite army facing west. A Spanish visitor was trying to make sense of the compass symbol in the top right-hand corner of the map while I smiled at the unexpected irony. Whoever had stuck the map on the window had the battle fought on the original site chosen by Colonel John O'Sullivan.

Beyond picturesque Leanach Cottage and the red flags of the government lines is a graveyard. Low, small boulders crudely inscribed on one face mark where the dead were buried. The first and only one to commemorate government casualties reads: 'Field of the English. They were buried here.' That wording helps keep a myth alive – that the battle was fought between Scotsmen and Englishmen. This misleading notion is further fed by a broch-like structure nearby. It carries another inscription:

The Battle of Culloden was fought on this moor.
16th April, 1746.
The graves of the gallant Highlanders who fought for Scotland and Prince Charlie are marked by the names of their clans.

It is the use of 'Charlie' instead of Charles that is perhaps most eloquent. After the romancing of the clans, the bens and the glens by Walter Scott and the cloying Balmorality of Queen Victoria, Charles Edward Stuart became Charlie, bonnie boats sped over the sea to Skye and all Highlanders became gallant. In fact, the battle lines at Culloden were not drawn between Scotland and England. At least a third of Cumberland's army were Scots, probably more, and several clans, such as the Campbells, Grants and Mackays, were loyal to the Hanoverians and sent men to fight for them. German, French and Irish troops were also on the field.

Beside the path are two more telling details. At *Cuil Lodair*, there are still little pools. Not far from the red flags of the government positions is a wide patch of boggy ground and the dark, peaty waters of a pool perhaps twenty yards long and ten yards wide – a genuine obstacle. And close by is the only memorial to a single individual I found on the moor. The inscription on the small stone reads:

Well of the Dead.
Here the Chief of the MacGillivray fell.

*

Some men pray before battle, others sing psalms. Along the long lines of clansmen, from the MacDonald regiments to the Atholl Brigade, some men did close their eyes and begin to chant. But they were not invoking God's protection before they charged across the moor. They were summoning the Army of the Dead. In a low, rumbling murmur, clansmen observed the ancient ritual of the *sloin-neadh*, 'the naming of the names'. Each recited his genealogy: *is mise mac Iain, 'ic Sheumais, 'ic Iain Mor, 'ic Ruaridh*. Many men could go back twenty generations and more and they did this to centre them-selves, to remember who they were, where they had come from and why they had come to the moor to fight. Men were summoning ghosts, to add their ancestral courage, their fabled prowess to their own. As they looked out over Culloden, the little pools and the marsh grass and the icy sleet blew in their faces, they watched the government army take up its position. And the clansmen felt the breath of great warriors on their necks, whispering to them, remem-bering the glories of the past.

Sometime after midday, the Duke of Cumberland sent forward Lord Bury across no-man's land. At the northern edge of the moor, the armies were about 1,000 yards apart but, on the southern, only 500 or 600 yards from each other. Bury was a brave man for he rode to within 100 yards of the Highland army and could, no doubt, hear their jeers and insults. Cumberland wanted him to assess how many cannon his enemy had. Soon after Bury reined his horse around,

Jacobite batteries opened fire. Their cannonade was met with an immediate response and events began to accelerate. At such long range, it is unlikely that either had much effect, except in one sense. The roar of the government cannon prompted Prince Charles to issue the *claideamh mor*, the order to charge. The war pipes echoed over the moor as the battle rants played and the order was given to a messenger. But it never reached the front line. As he ran forward from the prince's position, MacLachlan of Inchconnel was decapitated by a cannonball. Colonel Harry Ker retrieved the order and, so that the Jacobite line would straighten and all would charge at once and at the same distance from the enemy, he rode up first to the MacDonald regiments. As they advanced, Ker went down the line until he reached Clan Chattan. Once they were away, Clan Cameron and the Atholl Brigade both broke into the charge on the right wing.

It was at that moment the carnage began.

*

The ground between the Jacobite left wing, where the MacDonalds began to advance, and the government lines is still very boggy in places and I saw several dark little pools. Testing the ground around them, it was spongy and very tussocky, easy either to sink into or turn an ankle. Even though the moor was grazed in the 1740s and there would have been much less heather or willow and birch scrub, the footing would have been very boggy, cloying and uncertain, especially after a winter's rains. In an effort to return the part of the battlefield they own to how it was in 1746, the National Trust for Scotland has reintroduced shaggy Highland cattle and goats. Behind a very robust enclosure were half a dozen of these great beasts, three black and three an oatmeal colour, their horn-spreads splendid. But, even in November, the churned mess they had made of the ground was at least a foot deep. Black, peaty mud was everywhere and the idea of a charge of any speed, any velocity across ground half as deep is hard to imagine – even if it was only patchy. Progress would have been halting at best.

A chill breeze began to blow down from the north and I saw that it had shifted the low cloud off the Moray Firth and that beyond it the Sutherland mountains were snow-capped. I passed more memorial stones – MacLachlan, Maclean, MacGillivray and Mixed Clans were all inscribed. A wide tarmac track allowed me to move south, following Colonel Harry Ker of Graden as he gave the order to charge. Like me, he was a long way from home. His ancestors were Border reivers and the family stronghold is only a few miles south of Kelso, where I was born. The Kers eventually became Marquises of Lothian and the family never gave up their Catholic faith.

As I walked down the track I passed low stone plinths that marked the positions of the clans and gave their numerical strength. When I reached Clan Cameron and the Atholl Brigade, I looked across the moor to the flags showing the government lines. They seemed a long way off but what struck me forcibly was how uneven the ground was. Less than 100 yards from where Lord George Murray sat on his grey horse, there was a deep dip. From the bottom, I could see neither set of flags and impeding my advance there was an enclosure formed with turf dykes, what are also known as fail-dykes. No force of clansmen could have moved quickly until they breasted the rise on the far side.

The drystane dykes of Culwhiniac Farm are much cast down and a wire-stock fence now borders the moor, a ploughed field sown with winter barley on the far side. On the top wire perched a robin, his red breast puffed out. He sang his winter song and, as I walked up out of the deep dip, he hopped along beside me.

*

When George Murray spurred his horse up the same slope, his Atholl Brigade and Clan Cameron behind him, they were met with withering fire. Government artillery began to fire not cannonballs but canister shot, also known as grapeshot. Inside metal canisters scores of musket balls were packed and, when the clansmen ran within 300 yards of the gun emplacements, the gunners began to fire round after murderous round. With grapeshot scattering in an arc, like pellets from a shotgun, it was not necessary to aim and sight and so the government batteries could get off many more rounds much more quickly. Clan Chattan appeared to lead the charge and came within range before any other clan or regiment. When the air grew thick with whizzing musket balls, the whole brigade of 500 and Clan Fraser's men slewed suddenly to the right, swerving to avoid the bombardment. They crashed into Clan Cameron and the Atholl Brigade and the disciplined charge instead became a huge mob of men perhaps twenty or thirty deep. The government gunners reloaded quickly and one eyewitness, Michael Hughes, later wrote: 'The grapeshot made open lanes quite through them, the men dropping down by wholesale.'

There was no room. No organisation, little sense of command to enforce and follow the well-tried practice of advancing to within twenty or so yards, firing a volley and then forming wedges.

The hail of grapeshot had, in effect, decapitated the clans because their commanders and chiefs, men who always led from the front, were directly in the firing line. Cameron of Lochiel had both his ankles broken by musket balls and Charles Fraser of Inverallochy was brought down. Alexander MacGillivray was badly wounded as he led the charge of Clan Chattan but still managed to fight on. He broke through the redcoat ranks, jumping over the bodies of those who had fallen. But a blow to the head half-blinded him and the chief was brought to his knees. He managed somehow to crawl back through the melee to the Well of the Dead, where he died. His memorial was raised close by.

MacGillivray's second-in-command, Major Gillies MacBean, showed extraordinary courage. It may be that he managed to get the men around him into a wedge formation for he and others broke through the government lines in the same place. Even though he had been stabbed several times by bayonet thrusts and suffered a terrible, slashing cut across his face, he fought like a fury, killing several redcoats. John MacGillivray, who may have been part of MacBean's wedge, killed twelve men with his sword and dirk before he was cut down by a reserve battalion behind the front line.

On the Jacobite right wing, the battle hung in the balance for a few chaotic minutes. As Clan Cameron and the Atholl Brigade rushed forward, despite fearful casualties, they attacked Barrell's Regiment and the government line suddenly bulged. At Prestonpans, the shock of impact had quickly turned redcoat ranks and a rout immediately followed as the whole army disintegrated. But at Culloden, the soldiers stood fast. Better training and better tactics gave confidence and resolve. In ranks three deep, the government troops managed to complete several rounds of platoon firing at close range. When the front rank had fired a volley, instead of fumbling to reload before the charging Highlanders were on them, they quickly fixed bayonets to form a bristling rampart of steel. They may have gone down on one knee and held their muskets at an angle, like stakes driven into the ground. Behind the front rank, protected, the second and third ranks continued to fire and reload, getting off several close-range volleys at the clansmen. The rate and breadth of musket fire was tremendously destructive, with perhaps 1,400 men shooting at the densely packed mass of Clan Chattan, Frasers, Appin Stewarts, Camerons and Atholl men. A corporal in one of the government regiments on their left wing remembered: 'When we saw them coming towards us in great haste and fury, we fired at about fifty yards distance, which made hundreds fall; notwithstanding which, they were so numerous, that they still advanced, and were almost upon us before we had loaded again. We immediately gave them another full fire.'

When the Highlanders did manage to engage, they found that the government soldiers' bayonet drill had changed. Instead of stabbing at the man directly in front, they thrust at the clansman on their right as he raised his sword arm. In the ruck of close-quarter fighting, when a multitude of things happened in a moment and the noise was deafening, this will not always have been possible but several men, like Alexander MacGillivray, were badly wounded by bayonets and the short, spear-like halberds known as 'spontoons'.

Despite all of this murderous and more or less continuous fire, the Jacobite right, Clan Cameron in the van, pushed hard to break through. Barrell's Regiment suffered terrible casualties, including their commanding officer, and they lost their colours. But, on the point of breakthrough, when the clans might have been able to get behind the government lines and roll them up from the south, perhaps inducing a rout, Major General John Huske quickly organised a counterattack. James Wolfe – later the general who won a posthumous victory at the Plains of Abraham in Canada in 1759 – was a captain in Barrell's Regiment and he recalled:

> The regiment behaved with uncommon resolution. They were however surrounded by superiority, and would have been destroyed had not Col. Martin with his regiment (the left of the 2nd line of foot) moved forward to their assistance, prevented mischief, and by a well-timed fire destroyed a great number of them.

Huske's prompt intervention in bringing up the second line was the decisive moment in the battle of Culloden. The charge had failed and not only because of the ground. The future had at last defeated the past. A modern army using artillery and well-drilled, rolling musket fire had kept at bay a force of immensely courageous warriors armed with bladed weapons, and then destroyed them.

*

When I reached the place where so many had fought so furiously, where they had died and where the fate of a dynasty and of an ancient culture was decided, there was nothing but a flat expanse of old pasture. But what else could there be? More mute monuments? More information? Perhaps the silence and the emptiness were eloquent. My robin had flown off and, as the air grew chill in the late afternoon, I saw mist rising in the valley of the River Nairn.

Behind me lay a field of blood. When the Highlanders retreated and Prince Charles fled, the government soldiers committed terrible atrocities, bayoneting or shooting the wounded lying on the moor, riding down men who could only attempt to stagger to a place of safety. But then the clansmen did dreadful, cruel things in the aftermath of the battles at Tippermuir, Aberdeen and Prestonpans. What was different in 1746 was the scale and the intensity of the reprisals. On the express orders of the Duke of Cumberland, a programme of genocidal actions began as the Highland landscape was despoiled, its people murdered, attacked or raped, their cattle stolen, their farmhouses fired. While the flight of the prince across the heather, the courage of Flora MacDonald and the persistence of his pursuers became the stuff of romance and even legend, the clans who had supported him suffered appallingly. Their way of life had been changing before Culloden but, after what the Highlanders called *Am Bliadhna Thearlaich*, 'The Year of Charles', history accelerated.

The physical bravery of these warriors will never fade. Even in the hours after the battle at Culloden was lost, some fought beyond the end of their strength and courage. His leg broken by grapeshot and very badly wounded, Major Gillies MacBean of Clan Chattan had somehow made his way out of the ruck of the fighting near the Well of the Dead. When his clan began to retreat, he could not follow them. Dragoons caught up with the wounded man at the Culwhiniac dyke. Hemmed in on three sides, MacBean managed to get his back against the dyke and he fought like a man possessed, slashing at the riders with his sword. Spurring their horses, the dragoons trampled him to the ground and rode over his body. Lord Ancrum, one of Cumberland's staff officers, roared for MacBean to be spared but, in their crazed rage, the soldiers ignored him. Still he was not dead. Still he refused to stop fighting. When the dragoons wheeled away, distracted by something else, MacBean crawled to a barn where an old woman hid him under her store of winter hay. Some hours later, as darkness descended on the moor and silence fell at last, this great warrior was finally defeated, overcome by his terrible wounds. But his courage was not forgotten.

The Old Road

Arisaig to Morar

It was a last resort. The Met Office forecast had promised a day of West Highland rain, sheeting down in heavy showers off the ocean, making my plans impossible. All the battlefields I'd walked and their approaches had been seen on days of sunshine, with only the odd squall to send me scurrying back to my car for shelter. The reason for choosing only good weather to follow in the footsteps of the clans had less to do with a natural aversion to a soaking and was more concerned by how I record these journeys back into the darkness of the past.

I use a phone camera to record much of what I see, its photos often far clearer, more atmospheric aides-memoire than only memoir. When an observation occurs to me or I remember a fact or a date related to what I see, I scribble those down on an old-fashioned police notebook, complete with an elastic band on the bottom to mark the page. When I climbed the rocky, steep, rhododendron-blocked knoll by the main road at Glenfinnan to look for the inscribed stones that claimed that Prince Charles's standard was raised there, I made a breathless note. If the arthritic and old Marquis of Tullibardine needed two men to help him hold the flag's pole upright, then how did he manage to get up here? Both of these means of making notes on what I see are made well-nigh impossible in continuous rain.

What I'd hoped on this, my final day, as I completed my series of journeys at last, was to walk the road that had first kindled in me a love of the Highlands and Islands, a place I have returned to again and again. It is a true place of spirits, somewhere I could not only sense the ghosts of clansmen walking beside me but also hear the whispers of their stories and the plaintive echoes of their music on the edge of the sea wind as it whistles off the ocean, driving the banked clouds in from the west to collide with the grey, glowering mass of the mighty mountains.

The road runs from Arisaig to Morar, the old road that winds up and down the rocky shore, around hummocky mosses and sudden corners, the road that reveals the glories of the western strands, the white sand of the Morar estuary, the sweep of Camusdarach beach, the machair at Bunacaimb and Back of Keppoch. But the morning's rain would veil these precious places and, as always happened when a day-long downpour comes, a walk would become a trudge, eyes downcast, the wet inevitably seeping into what promised to be a journey through the past, my own as well as the centuries of the clans. It would become something to be endured.

So, my plan had to change. Instead of walking, I'd drive to a handful of places I knew well and walk a mile or two before retreating to the car and its heater and moving on. But that didn't work either. I parked on the shore at Arisaig at the back of 8 a.m., when the grey light had lifted a little and I could see the dark blues of the sea and the land. Out to the west, the humps of the islands of Rum and Eigg were strewn with mist and I waited a few minutes to see if the rain might ease.

When I first came to Arisaig as a teenager in the 1960s, it struck me as a beautiful, busy little fishing village, the clutter of nets, fish boxes and lobster pots piled against the low sheds by the quay. Beyond its bay, I had seen the islands for the first time, their silhouettes sharp against the blue ocean. And when I walked up the rising road north of the anchorage, the jagged ridge of the Cuillin loomed dark on the far horizon. I had arrived in Arisaig on a school trip with a chattering gaggle of fourteen-year-olds who had never seen the West Highlands and never gazed over the Atlantic Ocean before. It would be untrue to say that I was awed by the elemental majesty of what I saw on that first morning when we got off the train from Glasgow. Like many boys and some girls at that age, I pretended not to be impressed by anything. But I do remember looking, staring over the shoulders of whoever was talking about goodness knows what. Without acknowledgement, at least at the time, the old road, its vistas, its history and the mountains behind it made an indelible mark.

I was drawn back again and again. As a student and then when I worked in television, I found myself driving and walking on the road, understanding more and more of its place, what I have come to believe is a pivotal place in the story I've attempted to tell in this book. The longest time I spent in Arisaig was when I was making a documentary film about a film, Bill Forsyth's lovely, magical *Local Hero*. The plot revolved around the efforts of an American oil company to buy the beach near the imaginary Highland village of Ferness. What made it all work was another kind of magic. Bill chose to film important sequences on the beach at Camusdarach, 'the Oak Bay'. Its pale-yellow sand lies only a few hundred yards off the old road. Defined by the horns of rocky promontories that reach into the sea at either end, it seemed to be a place apart, entire and powerful, possessed of an extraordinary spirit of place. Bill's story caught that as the beach worked its magic on all who saw it, spoke to them, changed them and made them fall in love with it.

On a still summer evening in 1964, I suggested, very tentatively, to Jennifer Wilson that we go for a walk on Camusdarach beach. Just the two of us. Our school party was staying at the Garramore Youth Hostel on the landward side of the road, now, sadly, no more. Once we had scrambled up the dunes, we found somewhere to sit and watch the sun set over the ocean, making the Cuillin seem to glow. As the monochrome of gloaming fell, I told Jennifer Wilson that I loved her.

I've no doubt at all that, at that moment and in that place, I did. Its magic was working on me. The puberty-stricken, testosterone-driven reality might have been quite different but I don't think so. I didn't lunge at her or even touch her at all. I just sat on the dune, staring out over the darkling ocean, not at all sure what to say next. Jennifer said nothing. She just turned and looked at me. Blankly. And said nothing.

When I parked at Arisaig, a lifetime later, I had hoped to find somewhere warm and welcoming to have breakfast, some reviving coffee and make some notes to get the rain-soaked day on the old road started. The only place that seemed to be open was the brightly lit Spar grocery.

'It's a disgrace!' said the kind lady behind the counter. 'There's nowhere open in the village. Nothing for people at all. Just a disgrace. We need people to come here but we just don't look after them. If you want some breakfast, you'll have to drive up to Mallaig. There's a cafe near the ferry terminal.'

I followed the fast, straight new road and parked outside the Co-op. The new road was built some way inland from the old winding trail I planned to follow in a series of short journeys.

It was the last resort. The Jac-o-Bites cafe turned out to be a strip-lit, square room with white plastic chairs and excellent bacon rolls. Once I'd brushed yesterday's crumbs off the table, I sat down, glad to be out of the penetrating rain that had been falling all morning, to make a plan and write some notes.

All of my own ancient experience of magic fled to the back of my mind as I realised that it was something else that had drawn me back – something I'd learned in the process of telling this story. When the clans gathered up all their ancestral courage and their chiefs raised their swords, shouted the *claideamh mhor*, the order to charge, their men roared their war cries. They were often the names of their places, the home-places of their people, the reason they had come to all those battlefields to fight. And the road that threads its way from Morar to Arisaig understands all that ferocious love and all those bonds that only death could break. There is a Gaelic word, *duthchas*, that does not translate well into English. German has an equivalent. Both *Heimat* and *duthchas* can mean something like home-ness but much more powerful than anything merely domestic. A clan's home was where their people were, where their history had happened across centuries and they saw themselves and their land as indivisible.

When Gaelic speakers meet someone they don't know, they don't ask what the other person does or where they live. They ask *Co as a tha thu*? It means 'Who are your people?' And before the catastrophe at Culloden, the reprisals and the bitter years of the Clearances, the answer always included a place, the place where they are, where they are themselves.

That's why the old road seemed to me to be a fragile thread, part of a disappearing, unravelling tapestry of a lost, harsh, ruthless and beautiful past.

I looked out of the windows of the Jac-o-Bites to see that the rain had eased. Like most fishing ports and ferry terminals, Mallaig is a mess, a cluttered waiting room for those moving between the land and the sea. Both arriving at the end of a narrow coastal strip, little more than a shelf between the mountains and the sea, the road and the railway run cheek by jowl before remembering to end just before the pier. Passengers from the train who are travelling onwards to Skye, Canna, Eigg, Muck or Rum have only a few yards to walk to the waiting CalMac ferry. Beyond all that bustle is the fishing port and the stink of it, simultaneously stomach-turning and evocative. I walked past a small fish shop where, more than once, I'd bought something from the catch of the day or something smoked to take home.

Counting back through my often-faulty memory, I realised I'd last been in Mallaig a long time ago, in 1998, in another century. When I reached the northernmost quay, I looked across the Sound of Sleat and, through the grey sea mist, I could make out the reason I often used to drive up to Mallaig, always taking the old road. On the far shore stood a white beacon of hope. Skye is home to Sabhal Mor Ostaig. Now part of the University of the Highlands and Islands, it was then a Gaelic-medium further education college, somewhere unique in Scotland, a place where the language of the clans lived and worked. When I was Director of Programmes at Scottish Television, I supported it as much as was possible, helping to persuade my company to donate many hundreds of thousands of pounds to its development.

In 1998, I came to Mallaig to catch the Skye ferry to celebrate the opening of new buildings at the college – the *Arainn Chaluim Chille*, 'the Campus of St Columba'. The site is dominated by a hall of residence, a white tower known as 'the Broch', and, on the far side of the grey waters, I could make out its shape. Gaelic is dying fast. The number of native speakers who live in the language, use it every day and turn to English only when necessary is dwindling alarmingly quickly. Perhaps only a little over 10,000 are left. Sabhal Mor Ostaig and its Broch are bulwarks as well as beacons.

The award of £9 million from the Conservative government of Margaret Thatcher for the production of television programmes that had taken me to Lewis had also meant frequent journeys to Skye. The annual grant would become a lifeline that propelled the language of the men who mustered at Glenfinnan from the margins of Scottish cultural life to the centre. Training in television production techniques for Gaelic speakers was urgently needed and I saw that Sabhal Mor Ostaig could take a pivotal role in that. And I was also certain that learners and non-native speakers would keep the language alive. To put my mouth where the company's money and my opinions were, I began to learn the language. For two mornings a week over several months I went for lessons to the house and kitchen table of a wonderful teacher in Kilbarchan in Renfrewshire. It was as much of an immersion course as time would allow.

It turned out to be a mind- and eye-opening journey. I began to understand the Highlands and Islands in a different way. Even something as simple as knowing what placenames and the names of mountains, rivers and lochs meant was a way of understanding a past that was fast disappearing At the head of Glencoe stands the imposing mass of *Buachaille Etive Mor*. It means 'the Great Herdsman of Etive' – both a metaphor and a memory. On its lower slopes, the cattle, sheep and goats of the MacIains, Clan Donald, grazed for centuries. The Great Herdsman watched over the animals and the

people who walked their lives in his shadow, generation after generation, in the glen below.

Gaelic is a beautiful language, mouth-filling and mellifluous. Its
flowing syllables make the landscape come alive. In Donald MacIver's
great lyric, '*An Ataireachd Ard*', 'The High Surge of the Sea', he uses
a verb that almost translates as 'the action of the waves washing back
and forth on the sand'. It is one word, *sluaisreadh*. Approximately
pronounced as slewashriv, it is more than onomatopoeic – it is
poetic.

Even a little of the language unlocks the body warmth of Highland
and Islands society. There are everyday and obvious examples like
the long list of terms of endearment, much longer than in English,
all expressed in the vocative case, something now sadly lost to us.
When my teacher's mother came down from Lewis to visit, I inflicted
my rudimentary Gaelic on her.

'*A' ghraidh*,' she said, smiling, '*tha sin gle mhath*.' – 'My dear, that's
very good.'

Further up the scale is *a' ghaol* for 'my love', then *mo leannan* for
'my love(r)'. There are no fewer than twelve near-synonyms for
'darling' and the term for 'my most fond', 'my most beloved' is *m'
eudail*. It reeks of the past and it also makes me laugh. It literally
means 'my cattle' and is usually translated as 'my treasure'. For a
clansman, his most treasured possessions were his cattle, how his
wealth was measured. If you called a woman a cow in English, the
reaction would perhaps not be the same.

Continuity as much as history is embedded in the language. Just
as the clansmen at Culloden recited the *sloinneadh*, 'the naming of
the names of memory', – their genealogy – Gaelic speakers still do
that. It is a means of locating someone in a different sort of world-
wide web and also characteristic of a rural society. Until Inverness
recently acquired the designation, there were no cities or large towns
in the Highlands or Islands. Gaelic speaks of the land, its plants and
animals, the people who tend them both and it is also an echo of
fast-disappearing memory. When emigrants moved away, either
across the oceans or to the cities of the south, out of the body warmth

of their native places, they lost the language quickly, rarely passing it on. It had no relevance and little application to the new places where they found themselves – Glasgow, New York or the vastnesses of Canada and Australia.

The Broch on the shore of the Sound of Sleat is defiant in another way. It was built on the site of some of the first departures. In 1773, the grumpy Samuel Johnson and his long-suffering travelling companion, James Boswell, came to Ostaig to stay for a few days. It was there, where the college now stands, that they saw and took part in the dance called America. Boswell noted:

> We performed, with much activity, a dance which, I suppose, the emigration from Skye had occasioned. They call it America. Each of the couples, after the common involutions and evolutions [turns], successively whirls around in a circle, till all are in motion, and the dance seems intended to show how migration catches, till a whole neighbourhood is set afloat.

After Culloden, the age of departure and Clearance began. The land emptied and fell silent, a working landscape degenerating into mere scenery. The language that described it became a distant echo.

In 1989, with a Gaelic TV schedule to create, I felt that we could not listen only to echoes, deal only in memory, the past and often a past whose edges were tinged with tears and sometimes great resentments. By chance I'd heard a haunting, memorable song called '*An Ubhal as Airde*', 'The Highest Apple'. It was sung by Donnie Munro and performed by Runrig, a band formed by Rory and Calum MacDonald, two native Gaelic-speaking brothers from Skye. It is an anthem of memory, continuity, religious belief and education, all of it wrapped up together and profoundly influenced by the swirling cadences of the Gaelic psalmody. Above all, it was authentic and new. And it told me that the language might have a future in a modern Scotland if it could remember and reinterpret its past and shine a light on the present in powerful ways that would reach out to all Scots.

I bought several of Runrig's albums – on cassettes in those far-off days – and played them on car journeys. The band sang of a Highland and Islands experience of life, of history and the land, and occasionally in Gaelic. One of their most striking and powerful compositions was 'Dance Called America', its verses and sentiment deriving directly from what James Boswell saw on Skye in 1773. Playing live concerts all over Scotland and in Europe, Runrig were uniquely popular. No Highland, Gaelic-speaking musicians had ever broken out of their heartland and enjoyed such widespread success, especially amongst younger people.

Politics was also at work, interacting with and refracted by popular entertainment. Since 1979, the Conservative government of Margaret Thatcher had won three United Kingdom general elections but was unpopular in Scotland. The number of Scottish Conservative MPs halved from twenty-two in 1979 to eleven in 1992 and, by 1997, they held no seats north of the Border. Runrig's success amongst non-Gaels in part stemmed directly from their origins and their culture. There was no part of Scotland that could be more different from England than the Highlands and Islands, nowhere more Scottish. And Gaels did not need to express themselves in English.

I decided we should make a film about the band, based on a concert they would give at Glasgow's Barrowland Ballroom. It was broadcast at peak time, 9 p.m. on 8 May 1990, on Scottish Television. And, to my amazement, it was watched by more than a million people – an unprecedented, staggering number – and the film's second song was 'Dance Called America'.

The concert was part of a turning moment in perceptions of Gaelic and the communities of the Highlands and Islands. The Thatcher government had done something that surprised many with their commitment of £9 million in 1989 to the production of Gaelic TV programmes. But, before these new, funded programmes could be produced, STV pioneered peak-time series in Gaelic with a cookery series, called *Haggis Agus*, and, a game show, *De Tha Seo?* These shows were subtitled and regularly watched by 250,000 to 300,000 viewers, six or seven times the size of the Gaelic speech community. In 1993, STV made and broadcast a Gaelic soap opera, *Machair*, and it achieved similar ratings. The net effect of all this concentrated exposure in a short period was to fast-forward Gaelic culture, bringing it from the margins into the mainstream of public life in Scotland. Where it has remained.

Throughout all of that period of intense work, I hoped that the dying language would leave a living legacy, one that would, of necessity, be carried on by learners as the native speech community shrank.

Driving down from Mallaig, I played Runrig's music again and remembered all the excitement, fun and creativity. I'm proud of what we achieved thirty years ago but I found myself filled with a sudden sense of regret, a strange melancholy I couldn't shake off.

I turned off the new road to follow the old one I'd loved so much, thinking of the past, of all that was lost and gone, the people who had gone. It was the sudden thunder that broke into my reverie. Down a steep brae from the village of Morar, the shortest river in Britain roars through a gorge. Swollen with rain, the River Morar was a roiling, foaming torrent. I parked by the side of the old road bridge as a train rattled over another, above me. The noise was deafening. Beyond them and the new road bridge stretched the white sands of Morar. But it was not the beach I was looking for.

At first I couldn't find Camusdarach. The winding road was as I remembered it but the landscape on either side was much changed. There were scores of new houses, many of them bright white in the rain, some large, others more standard bungalows. Many had spectacular views. Name plaques and driveway signs announced Dune Cottage and Taigh Geal. Some had stacks of white plastic chairs on decking outside their front doors and I guessed these were holiday homes. Others certainly were. Signs pointed the way to Carn Lodges and Traigh Lodges but there was nothing to tell me where Garramore Youth Hostel had been. On either side of the old road, it seemed to me that a community had grown up and the landscape had come alive again. That impression was confirmed when I had to pull into a passing place to allow an Amazon Prime delivery van to get past.

Reckoning I'd overshot Camusdarach, I turned and drove back north. Well waterproofed against the insistent rain, an older man was putting out his rubbish and his English accent told me that I was close, the car park for the beach was at the foot of the hill. I watched him walk back to a large and well-sited new house he had named *Sealladh na Mara*, Sea View. That lifted my melancholy spirits, to see that sort of commitment, naming where he lived in a language he probably didn't understand. It was not superficial, the old man in the waterproofs had committed himself to this place a century after most of its people had departed and he did that in the language they spoke. Its beauty and its magic still worked and not just for him but for the community that had clustered in South Morar in the twenty years since I'd last driven up the old road.

A path led over a wooden bridge to a sign: 'Welcome. Please Enjoy Beach Responsibly. Pick up after your dog. Take litter home. No fires close to sand dunes.' Attached to the uprights was an unexpected spark of memory. A sign directed visitors to 'Happer Inst.' And below that were two light blue-painted boards that had 'Sea' and 'Sky' on them. It was a memory from forty years ago. Played by Burt Lancaster, Felix Happer was the Texan oil tycoon in Bill Forsyth's *Local Hero*, the man who wanted to buy the beach. He was also obsessed by astronomy, constantly asking his staff about the night sky in Scotland.

Two people suddenly appeared, both wearing waterproof robes lined with thick towelling, the woman wearing a bathing cap and the man with wet hair. Wild swimming in the ocean on a day like this? Amazing. When I asked them about the beach and the sign, they told me that many people came each year to visit, brought to Camusdarach by Bill Forsyth's film. That cheered me. Stories, stories, stories, their enduring power is extraordinary.

I walked down a high-sided path, like a sandy tunnel, through the dunes. When I reached the beach, it was like a reveal in a film and it opened before me in all its heart-breaking beauty. Beyond a wide strand of perfect, pale-yellow sand, the waves gently shushed as the tide retreated. *Sluaisreadh*. And beyond the waves, framed by the horns of the dark rocks on either side, it seemed that infinity stretched across the ocean.

I stood for a long time, tears prickling and running down my cheeks, remembering all those people who had made me, many of them long gone, others dispersed. And I was glad to have come back to this blessed shore, to have set eyes on Camusdarach once more, a place of turning moments in my life. It felt to me that, almost sixty years before, I had begun a journey in this place and now it had ended. I knew I'd never come back. There would be no need to. It was as I remembered: magical, eternal, elemental, a place of spirits where the music of the wind whispered, where echoes of an immense past drifted over the waves.

The rain had stopped and, as I walked across the perfect, smooth sand, I saw that, behind me, I had left no footprints.

If this place could affect me so deeply, a man born and raised in the Borders, a world away, its rolling fields and sheltering river valleys very different from the majesty of Morar, how did it seem to Allan MacDonald and the 150 clansmen he led from here to the muster at Glenfinnan? Beautiful is not enough and yet it is everything. This bay of intimate loveliness and vaulted grandeur was empty when I came. But, to MacDonald and the generations before him and his men, it was home. Some were on this shore every day, fishing, catching scuttling crabs, prising limpets off the rocks, collecting cockles, mussels, playing, learning, travelling up and down the old road, sitting in the evening dunes watching the sun settle in the west, silhouetting the far Cuillin, exchanging words of love. And, when they began to leave and the white-sailed ships slipped over the horizon, its beauty tore at their hearts.

At Camusdarach I could hear more clearly than anywhere on my journey what Gaelic speakers call 'the music of the thing as it happened'. Here in the horned bay, the shadows of the Army of the Dead flitted and flickered in the clear air, passing across the sand, leaving no trace, swirling around me. I picked up a piece of stone. Shaped like a large arrowhead and glinting with scintillas of crystal, it was red and heavy, a piece of red granite or perhaps Lewisian gneiss, one of the oldest rocks on earth. I washed the sand off it in a rock pool and put it in my pocket. All the time I have been writing these passages about Camusdarach, I have clutched the stone in my left hand.

It was late afternoon when I left. The rain was falling once more and I draped my waterproof over the back seats of my car, turning the heater up to maximum. Before I could leave, I needed to gather myself and try to make sense of the unexpected and overwhelming churn of emotions that had overtaken me. Even though the day was ending, the rain-cloud sky growing dark, I didn't want to leave, but I had to. I needed to go home, back to my own home-place.

Half an hour later, I stopped at a lay-by at a sign for The Prince's Cairn. It was built near the head of Loch nan Uamh by The Forty-Five Association and the sign said in Gaelic and English:

This cairn marks the traditional spot from which Prince Charles Edward Stuart embarked for France, 20th September 1746.

The cairn itself is at the bottom of a path down to a very rocky and wild shore and is not easy to reach, especially in wet weather. It looks west, out to the ocean and the setting sun. It was the place where it all began to end, not just the Jacobite dream of restoration but also the clan society whose extraordinary courage and sacrifice had almost made the impossible possible. I didn't want to linger long in the rain but it felt disrespectful to hurry away into the warmth. So I stood for a time looking down the loch, feeling the sea wind freshen on my face and watching night fall.

Epilogue

King Charles III

My old friend George Rosie wrote a brilliant and elegiac postscript to *Am Bliadhna Thearlaich*, 'The Year of Charles'. In 1992, his award-winning play, *Carluccio and the Queen of Hearts*, premiered at the Edinburgh Festival Fringe. It told a sad and surprising story – the end of almost five centuries of dynastic history.

After his flight from Highland Scotland in the late summer of 1746, Prince Charles lived for another forty-two years. The charismatic and handsome young man who sat down next to Alasdair Mac Mhaighstir Alasdair on the deck of *Le du Teillay* gradually became an embittered, drunken and embarrassing figure. Charles began what he saw as his exile in Paris, a place where he might have found allies and support. But it all turned out very differently. By 1749, Louis XV and his ministers had agreed the Treaty of Aix-la-Chapelle. It brought to an end the War of the Austrian Succession between Britain and France. The Hanoverian government was determined to extinguish any possibility of yet another Jacobite rebellion and one of the treaty's terms was the immediate arrest of Prince Charles and his expulsion from France. All was done very publicly, designed as a deliberate humiliation. While at the opera at the Theatre du Palais-Royal with his mistress, Charles was forcibly removed from his box, arrested, bound hand and foot with 'silken rope' and imprisoned at the Chateau du Vincennes. Soon afterwards he was run out of Paris and the prince took temporary refuge in the papal territory of Avignon.

But hope still flickered and in 1750 Charles crossed the Channel to make a secret and very dangerous visit to London, staying at various safe houses belonging to Jacobite supporters. Realising that his rapidly diminishing chances of regaining the throne for the Stuarts were fatally weakened by his continued adherence to Catholicism, the prince became an Anglican. Bishop Robert Gordon probably presided over the celebration of the first communion – what formally confirmed his conversion. Despite staying for several weeks in London, at great personal risk, Charles was unable to rally much support.

With the outbreak of the Seven Years War, Britain and France once again became enemies. In 1759, the Duc de Choiseul, Louis XV's foreign minister, led preparations for an invasion across the Channel with a huge army of 100,000 men. He sent for Prince Charles and proposed he lead a force of exiled Jacobites and attempt to raise the clans once more. But, by that time, it seems that the prince had begun to drink to excess and his meeting with the duke was so fractious and bedevilled by unrealistic demands and aspiration that the notion of Charles's involvement was summarily dismissed. The invasion never took place but it was the last realistic chance for the restoration of the Stuarts – and the prince's own behaviour made his involvement impossible. By that time, he had entered a twilight life of bitter delusion and domestic upheaval that eventually descended into embarrassing farce.

In January 1766, James III and VIII, the Old Pretender, at last died in Rome. Charles immediately styled himself Charles III of England, Scotland and Ireland and demanded always to be addressed as 'Your Majesty'. Few did and, when he moved to Rome, the Pope ordered that the royal coat of arms be removed from above the gates of the residence he inherited from his father, the Palazzo Muti. Hope was fading fast if he could not rely on papal support for the restoration of the Catholic Stuarts. An English diplomat, William Hamilton, wrote dispatches describing the new king's increasing isolation. An English lady told him that he had 'all the reason in the world to be melancholy, for there is not a soul goes near him, not knowing what to call him'.

The Queen of Hearts in the title of George Rosie's play was a beautiful young German aristocrat, Louise de Stolberg-Gedern. In the fantasy world that Charles's delusions had created, he felt he needed an heir and this woman, his queen, would produce one. They were married in 1772 and attempted to create a court in exile where they received guests and visitors. Not many were willing to play the game and high society in Rome referred to them as the Count and Countess of Albany. Louise's good looks earned another title, long before Princess Diana coined it on television. As an alternative to being Queen of Scotland and England, a prospect that was rapidly disappearing, Louise was known as the Queen of Hearts.

Despite all these outward signs of Charles's decline, the British government remained watchful and a great deal is known about the last years of his life because of the dispatches sent to London by another diplomat, Sir Horace Mann. In the face of ridicule and snubs, the Pretender King became moody, morose and increasingly drunken. According to the servants of the royal household bribed by Mann, he was consuming up to twelve bottles a day of fortified Cyprus wine, something like sherry or port. As her husband slid into alcoholism, grew fat and became chronically breathless, the Queen of Hearts began to take lovers.

After they abandoned Rome and moved to Florence, to the Palazzo Guadagni, their marriage began publicly to disintegrate. On the night of 30 November 1780, matters spilled over into violence when Charles attacked his wife in front of servants. Some said he tried to rape her. Louise fled the palazzo to take refuge in the Convent of the White Nuns in the nearby Via del Mandorlo. King Charles followed her and, when he tried to force his way into the convent and was physically ejected, he stood outside in the street shouting insults and waking the neighbours. It was the embarrassing end of the marriage and Sir Horace Mann was delighted. 'The mould for any more casts of Royal Stuarts has been broken, or what is equivalent to it is now shut up in a convent of nuns,' he wrote to London.

On 30 January 1788 the delusions finally came to an end. Charles III of England, Scotland and Ireland died in Rome with only a belatedly legitimised bastard daughter as his heir. The Pretender King's brother, Henry, who had become a cardinal, said a requiem mass over the coffin. Charles had been dressed in royal robes with the insignia of the Order of the Thistle and the Order of the Garter, a replica of the English crown on his head and in one hand there was a sceptre and in the other the sword of state. The dream was played out to the last.

Looking back over a century of rebellion, it occurred to me more than once that the Stuarts did not deserve the bravery of the clans and their immense blood sacrifice. As kings of England, Scotland and Ireland, they were a feckless, reckless dynasty whose actions and inactions doomed them to eventual and perhaps inevitable failure. Charles I's haughty obduracy ignited the Wars of the Three Kingdoms and cost him his head. James II and VII's insistence on remaining a Catholic and trying to foist his religion on two overwhelmingly Protestant nations made his abdication and flight all too predictable. His exiled son's diplomatic skills were negligible and his failure to raise the morale of the rebels of 1715 abject. But it is the self-pitying, embarrassing decline of Prince Charles that rankles most. The bright hope that raised the standard at Glenfinnan faded fast in the fetid, petty politics of exile and failure in the crumbling palaces of Rome and Florence. The raw courage of Gillies MacBean at Culloden and countless other brave men was wasted on this lot, it seems to me.

More than that, there is something noble and profoundly attractive about the men who raised their claymores and raced across the heather. They were fighting for more than the restoration of a failed and useless dynasty. They charged headlong at their enemies to defend memory, to renew all their prowess, their ancient honour and their war glory. When the clans summoned the Army of the Dead at Culloden, it was as though the wind of history blew at their backs and carried their war cries clear across the snows of eternity and on to immortality. They were warriors to the very last.

Further Reading

Barthorp, M., *Jacobite Rebellions, 1689–1745*, Oxford 1982

Craig, Maggie, *Bare-Arsed Banditti: The Men of the '45*, Edinburgh 2010

Craig, Maggie, *Damn' Rebel Bitches: The Women of the'45*, Edinburgh 1997

Devine, T.M., *To the Ends of the Earth:Sotland's Global Diaspora, 1750*, London 2011

Fforde, Catherine, *A Summer in Lochaber*, Colonsay 2002

Hastings, Max. *Montrose, The King's Champion*, London 1977

Hill, J.M., *Celtic Warfare, 1595–1783*, Alabama 1986

Hopkins, Paul, *Glencoe and the End of the Highland War*, Edinburgh 2001

Hunter, James, *The Appin Murder: The Killing That Shook a Nation*, Edinburgh 2022

Hunter, James, *Culloden and the Last Clansman*, Edinburgh 2010

Hunter, James, *The Last of the Free: A History of the Highlands and Islands*, Edinburgh 2010

Innes, Bill ed., *St Valery, The Impossible Odds*, Edinburgh 2004

MacDonald, Donald, *Lewis: A History of the Island*, Edinburgh 1978

MacKay, John, *The Life of Lt. General Hugh Mackay*, Edinburgh 1836

Moffat, Alistair, *The Highland Clans*, London 2002

Moffat, Alistair, *Scotland: A History from Earliest Times*, Edinburgh 2015

Oates, Jonathan, *Battles of the Jacobite Rebellions*, Barnsley 2019

Prebble, John, *Culloden*, London, 2002

Prebble, John, *Glencoe*, London, 2005

Prebble, John, *The Lion in the North*, London 1971

1745 Association Quarterly, Autumn 1981

Reid, Stuart, *Culloden, 1746*, London 2018

Royle, Trevor, *Culloden: Scotland's Last Battle and the Forging of the British Empire*, London 2016

Scott, Jenn, *I Am Minded to Rise: The Clothing, Weapons and Accoutrements of the Jacobites from 1689 to 1719*, Coventry 2020

Sears, Stephen W. *Gettysburg*, New York 2004

Stevenson, David, *Highland Warrior: Alasdair MacColla and the Civil Wars*, Edinburgh, 2014

Thomson, Derick S., *Alasdair macMhaighstir Alasdair, Selected Poems*, Edinburgh, 1996

Index

Acharacle 13–15
Act of Union 155
Afghanistan, British Army in 65–6
Agassiz, Louis 82
Age of the Forays, the 38, 95
'Alasdair Mhic Cholla Ghasda' (song) 47–8
Allt na Larach pass 80–1
Am Bliadhna Thearlaich ('The Year of Charles') xxi–xxii
Anderson, Robert xiv
Anne, Queen 155
Argyll, John Campbell, Duke of 162–4
Arisaig 198–200
Atholl Brigade 187
Atholl clans, and Montrose 53–5
atrocities after battles 195–6
Auchinbreck, Sir Duncan Campbell of 80, 84–8

bagpipes 126–7
Balfour of Burleigh, Lord 72–3
Balmorality 189

bardic tradition, Gaelic 4–5, 91–3
See also Lom MacDonald, Iain; Mac Mhaighstir Alasdair, Alasdair (Alexander MacDonald); Sileas of Keppoch
Barrell's Regiment 195
Bearasaigh 41–4
berry picking 58–9
birlinns 18–19
Blair Castle 54
Boswell, James 204
Bothwell Bridge, Battle of 135–6
Bradstreet, Captain Dudley 168–70
Braemar, muster at 156–7
British Army, modern 65–7
brogan (brogues) 78–9
Brown, James (History of the Highlands) 149
Bury, Lord 190

Cameron, Clan xiii, xv–xvi, 20–1
Cameron, David (the 'Lion of the Covenant') 136–7
Cameron Highlanders (regiment) xx–xxi

Cameron of Glendessary, Jeanie
   21
Cameron of Lochiel, Sir Donald
   21
Cameron of Lochiel, Sir Ewen
   110, 127–8, 193
Cameronians, the 137–8,
   142–51
Campbell, Archibald, Marquis of
   Argyll 50–2, 77–8, 85
Campbell, Clan 77–9, 84–7
Campbell, John, Duke of Argyll
   162–4
Campbell of Auchinbreck, Sir
   Duncan 80, 84–8
Camusdarach beach 199, 206–9
Cannon, Colonel Alexander 143,
   145, 146–7, 150
Cardross, Henry Erskine, Lord
   145–6, 150
cavalry xvi, 73, 123, 174, 179
charge, Highland
  at Aberdeen 73
  at Clifton Moor 170
  at Culloden 191, 192–5
  at Dunkeld 147, 149
  at Glenmaquin 50–1
  at Inverlochy 86
  at Killiecrankie 127, 129
  at Mulroy 101–4
  at Prestonpans xv–xvi
  at Sherrifmuir 164, 172
  at Tippermuir 63–4, 67–8
Clanranald xiv, 17, 18–19, 36,
   95

clans
  battles 95
  feuds 34–9
Clearances 39, 204
Cleland, William 133–6, 137,
   138, 142–51
Clifton Moor 170
Cobham's 10th Dragoons 174
Coll (Coll Ciotach Mac
   Dhomnhaill, Colkitto) 48–9
Confederate Catholics of Ireland,
   Association of 49–52
Convention of the Scottish Estates,
   the 108–10
Cope, Sir John xiii–xv
courage 64, 66, 67
Covenant, Army of the 135–6. *see
   also* Cameronians, the
Covenanters 61–4, 131–8
Culloden 126–7, 185–96
Cumberland, Duke of 185, 190, 196

Dalilea, Loch Shiel 9–10, 15–16
Dalmore 40–1
'Dance Called America' (dance and
   song) 204, 205
Derby 167–70
Disarming Acts 126
Douglas 137–8
Douglas, Rev. Thomas 131, 134–5
Drumclog, Battle of 109, 134–5
Drummond, David, Master of
   Madertie 62–3
Drummond, James, Duke of Perth
   xiv–xvi

Drummond, Lord James 157
Drummond, Lord John 170–1, 175
Drummond, Sir John 60
Dubh, Alasdair (Black Alasdair of Glengarry) 111 See also Lom MacDonald, Iain
Duke of Perth xiv–xvi
Dundee 72
Dundee, John Graham of Claverhouse, Viscount 109–10, 118–19, 121–2, 125, 129, 135–6
Dunkeld 139–51
Dunkirk xx–xxi
duthchas 200–1

Edinburgh 108–9, 157
Eigg, massacre on 39
Eilean Fhionnan (Loch Shiel) 4, 16–17
El Alamein 126
Elcho, Lord (John Wemyss, the Earl of Wemyss) 61–4
emigration 72–3
endurance (martial virtue) 78
equipment
    of clansmen 124–7
    of Gallowglasses 123–4
Equivalent, the 155

Falkirk Muir 171–81
farming, traditional (transhumance) 96
feuds, clan 34–9

Field of the Shirts, the (*Blar na Leine*) 95
Fire and Sword, Letters of 36, 43, 94–5
Forsyth, Bill (*Local Hero*) 199, 207

Gaelic, learning 8, 14–15, 29–30, 201–4, 206
Gaelic place names 115, 200
Gallowglasses 122–4
Gathering Stone, the, Sherrifmuir 159–60
Gentleman Adventurers for the Conquest of the Isle of Lewis 32–4, 41
George I, King 155–6
George IV, King 111–12
Glen Roy 81–3, 110, 114
Glenaladale 19–20
Glenfinnan 20–7
Glenmaquin 50–1
Gordon, Duke of 109–10
Gordon, Lord Lewis 171
government soldiers xvi–xvii, 120–1, 189, 192–5
Graham of Claverhouse, John, Viscount Dundee 109–10, 118–19, 121–2, 125, 129
Grameid, The (Dr James Philip) 110–11, 113–14, 129
grapeshot 192–3
graves at Culloden 189–90
Gregory, James 93–4

Hackston, David 136
Hamilton, Robert 135–6
hand-to-hand fighting 64–6, 114
Harry Potter 24
Hawley, General Henry 171–3,
　175, 176, 179
hermitages (*diseart*) 16
Highland Army at Dunkeld
　143–51
Highland Companies (clans
　opposing Prince Charles)
　171
Highland Host in South-west
　Scotland 134
Highlanders
　cultural life 91–3
　dress and appearance 110–14,
　122
　training in fighting 64–5
Home, John (*History of the
　Rebellion in the year 1745*) xiv
honour 66
Huske, Major General John 195

Inveraray 77–9
Inverlochy, Battle of 84–7
Inverlochy Castle 84, 89
Inverurie, Battle of 171

Jacobite army, nationalities of 189
Jacobite cause, romance of 89
　84–7
Jacobite rebellion, 1715 156–64
James IV of Scotland 34
James V of Scotland 35

James VI of Scotland and I of
　England 32–3, 133
James VII of Scotland and II of
　England 105–9, 213
James VIII of Scotland and III of
　England (the Old Pretender)
　156, 164–5, 211, 213
Johnson, Samuel 204
Johnstone, James xvi–xvii

Keppoch 96
Ker of Graden, Colonel Harry
　xiii–xiv, 67, 185, 191, 192
Killiecrankie 114–30
Kilmarnock, Lady Anne 173
Kilmarnock, Lord 173
Kilpont, Lord 60, 71–2

Laggan Army, the 50–1
Laidlaw, Daniel 126
Lauder, Colonel George 116–17
Leslie, Alexander, General 51, 53
Lewis, invasion of 32
Local Hero (Bill Forsyth) 199,
　207
Loch Shiel Cruises 10–20
Lom MacDonald, Iain 79, 86, 88,
　92, 112–13, 125
Lordship of the Isles 35–6, 38, 49,
　95
Loudon Hill 131, 133
Love, Peter 42–3

Mac Colla, Alasdair 47–55, 67–8,
　73–4, 75–81, 84–8

Mac Mhaighstir Alasdair, Alasdair
(Alexander MacDonald)
1–5, 7–9, 23, 92–3
MacBean, Major Gillies 193, 196
MacDonald, Alexander (Alasdair
Mac Mhaighstir Alasdair)
1–5, 7–9, 23, 92–3
MacDonald, Coll 93–5, 100–2,
111
MacDonald, Iain Lom 79, 86, 88,
92, 112–13, 125
MacDonald of Morar, Allan 20,
24, 208
MacDonnell of Tiendrich, Donald
21
MacGillivray, Alexander 190, 193,
194
MacGillivray, John 193
MacGregor regiment at
Prestonpans xvi
Mackay, General Hugh 114,
117–20, 122, 128, 143
Mackenzie, Ruaridh (the Tutor of
Kintail) 43–4
Mackenzie of Suddie, Kenneth
95, 100–1, 102
Mackenzies of Kintail 36, 38,
42–4
Mackintosh, Lachlan 94–5,
99–102
Mackintosh of Borlum, Brigadier
William 101–2
MacLean of Duart, Lachlan Mor
39
Maclean of Duart, Sir John 110

Macleod, Murdo 41
Macleod, Neil 41–5
Macleods of Lewis 32–3, 34–8
MacRae monument, Sherrifmuir
153–4, 163
Mallaig 200–1
Mann, Sir Horace 212
Maol Ruadh (Mulroy) 97–101
maps, Ordnance Survey 96–7
Mar, John Erskine, Earl of 155–65
McBane, Donald 103–4, 127,
129–30
Menzies, Sir Alexander 60
mercenaries 52, 122–4
Mingary Castle 53
Monmouth, James, Duke of 135–6
Montrose, James Graham, Earl of
Battle of Aberdeen 72–4
Tippermuir 53–5, 60–4, 67–8,
70–2
winter campaign 75–81, 84–7
Mulroy, Battle of 95–103
Munro, Captain 148–9
Murray, Lord George xiii–xvi, 67,
167–70, 173–5, 177–9,
184–7
Murray, Lord, Marquis of Atholl
117
Murray, William, Marquis of
Tullibardine 8–9, 22–3, 26
muskets 124–5

naming of the names (*sloinneadh*)
190, 203

O'Cahan, Manas 51, 52, 85, 86
Old Rory (Ruaridh Macleoid,
      Rory MacLeod) 34–8
O'Neill, Phelim 49, 50–1
operational paralysis 66
O'Sullivan, Col. John 9, 20–2,
      175, 184–7

Parallel Roads, Glen Roy 81–3
Perth 55–65, 68–70
Philip, Dr James (*The Grameid*)
      110–11, 113–14, 129
piracy 42–3
place, love of 200–1
place names, Gaelic 200, 201–2
Prestonpans, Battle of xiii–xx, 67
Prince's Bay, the 20
Prince's Cairn, the 209

Queen of Hearts, the (Louise de
      Stolenberg-Gedern) 211–12

raising the standard at Glenfinnan
      9–10, 21–2
Raleigh, Sir Walter 33–4
Red Harlaw, Battle of 78
Reid, James 126–7
retreat from Derby, Jacobite
      169–70
rosehips 58–9
Rosie, George (*Carluccio and the
      Queen of Hearts*) 210,
      211–12
Roy Bridge 96, 98
rugby 67

Runrig (band) 30–1, 204–5

Sabhal Mor Ostaig 201–2
Sanquhar Declaration, the 136–7
Scott, Sir Walter 39, 111–12, 189
Seaforth, Earl of 79–80
Seven Men of Moidart,the 8–9
sheep lawns 98–9
Sherrifmuir 153–4, 157–65
Shiel, Loch, cruise on 10–20
shields (targes) 125–6
Sileas of Keppoch 91–3
Soldier's Leap, the, Killiecrankie
      129–30
Spean Bridge 84
Stewart, Lieutenant 147–8
Stewart of Ardvorlich, James 71–2
Stewarts, Appin 147–8
Stirling 59–60, 170–2
Stolenberg-Gedern, Louise de
      211–12
Stornoway 28–9, 31–2
Stornoway Castle 32–3
Stuart, Charles Edward, Prince
      early life 5–7
      Jacobite Rebellion xiii–xvii,
         7–10, 18–20, 167–70, 209
      later life 210–13
      romanticising of 189, 196
Swettenham, Captain 21–2
swords 125

tartan 110–13
television, Gaelic 28–31, 201–2,
      204–6

Telford, Thomas 139
terrain
  at Culloden 184–5, 186, 191
  at Falkirk Muir 178
  at Sherrifmuir 161–2
  at Tippermuir 61–2
  significance of 51, 67
Thatcher, Margaret 28, 202, 205
Tippermuir, Battle of 55–8, 61–4,
  66–70
Tories 154–6
Torloisk, feud at 39
transportation 136
trees, language of 91–2
Tullibardine, William Murray,
  Marquis of 8–9, 22–3, 26

Ulster, rebellion in 48–9

Wallace, Ben (MP) 66
war cries 200
War of the Austrian Succession 7,
  210
War of the Three Kingdoms 49
waulking songs 47–8
Well of the Dead, Culloden 190
William of Orange (King William
  III) 106–8
Wolfe, James 195
World War I 126
World War II 126

Year of Miracles, the 54

Islands of the Evening
Journeys to the Edge of the World

A *New Statesman* Book of the Year

Fourteen centuries ago, Irish saints journeyed to the Hebrides and Scotland's Atlantic shore. They sought solitude in remote places, but their mission was also to spread the word of God to the peoples of Scotland. Columba was the most famous of these pioneers who rowed their curraghs towards danger and uncertainty in a pagan land, but the many others are now largely forgotten.

Alistair Moffat sets off in search of these elusive figures. As he follows in their footsteps, he finds their traces not so much in tangible remains as in the spirit and memory of places that lay at the very edge of the world.

'An exploration of Scotland's past through the eyes of a scholarly hiker . . . magnificent'

New Statesman

'Delightful . . . Moffat's writing is at its most fascinating when he writes about his own experience'

Church Times

Scotland: A History from Earliest Times

Alistair Moffat brings vividly to life the story of this great nation, from the dawn of prehistory through to the twenty-first century.

An ambitious, richly detailed and highly readable account, *Scotland: A History from Earliest Times* offers a comprehensive view for the general reader, skilfully weaving together a dazzling array of facts and details which reference a vast range of sources, from the lives of saints, medieval documents and great works of literature to reports of sporting events and contemporary popular culture. The result is an imaginative, informative, balanced and dazzlingly varied portrait of Scotland over the centuries, seen not just through the experience of the kings, saints, warriors, aristocrats and politicians who populate the pages of most conventional history books, but also the ordinary people who have lived Scotland's history, and, in their own way, have played an inestimable role in shaping its destiny.

'What brings Moffat's history to life is his ability to see significance in detail, to seize on the historical anecdotes that really count'
The Scotsman

'Rattles along with complete narrative certainty'
Scottish Review of Books

'This is a very readable, well-researched and fluent account'
Scotland on Sunday

'Moffat plunders the facts and fables to create a richly detailed and comprehensive analysis of a nation's past and references a huge number of sources'
Scotland Magazine

The Scots: A Genetic Journey

History has always mattered to Scots, and rarely more so than now. But whilst traditional views of the past are shaped by documents, events and physical remains, we have until recently overlooked the fact that an almost limitless archive of history lies hidden inside our own bodies, and that the ancient story of Scotland is carried around within us. The recent mushrooming of genetic studies and of DNA analysis is rewriting our history in spectacular fashion.

In *The Scots: A Genetic Journey*, Alistair Moffat explores the history that is printed in our genes, and in a remarkable new approach, comes to some fascinating conclusions about who we are and where we come from.

'Packed with genetic revelations'

Scotland Magazine

'[Moffat] is wonderfully able to communicate the epic elements of the story'

The Scotsman

'Highly readable and extremely educational – will make you look afresh at both Scotland and the Scots'

Scottish Field

The Borders
A History of the Borders from Earliest Times

Alistair Moffat tells the story of a part of Scotland that has played a huge role in the nation's history and moved poets, painters and writers as well as ordinary visitors for hundreds of years.

The hunter-gatherers, who first penetrated the virgin interior, the Celtic warlords, the Romans, the Northumbrians and the Reivers, who dominated the Anglo-Scottish borderlands for over 300 years, have all had their part to play in the constantly evolving life of the area. It is the people of a place that make its history, and this book is a testament to those who have made the Borders their home and who have created the traditions, myths and romance that define it so strongly.

'Quirky, learned and utterly absorbing'

Allan Massie

'Highly readable'

Northern History

'Beautifully written, a fine book'

Sunday Herald

The Reivers
The Story of the Border Reivers

From the early fourteenth century to the end of the sixteenth, the Anglo-Scottish borderlands witnessed one of the most intense periods of warfare and disorder ever seen in modern Europe. As a consequence of near-constant conflict between England and Scotland, Borderers suffered unimaginably at the hands of marauding armies, who ravaged the land, destroying crops, slaughtering cattle, burning whole settlements and killing indiscriminately. Forced by extreme circumstances, many Borderers took to reiving to ensure the survival of their families and communities.

For the best part of 300 years, countless raiding parties made their way over the border, from Dumfriesshire to the high wastes of East Cumbria, from Roxburghshire to Redesdale, from the lonely valley of Liddesdale to the fortress city of Carlisle. Often they returned under the cover of darkness, leading their precious cargo of stolen livestock through desolate landscapes in order to avoid detection.

The story of the Reivers is one of survival, stealth, treachery, ingenuity and deceit, expertly brought to life in this acclaimed book.

'Exciting and dramatic

Cumberland News

'Compelling, thought-provoking and entertaining

The Herald

'A definitive piece of research, colourfully and humorously written'

Scots Magazine